VIZ GRAPHIC NOVEL

Di Gi Charat

OL. 2

Di Gi Charat ™
Volume 2

English Adaptation by
Gerard Jones

Translation/Mari Morimoto
Touch-up & Lettering/Andy Ristaino
Cover & Graphic Design/Yuki Shimotoku
Editor/Eric Searleman

Managing Editor/Annette Roman
Editor-in-Chief/William Flanagan
Sr. VP of Editorial/Hyoe Narita
VP of Sales & Marketing/Rick Bauer
Publisher/Seiji Horibuchi

Published by VIZ, LLC
P.O. Box 77064
San Francisco, CA 94107

10 9 8 7 6 5 4 3 2 1
First printing, April 2003

store.viz.com

CONTENTS

Princess Gamers	by Koge-Donbo	7
What's Wrong with this Picture?	by PEACH-PIT	11
Usada Collapses?!	by PEACH-PIT	17
Fall Festival	by Kazuki Shu	21
Costume Panic	by Yuma Suzuka	32
Welcome	by Seara	47
Another Busy Day... Meow!	by Mami Urano	65
No Rice!	by Rina Yamaguchi	69
Dreams x Ambition x Retail	by Iru Isoshigaki	79
A Dangerous Couple	by Iru Isoshigaki	88
Summer Crime	by Yuki Nakano	89
Sentimental Puchiko	by Towa Ozora	95
Morning Fresh	by Mayumi Takayanagi	107
Puchiko's First Love	by Rocket-Brothers	113
The Great Detective Puchiko	by Tsukiko	125
Cinderella Syndrome	by Marumi Yamamoto	135
What I Love the Most	by Kanan	143
Puchiko's Hat	by Hina	155
Glossary		161

CHARACTERS

Di Gi Charat

NAME: DI GI CHARAT
NICKNAME: DIGIKO
AGE: 10 YEARS OLD
BIRTHDAY: FEBRUARY
    8TH (AQUARIUS)
HEIGHT: 4' 11" (INCLUDING
    CAT EARS)
WEIGHT: 84 POUNDS
MEASUREMENTS: SECRET
BLOOD TYPE: O
FAVORITE FOOD: BROCCOLI
SPECIAL POWER: LASER
    BEAMS FROM EYES
PERSONALITY: CUNNING o
    CHEEKY o A WEE BIT
    INSENSITIVE

THE CROWN PRINCESS OF
PLANET DI GI CHARAT,
CURRENTLY "STUDYING" ON
EARTH. WHILE WORKING AT A
STORE CALLED GAMERS SHE
SCHEMES TO BECOME AN
ACTRESS. HAS A HABIT OF
ADDING "MEOW" TO HER WORDS,
AN ODD ACCENT LEFT OVER
FROM PLANET DI GI CHARAT.

Gema

NAME: GEMA
AGE: ?
BIRTHDAY: JULY 13TH (CANCER)
BLOOD TYPE: O
FAVORITE FOOD: BROCCOLI
SPECIAL POWER: BLOW PIPE (DARTS)
PERSONALITY: HONEST o
    HARD-WORKING

DIGIKO'S GUARDIAN. DAY AND NIGHT,
HE STRUGGLES TO BRING HER
RAMPAGING ENERGY UNDER CONTROL.
ADDS "GEMA" TO HIS SENTENCES.

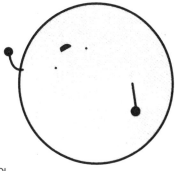

CHARACTERS

Rabi En Rose

NAME: USADA HIKARU
NICKNAME: USADA
AGE: 14 YEARS OLD
BIRTHDAY: AUGUST 30TH
    (VIRGO)
HEIGHT: 5' 6" (IN HEELS)
WEIGHT: SECRET
MEASUREMENTS: SECRET
BLOOD TYPE: A
FAVORITE FOOD: RICE BALLS o
    PERSIMMON SEEDS
SPECIAL POWER: BUNNY-
    COPTER
PERSONALITY: BOSSY

SHE ALSO WORKS AT GAMERS
AND YEARNS TO BE A STAR.
OUTWARDLY DIGIKO'S RIVAL,
SHE IS SECRETLY A LONELY
SOUL WHO WISHES SHE
COULD BE DIGIKO'S FRIEND.
HATES HER REAL NAME, SO
USUALLY CALLS HERSELF
"RABI EN ROSE," MEANING
(SORT OF) "PINK RABBIT."

Magical Kappas

NAME: KAPPA
AGE: ?
BIRTHDAY: ?
BLOOD TYPE: ?
FAVORITE FOOD: ?
SPECIAL POWER: MASTERY
    OF NUMBERS
PERSONALITY: ?

USADA'S SECRET WEAPON AGAINST
DIGIKO... BUT NOT A VERY EFFECTIVE
ONE. THOUGH USUALLY SEEN ONE
AT A TIME, THERE ARE MANY OF
THESE MAGICAL CREATURES.

CHARACTERS

Petit Charat

NAME: PETIT CHARAT
NICKNAME: PUCHIKO
AGE: 5 YEARS OLD
BIRTHDAY: JANUARY 21ST
    (AQUARIUS)
HEIGHT: 3 5" (INCLUDING
    CAT EARS)
WEIGHT: 40 POUNDS
MEASUREMENTS: ?
BLOOD TYPE: B
FAVORITE FOOD: RARE STEAK
SPECIAL POWER: LASER
    BEAMS FROM EYES
PERSONALITY: SPACEY

CAME WITH DIGIKO FROM
PLANET DI GI CHARAT. USUALLY
A GIRL OF FEW WORDS, SHE
ACTUALLY POSSESSES QUITE A
VENOMOUS TONGUE. SHE'S
ALWAYS STICKING TO DIGIKO,
BECAUSE (OR SO THE STORY
GOES) SHE FEELS INDEBTED TO
DIGIKO FOR SAVING HER FROM
A DEADLY TRAP. WHERE DIGIKO
ADDS "MEOW" TO HER WORDS,
PUCHIKO ADDS "MYEW."

Hokke-Mirin

NAME: HOKKE-MIRIN
AGE: ?
BIRTHDAY: ?
BLOOD TYPE: ?
FAVORITE FOOD(S): ?
SPECIAL POWER: WALKING ON
    HIND LEGS
PERSONALITY: ?

ONE RAINY DAY, IN THE MIDDLE OF
GROCERY SHOPPING, PUCHIKO PICKED
UP THE STRAY HOKKE-MIRIN. SHE'S A
FEMALE CALICO.

CHARACTERS

Pyocora Analog III

NAME: PYOCORA ANALOG III
NICKNAME: PIYOKO
AGE: 8 YEARS OLD
BIRTHDAY: OCTOBER 23RD
     (LIBRA)
HEIGHT: 4' 7"
WEIGHT: SECRET
MEASUREMENTS: SECRET
BLOOD TYPE: AB
FAVORITE FOOD: BUTTER
    SANDWICH
SPECIAL POWER: MOUTH
    BAZOOKA
PERSONALITY: PRECOCIOUS

BOSS OF THE DARK GEMA GEMA
GANG. IN ORDER TO REBUILD HER
EVIL ORGANIZATION'S TROUBLED
FINANCES, SHE SCHEMES TO
KIDNAP DIGIKO FOR RANSOM.
HAS A HABIT OF ADDING
"SQUEEK" TO HER WORDS, A
LEFTOVER FROM THE ACCENT
OF THE PLANET ANALOG.

Nazo Gema

NAME: NAZO ("MYSTERIOUS") GEMA
AGE: ?
BIRTHDAY: ?
BLOOD TYPE: ?
FAVORITE FOOD: ?
SPECIAL POWER: ?
PERSONALITY: ?

ALWAYS NEAR PIYOKO. THOUGHT
TO BE PIYOKO'S GUARDIAN AS
"GOOD GEMA" IS TO DIGIKO, BUT NO
ONE KNOWS FOR SURE.
SILENT.

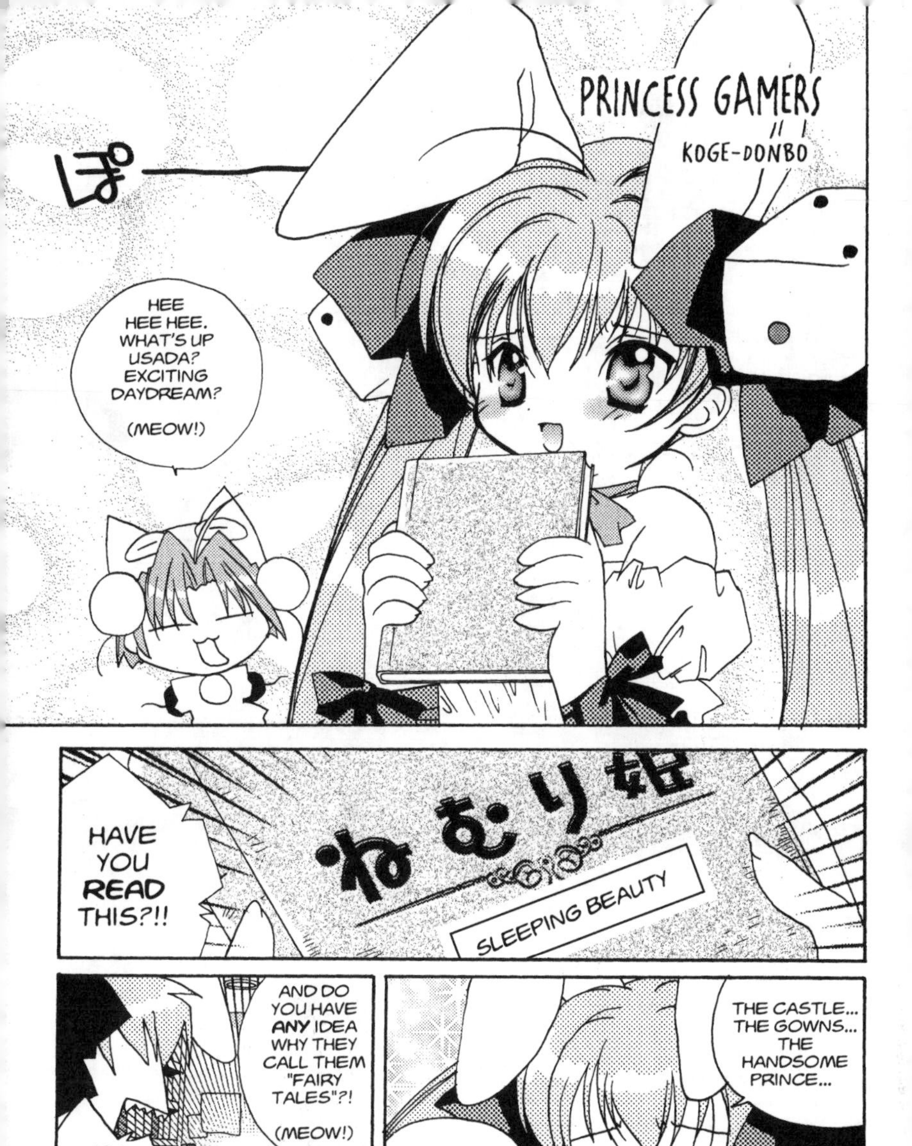
PRINCESS GAMERS
KOGE-DONBO
HEE HEE HEE. WHAT'S UP USADA? EXCITING DAYDREAM? (MEOW!)
ぽー
HAVE YOU **READ** THIS?!!
ねむり姫
SLEEPING BEAUTY
THE CASTLE... THE GOWNS... THE HANDSOME PRINCE...
PRIN-CESSES ARE **SO** COOL!!
AND DO YOU HAVE **ANY** IDEA WHY THEY CALL THEM "FAIRY TALES"?! (MEOW!)
YOU JUST DON'T HAVE A GIRLISH BONE IN YOUR BODY, DO YOU?!

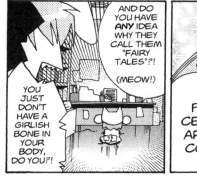

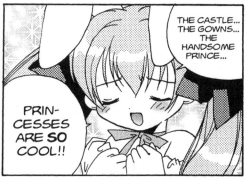

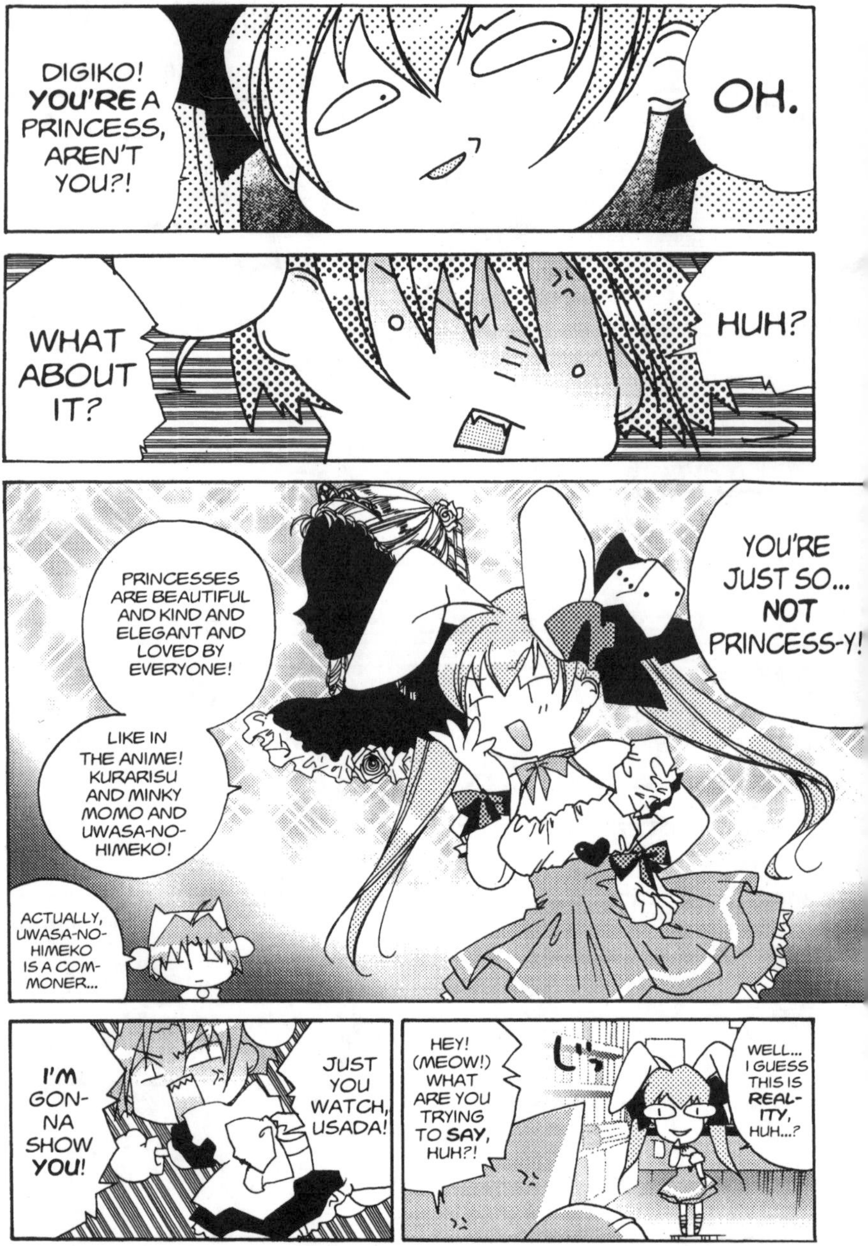
OH.
DIGIKO! YOU'RE A PRINCESS, AREN'T YOU?!
HUH?
WHAT ABOUT IT?
YOU'RE JUST SO... NOT PRINCESS-Y!
PRINCESSES ARE BEAUTIFUL AND KIND AND ELEGANT AND LOVED BY EVERYONE!
LIKE IN THE ANIME! KURARISU AND MINKY MOMO AND UWASA-NO-HIMEKO!
ACTUALLY, UWASA-NO-HIMEKO IS A COMMONER...
WELL... I GUESS THIS IS REALITY, HUH...?
HEY! (MEOW!) WHAT ARE YOU TRYING TO SAY, HUH?!
JUST YOU WATCH, USADA!
I'M GONNA SHOW YOU!

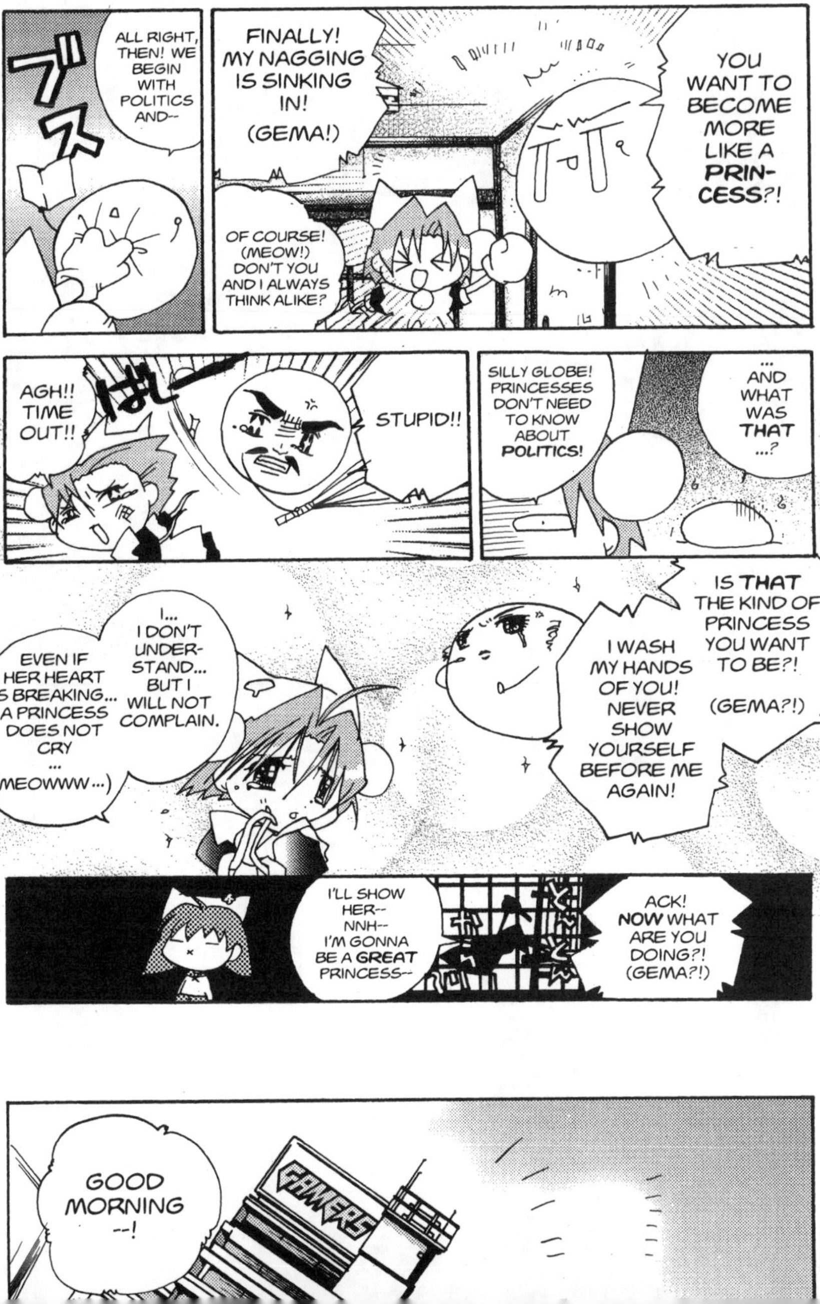
YOU WANT TO BECOME MORE LIKE A **PRINCESS?!**
FINALLY! MY NAGGING IS SINKING IN! (GEMA!)
OF COURSE! (MEOW!) DON'T YOU AND I ALWAYS THINK ALIKE?
ブス
ALL RIGHT, THEN! WE BEGIN WITH POLITICS AND--
... AND WHAT WAS **THAT** ...?
SILLY GLOBE! PRINCESSES DON'T NEED TO KNOW ABOUT **POLITICS!**
STUPID!!
ばし
AGH!! TIME OUT!!
IS **THAT** THE KIND OF PRINCESS YOU WANT TO BE?! (GEMA?!)
I WASH MY HANDS OF YOU! NEVER SHOW YOURSELF BEFORE ME AGAIN!
I... I DON'T UNDERSTAND... BUT I WILL NOT COMPLAIN.
EVEN IF HER HEART IS BREAKING... A PRINCESS DOES NOT CRY ... (MEOWWW...)
ACK! **NOW** WHAT ARE YOU DOING?! (GEMA?!)
I'LL SHOW HER-- NNH-- I'M GONNA BE A **GREAT** PRINCESS--
GOOD MORNING --!
GAMERS

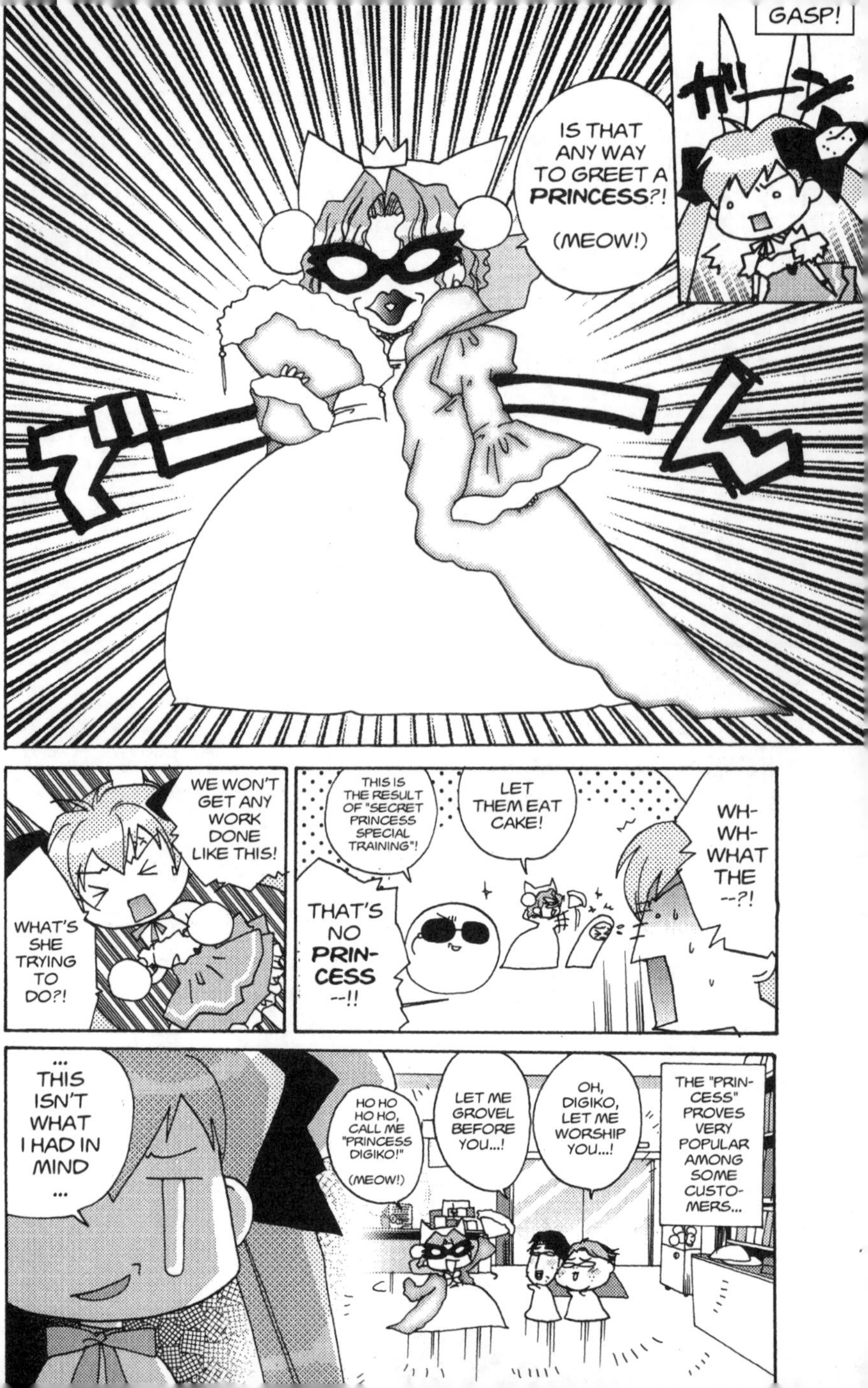
GASP!
IS THAT ANY WAY TO GREET A **PRINCESS**?! (MEOW!)
WH-WH-WHAT THE --?!
LET THEM EAT CAKE!
THIS IS THE RESULT OF "SECRET PRINCESS SPECIAL TRAINING"!
THAT'S NO **PRIN-CESS** --!!
WE WON'T GET ANY WORK DONE LIKE THIS!
WHAT'S SHE TRYING TO DO?!
THE "PRIN-CESS" PROVES VERY POPULAR AMONG SOME CUSTO-MERS...
OH, DIGIKO, LET ME WORSHIP YOU...!
LET ME GROVEL BEFORE YOU...!
HO HO HO HO, CALL ME "PRINCESS DIGIKO!"
(MEOW!)
... THIS ISN'T WHAT I HAD IN MIND ...

END

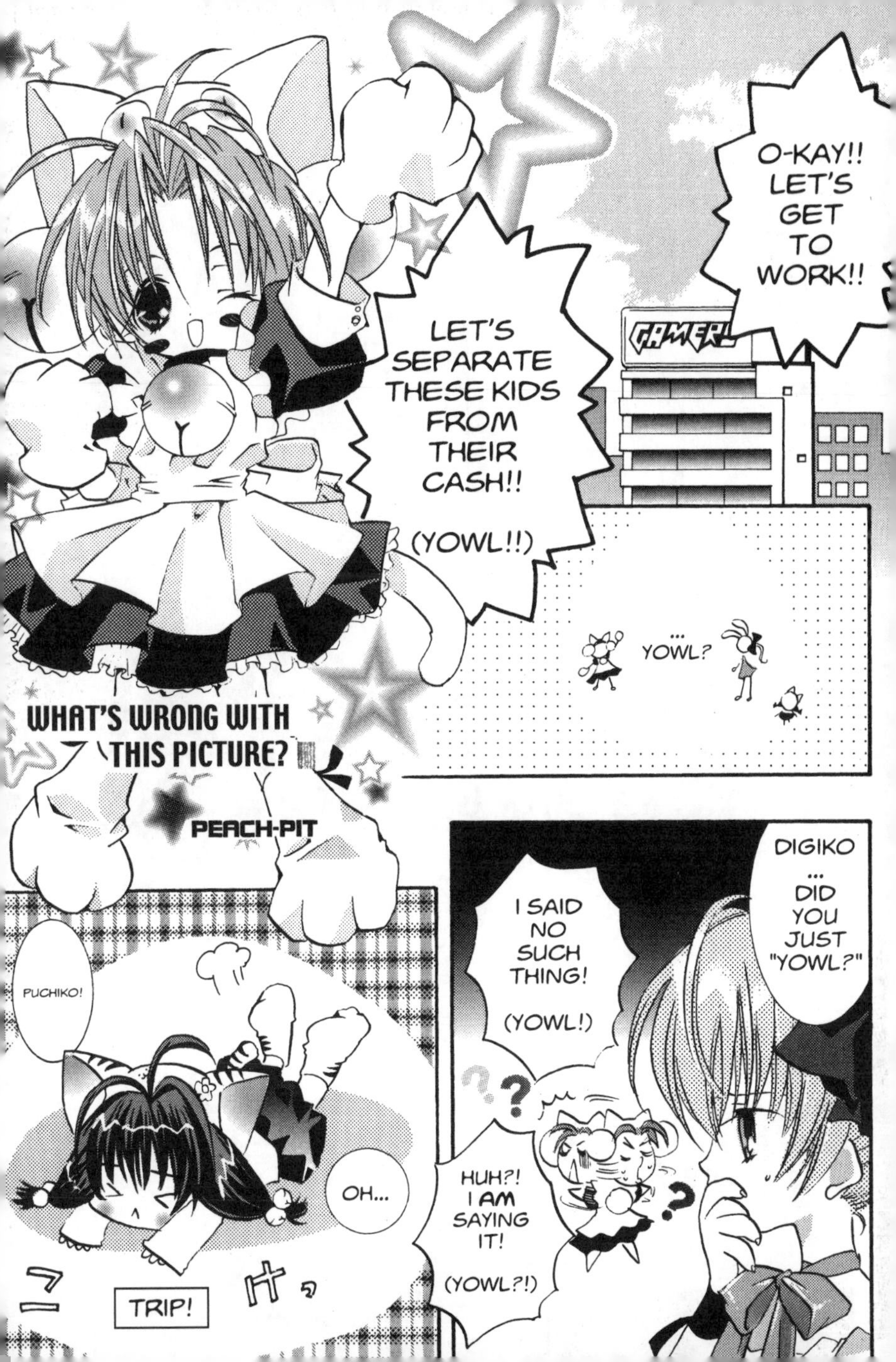
O-KAY!! LET'S GET TO WORK!!
LET'S SEPARATE THESE KIDS FROM THEIR CASH!! (YOWL!!)
WHAT'S WRONG WITH THIS PICTURE?
PEACH-PIT
... YOWL?
DIGIKO ... DID YOU JUST "YOWL?"
I SAID NO SUCH THING! (YOWL!)
HUH?! I AM SAYING IT! (YOWL?!)
PUCHIKO!
OH...
TRIP!

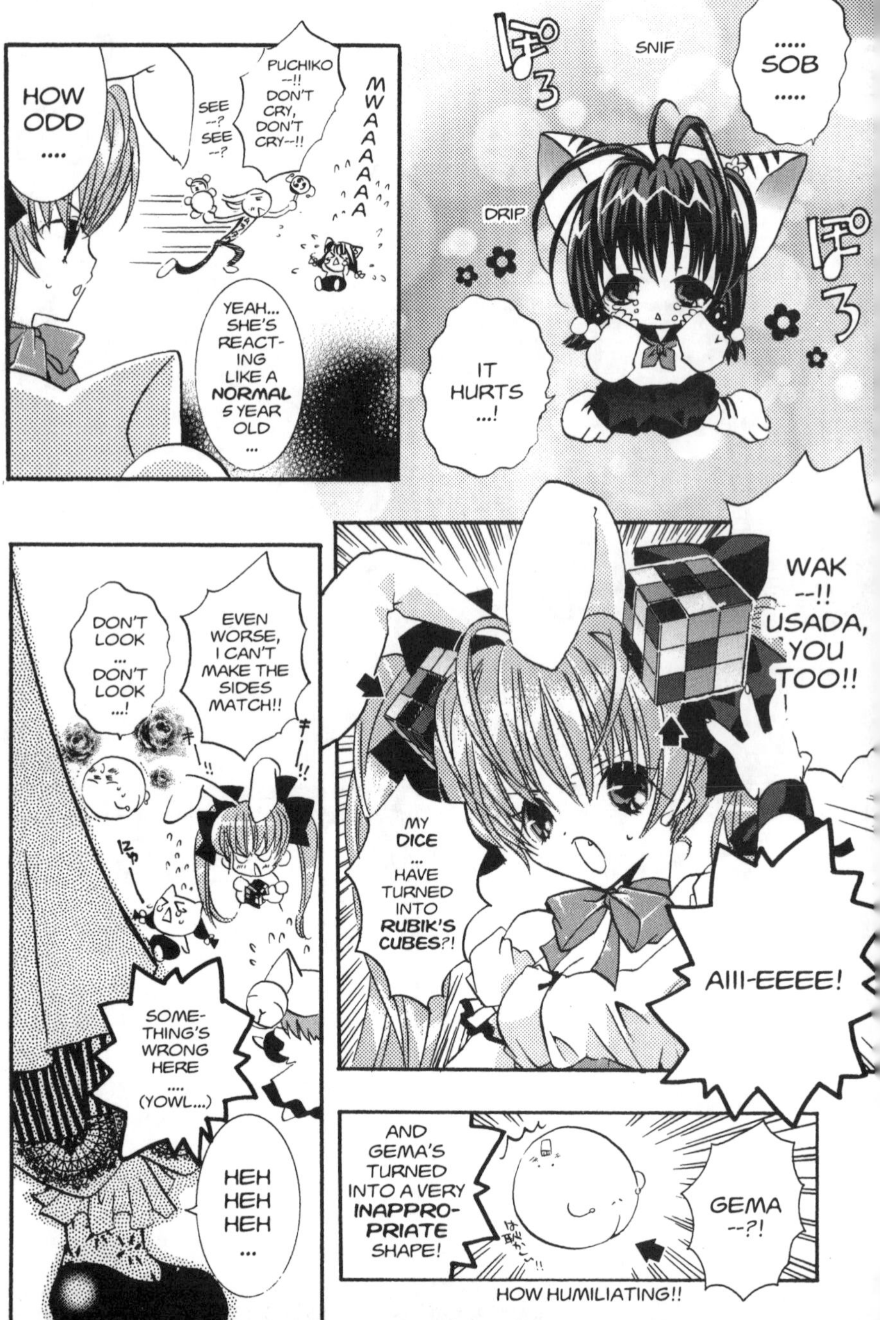
.....
SOB
.....
SNIF
ぽろ
ぽろ
DRIP
IT HURTS ...!
MWAAAAAAAA
PUCHIKO --!! DON'T CRY, DON'T CRY--!!
SEE --? SEE --?
HOW ODD ....
YEAH... SHE'S REACTING LIKE A NORMAL 5 YEAR OLD ...
WAK --!! USADA, YOU TOO!!
MY DICE ... HAVE TURNED INTO RUBIK'S CUBES?!
AIII-EEEE!
GEMA --?!
AND GEMA'S TURNED INTO A VERY INAPPROPRIATE SHAPE!
HOW HUMILIATING!!
EVEN WORSE, I CAN'T MAKE THE SIDES MATCH!!
DON'T LOOK ... DON'T LOOK ...!
SOMETHING'S WRONG HERE .... (YOWL...)
HEH HEH HEH ...

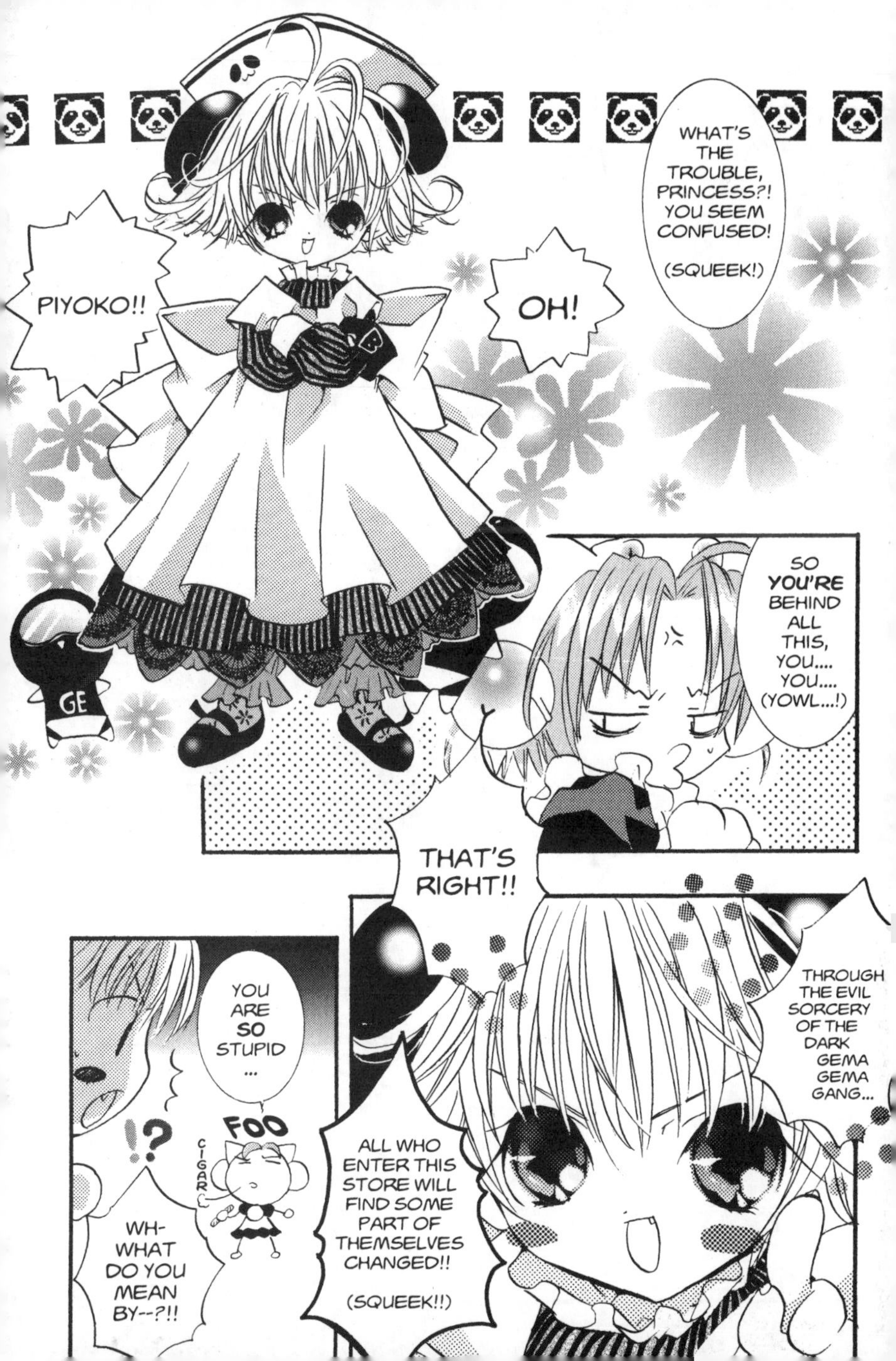
WHAT'S THE TROUBLE, PRINCESS?! YOU SEEM CONFUSED!
(SQUEEK!)
OH!
PIYOKO!!
GE
SO YOU'RE BEHIND ALL THIS, YOU.... YOU.... (YOWL...!)
THAT'S RIGHT!!
THROUGH THE EVIL SORCERY OF THE DARK GEMA GEMA GANG...
ALL WHO ENTER THIS STORE WILL FIND SOME PART OF THEMSELVES CHANGED!!
(SQUEEK!!)
YOU ARE SO STUPID ...
FOO
CIGAR
!?
WH-WHAT DO YOU MEAN BY--?!!

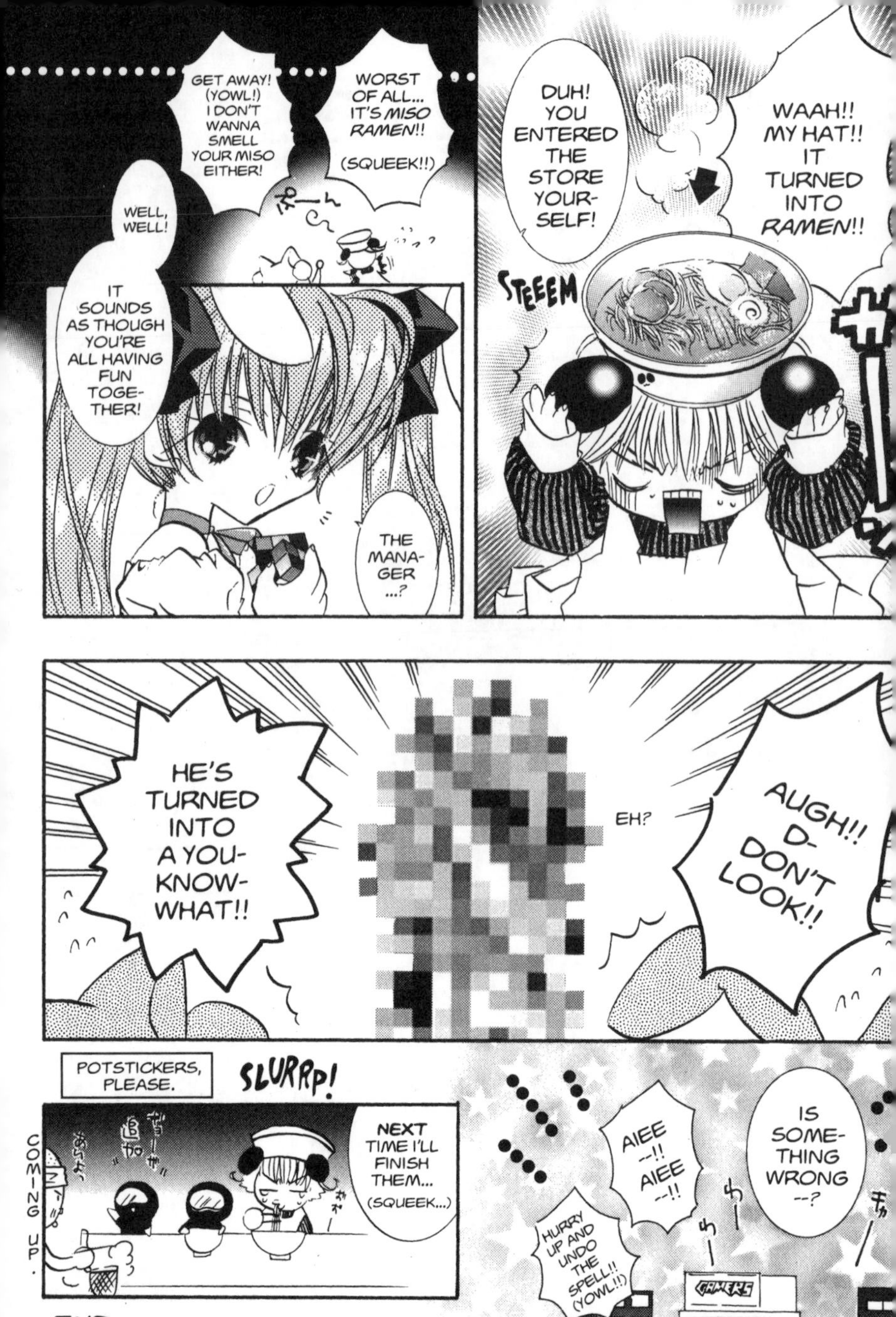
WAAH!! MY HAT!! IT TURNED INTO RAMEN!!
DUH! YOU ENTERED THE STORE YOURSELF!
STEEEM
WORST OF ALL... IT'S *MISO RAMEN*!! (SQUEEK!!)
GET AWAY! (YOWL!) I DON'T WANNA SMELL YOUR MISO EITHER!
WELL, WELL!
IT SOUNDS AS THOUGH YOU'RE ALL HAVING FUN TOGETHER!
THE MANAGER ...?
AUGH!! D-DON'T LOOK!!
EH?
HE'S TURNED INTO A YOU-KNOW-WHAT!!
IS SOMETHING WRONG--?
AIEE--!! AIEE--!!
HURRY UP AND UNDO THE SPELL!! (YOWL!!)
GAMERS
POTSTICKERS, PLEASE.
SLURRP!
NEXT TIME I'LL FINISH THEM... (SQUEEK...)
COMING UP.

END

WHAT WOULD YOU LIKE TO SEE HAPPEN AT GAMERS?

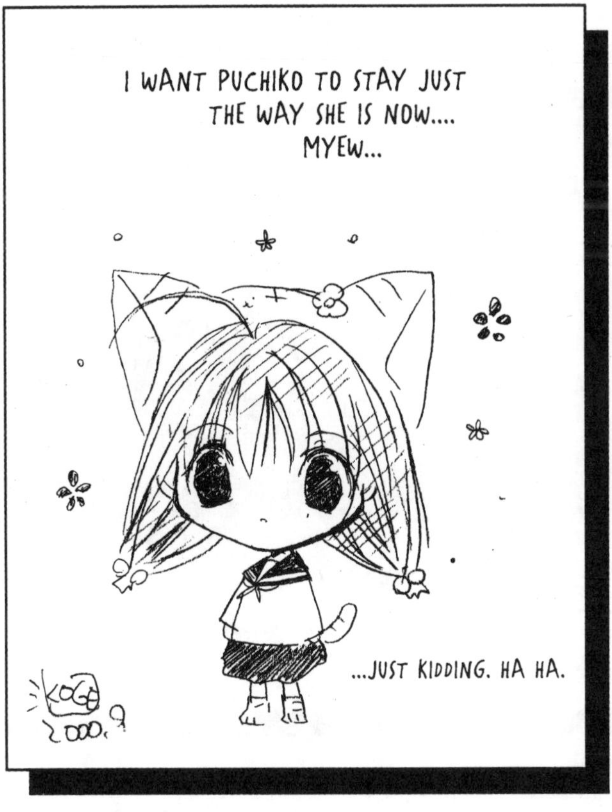
I WANT PUCHIKO TO STAY JUST THE WAY SHE IS NOW.... MYEW...
...JUST KIDDING. HA HA.
KOGE 2000.9

KOGE-DONBO

WHAT WOULD YOU LIKE TO SEE HAPPEN AT GAMERS?

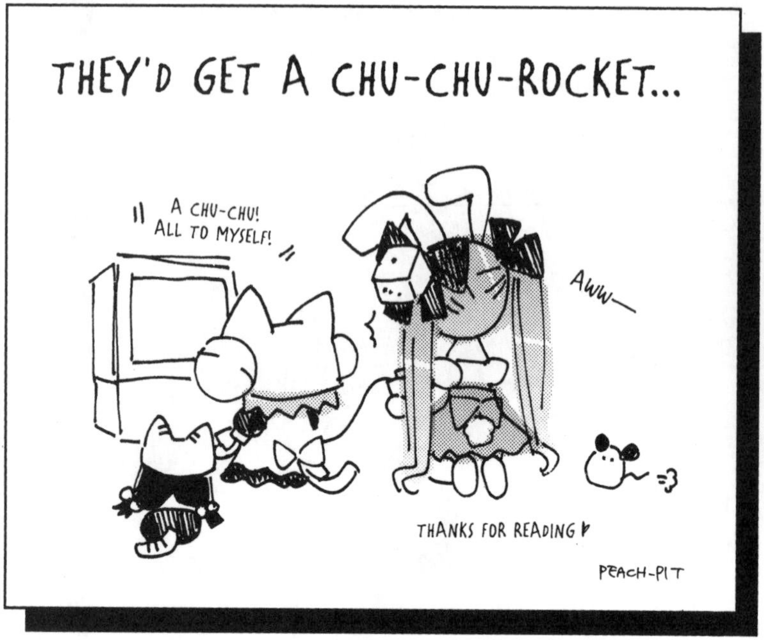
THEY'D GET A CHU-CHU-ROCKET...
A CHU-CHU! ALL TO MYSELF!
AWW—
THANKS FOR READING
PEACH-PIT

PEACH-PIT

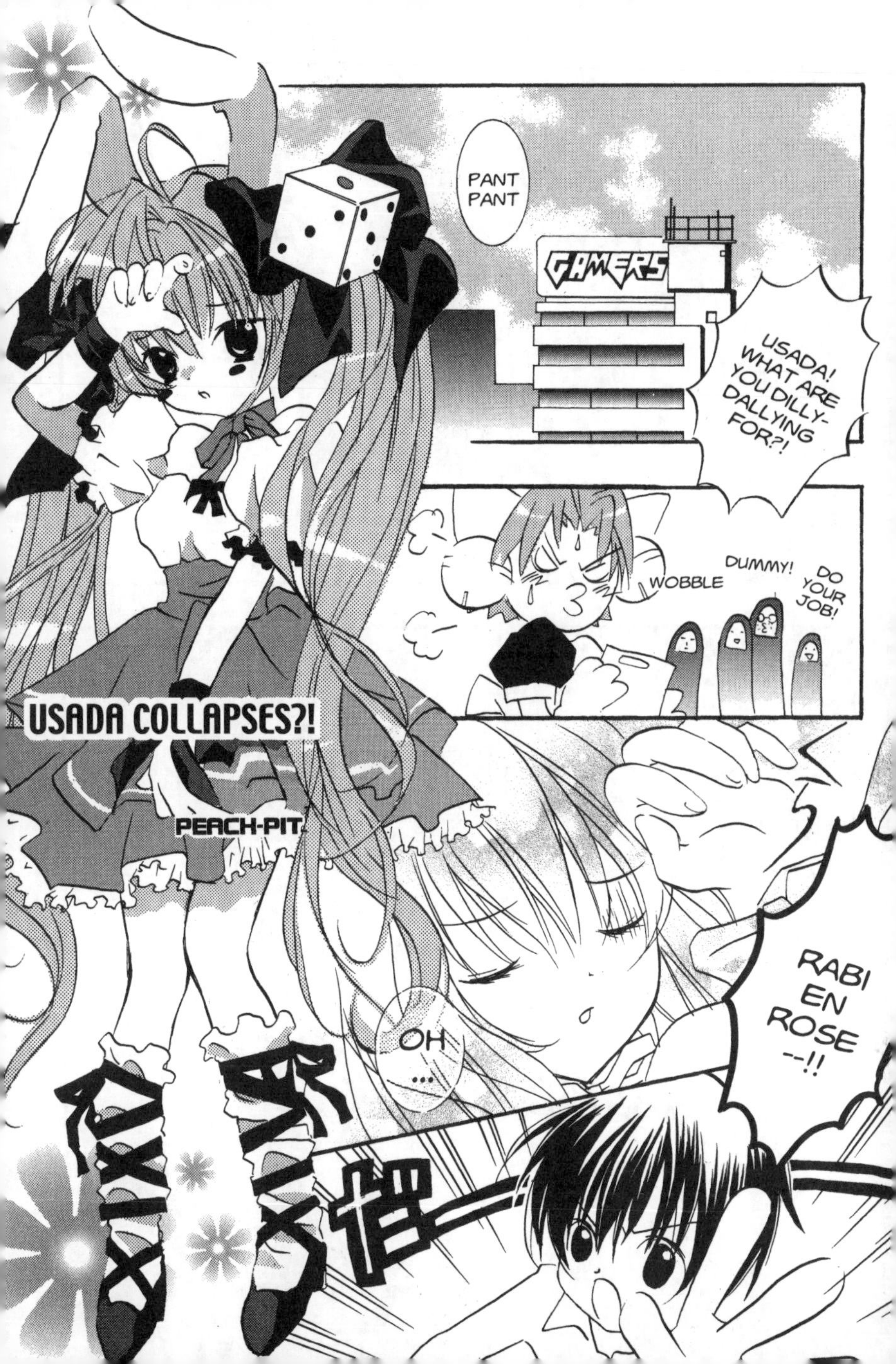
PANT PANT
GAMERS
USADA! WHAT ARE YOU DILLY-DALLYING FOR?!
DO YOUR JOB!
DUMMY!
WOBBLE
RABI EN ROSE--!!
OH...
USADA COLLAPSES?!
PEACH-PIT

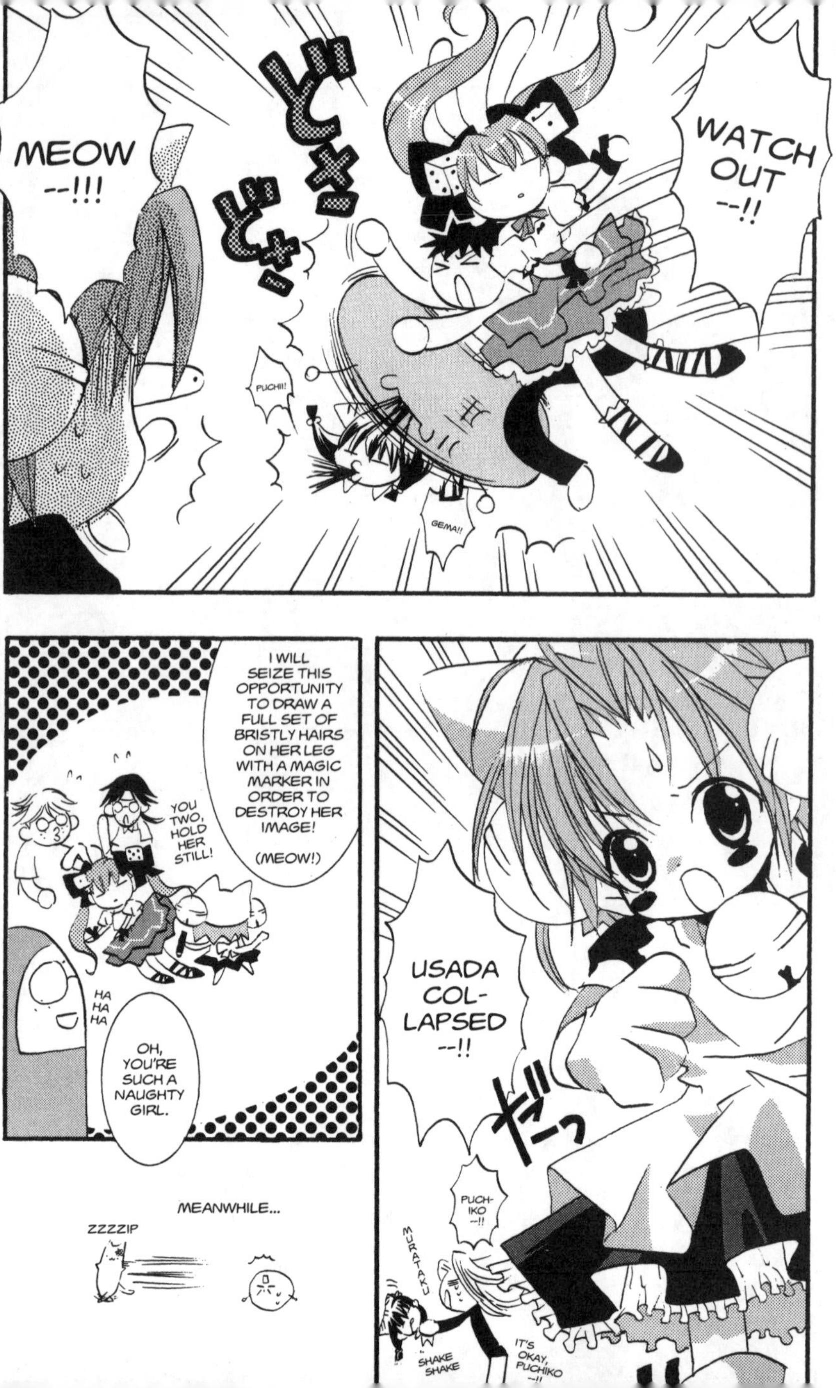
WATCH OUT --!!
PUCHII!
GEMA!!
MEOW --!!!
USADA COL-LAPSED --!!
PUCHIKO --!!
MURATAKU
IT'S OKAY, PUCHIKO --!!
SHAKE SHAKE
I WILL SEIZE THIS OPPORTUNITY TO DRAW A FULL SET OF BRISTLY HAIRS ON HER LEG WITH A MAGIC MARKER IN ORDER TO DESTROY HER IMAGE!
(MEOW!)
YOU TWO, HOLD HER STILL!
HA HA HA
OH, YOU'RE SUCH A NAUGHTY GIRL.
MEANWHILE...
ZZZZIP

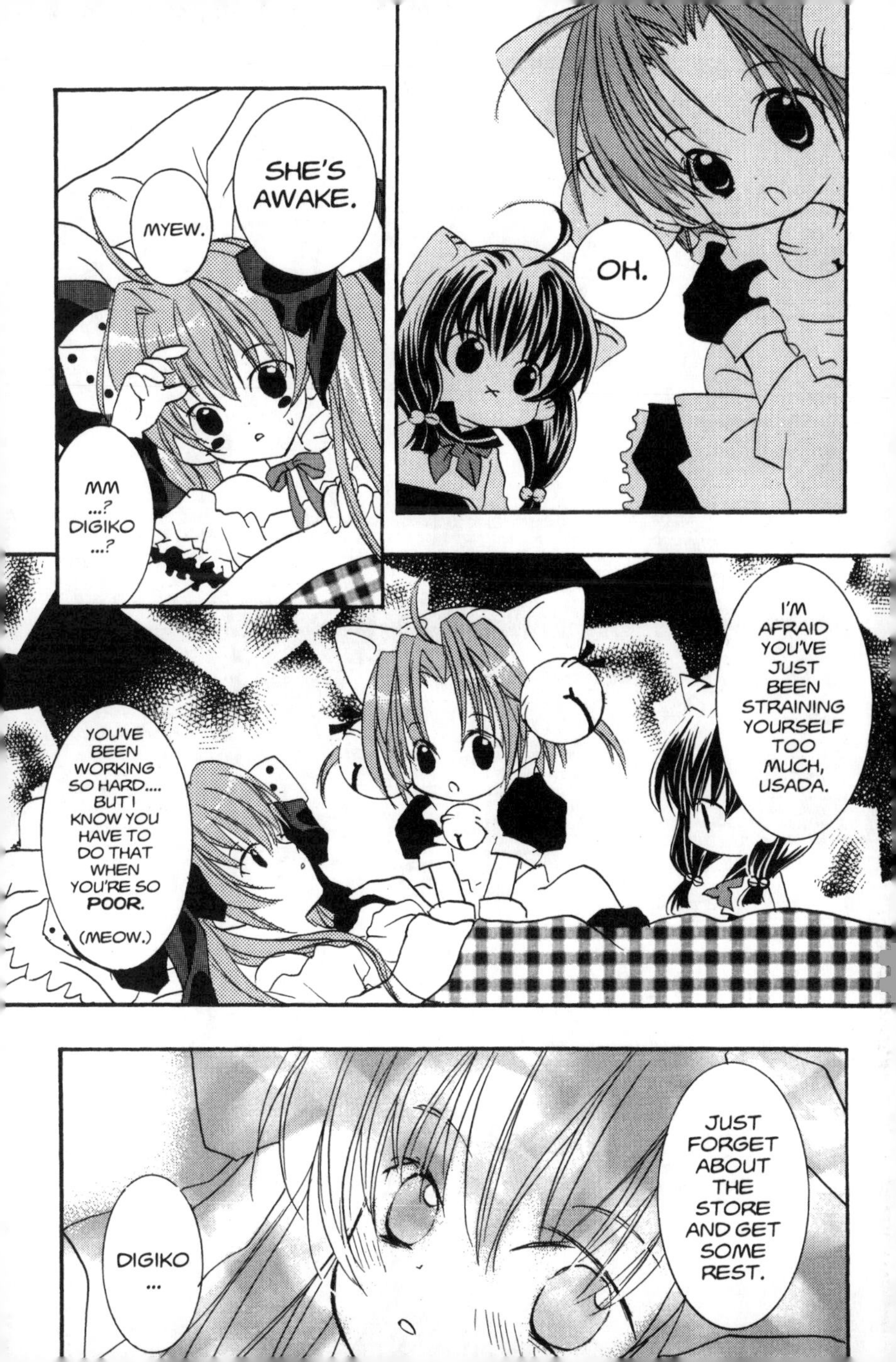
OH.
SHE'S AWAKE.
MYEW.
MM ...? DIGIKO ...?
I'M AFRAID YOU'VE JUST BEEN STRAINING YOURSELF TOO MUCH, USADA.
YOU'VE BEEN WORKING SO HARD.... BUT I KNOW YOU HAVE TO DO THAT WHEN YOU'RE SO **POOR**.
(MEOW.)
JUST FORGET ABOUT THE STORE AND GET SOME REST.
DIGIKO ...

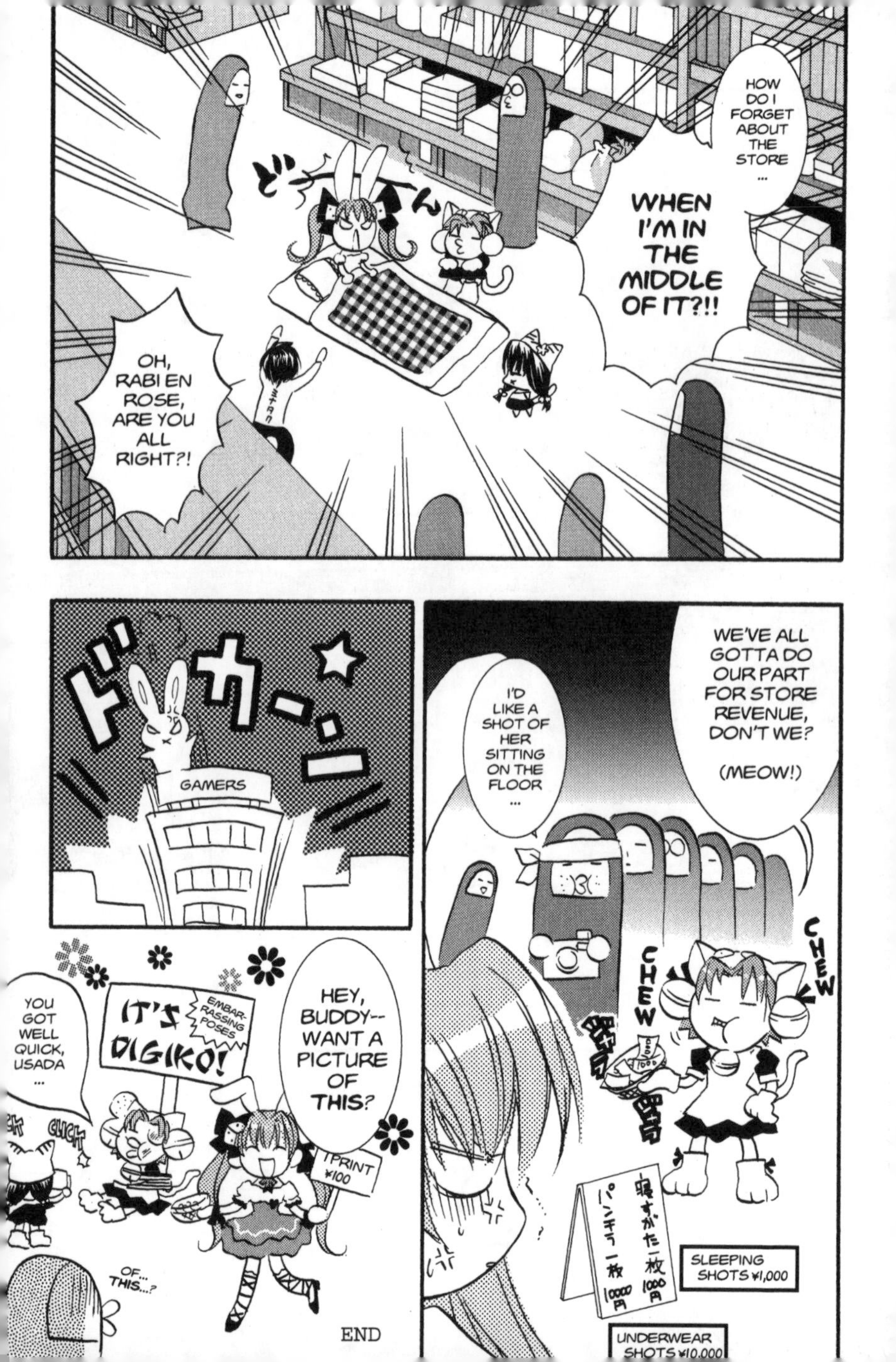
HOW DO I FORGET ABOUT THE STORE ...
WHEN I'M IN THE MIDDLE OF IT?!!
どてーん
OH, RABI EN ROSE, ARE YOU ALL RIGHT?!
WE'VE ALL GOTTA DO OUR PART FOR STORE REVENUE, DON'T WE?
(MEOW!)
I'D LIKE A SHOT OF HER SITTING ON THE FLOOR ...
CHEW
CHEW
寝すがた 一枚 1000円
パンチラ 一枚 10000円
SLEEPING SHOTS ¥1,000
UNDERWEAR SHOTS ¥10,000
ドカーン
GAMERS
HEY, BUDDY-- WANT A PICTURE OF THIS?
IT'S DIGIKO!
EMBARRASSING POSES
1PRINT ¥100
YOU GOT WELL QUICK, USADA ...
CLICK
OF... THIS...?

END

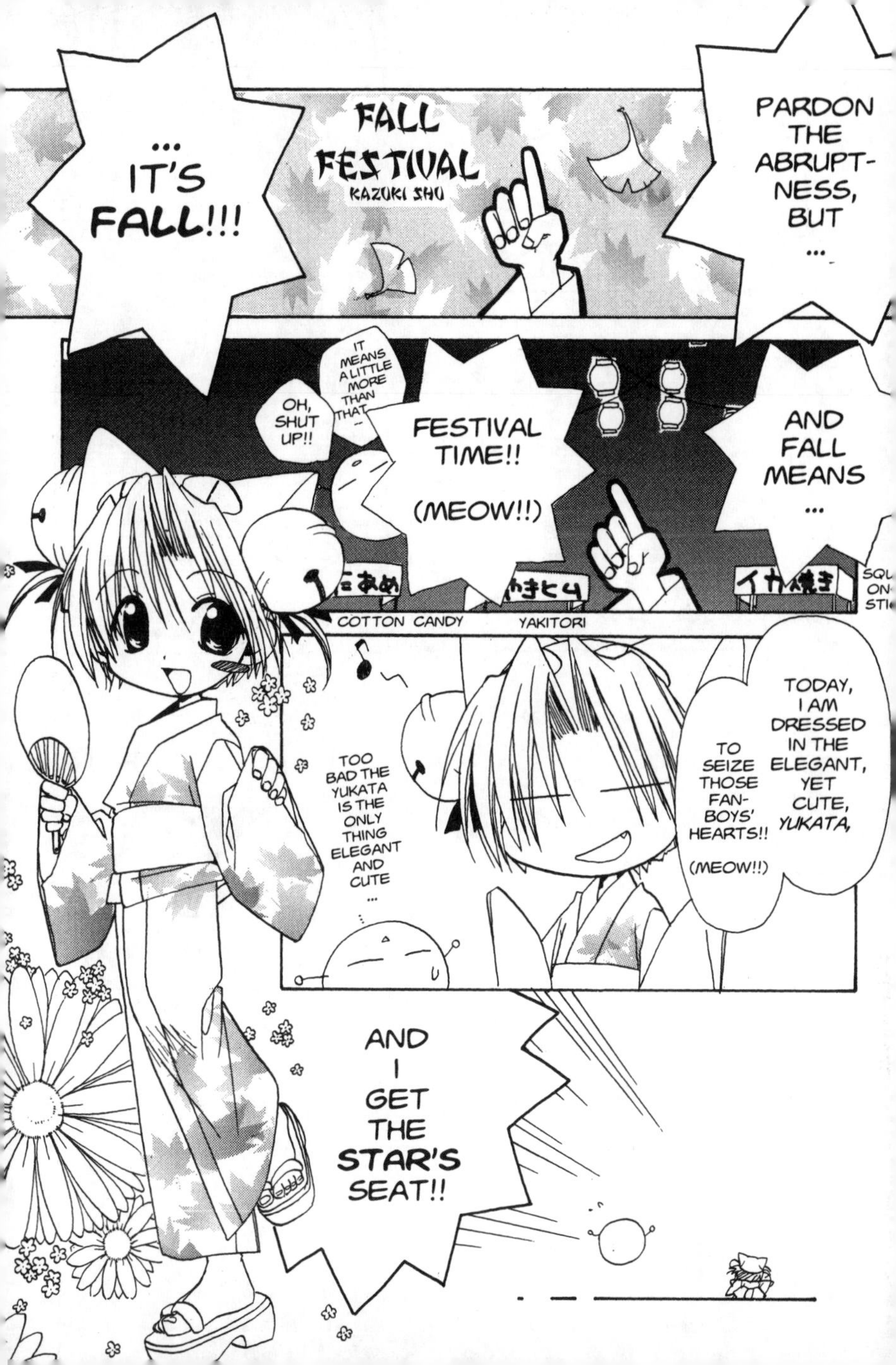
FALL FESTIVAL
KAZUKI SHU
PARDON THE ABRUPTNESS, BUT ...
... IT'S **FALL**!!!
AND FALL MEANS ...
FESTIVAL TIME!! (MEOW!!)
IT MEANS A LITTLE MORE THAN THAT --
OH, SHUT UP!!
イカ焼き
SQU ON- STI
やきとり
YAKITORI
COTTON CANDY
TODAY, I AM DRESSED IN THE ELEGANT, YET CUTE, *YUKATA,*
TO SEIZE THOSE FAN-BOYS' HEARTS!!
(MEOW!!)
TOO BAD THE YUKATA IS THE ONLY THING ELEGANT AND CUTE ...
AND I GET THE **STAR'S** SEAT!!

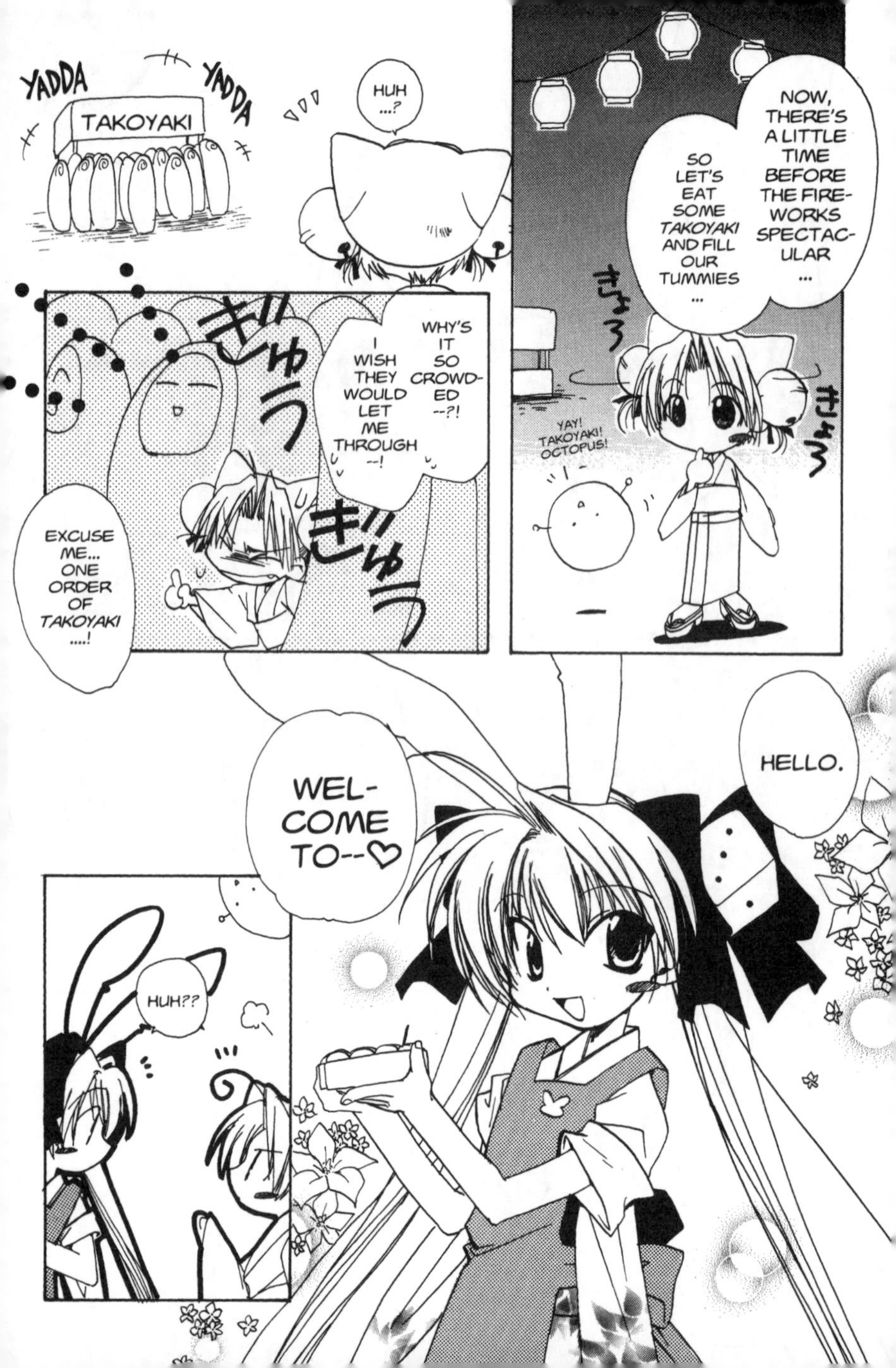
NOW, THERE'S A LITTLE TIME BEFORE THE FIRE-WORKS SPECTACULAR...
SO LET'S EAT SOME *TAKOYAKI* AND FILL OUR TUMMIES...
きょろ
きょろ
YAY! TAKOYAKI! OCTOPUS!
HUH...?
YADDA
YADDA
TAKOYAKI
WHY'S IT SO CROWDED--?!
I WISH THEY WOULD LET ME THROUGH--!
ぎゅう
ぎゅう
EXCUSE ME... ONE ORDER OF *TAKOYAKI*....!
HELLO.
WEL-COME TO--♡
HUH??

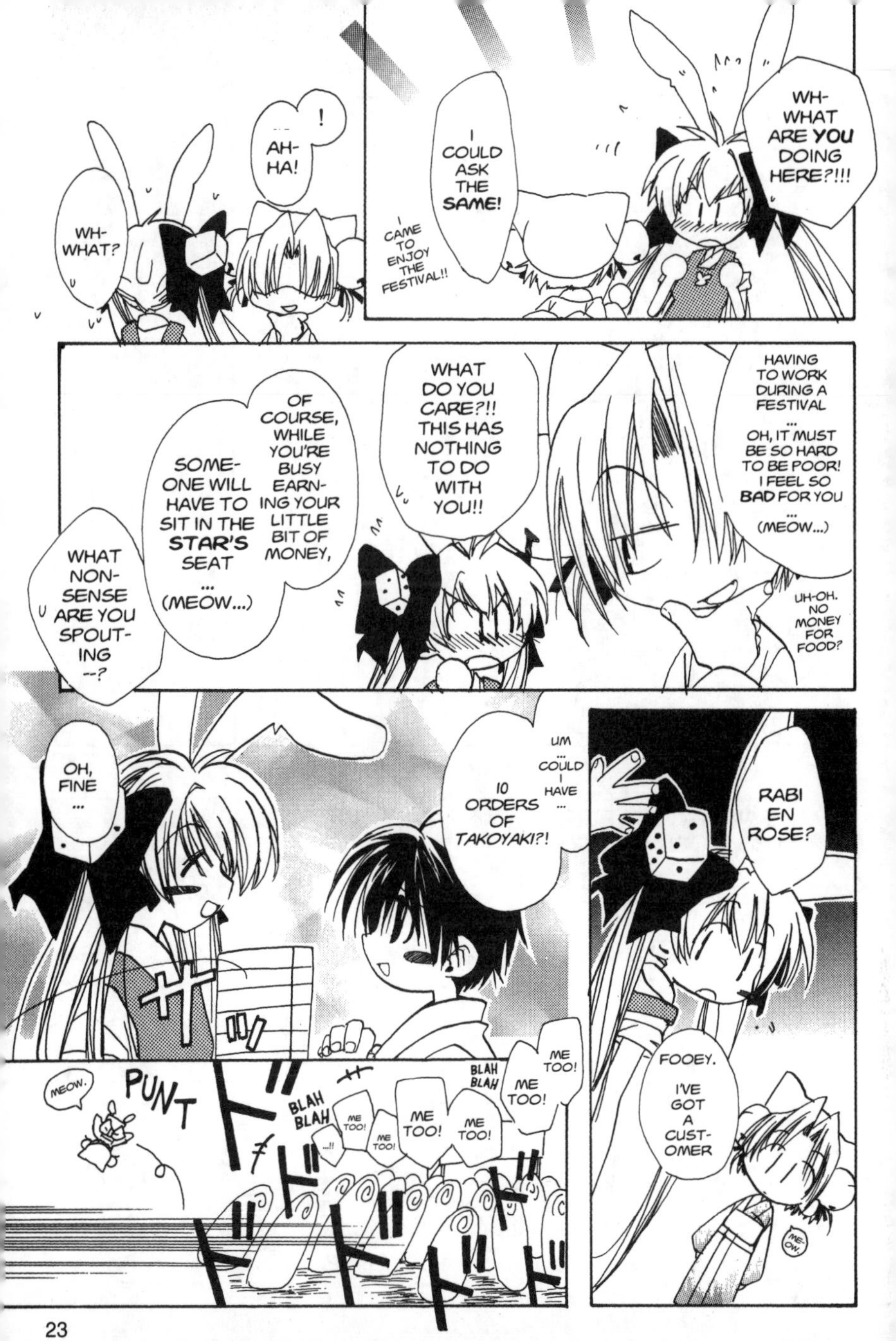
WH- WHAT ARE YOU DOING HERE?!!!
I COULD ASK THE SAME!
I CAME TO ENJOY THE FESTIVAL!!
!
AH- HA!
WH- WHAT?
HAVING TO WORK DURING A FESTIVAL ... OH, IT MUST BE SO HARD TO BE POOR! I FEEL SO BAD FOR YOU ... (MEOW...)
UH-OH. NO MONEY FOR FOOD?
WHAT DO YOU CARE?!! THIS HAS NOTHING TO DO WITH YOU!!
OF COURSE, WHILE YOU'RE BUSY EARN- ING YOUR LITTLE BIT OF MONEY,
SOME- ONE WILL HAVE TO SIT IN THE STAR'S SEAT ... (MEOW...)
WHAT NON- SENSE ARE YOU SPOUT- ING --?
RABI EN ROSE?
UM ... COULD I HAVE ...
10 ORDERS OF TAKOYAKI?!
OH, FINE ...
FOOEY. I'VE GOT A CUST- OMER
MEOW.
ME TOO!
BLAH BLAH
ME TOO!
ME TOO!
ME TOO!
ME TOO!
ME TOO!
...!!
BLAH BLAH
PUNT
MEOW.

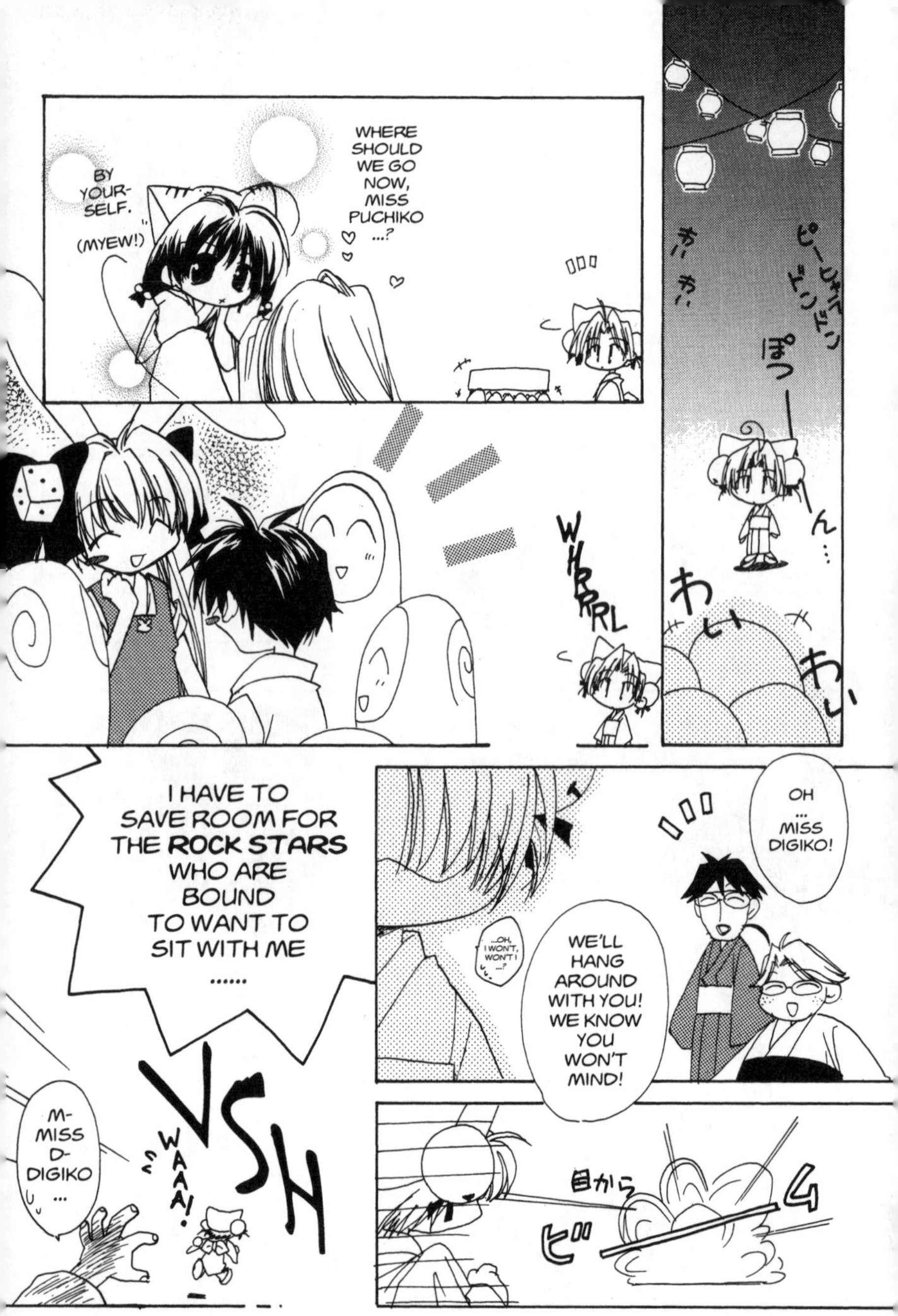

ピーヒャラ ドンドン
わいわい
ぽつーん…
わい わい
WHERE SHOULD WE GO NOW, MISS PUCHIKO ...?
BY YOURSELF.
(MYEW!)
WHRRRL
OH ... MISS DIGIKO!
WE'LL HANG AROUND WITH YOU! WE KNOW YOU WON'T MIND!
...OH, I WON'T, WON'T I ...?
I HAVE TO SAVE ROOM FOR THE **ROCK STARS** WHO ARE BOUND TO WANT TO SIT WITH ME ....
目から
ビーム
VSH
WAAA!
M-MISS D-DIGIKO ...

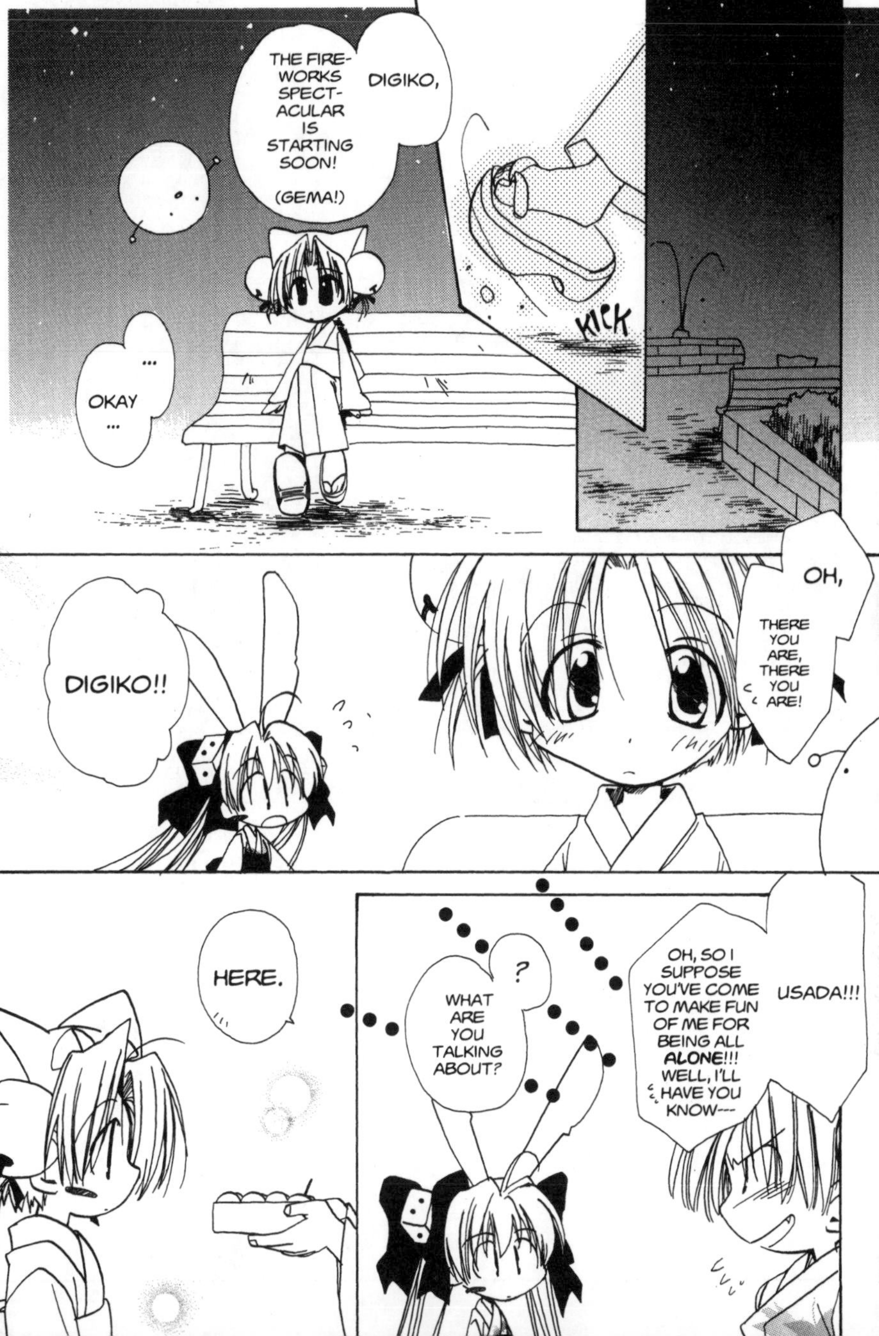
KICK
DIGIKO,
THE FIRE-WORKS SPECT-ACULAR IS STARTING SOON!
(GEMA!)
... OKAY ...
OH,
THERE YOU ARE, THERE YOU ARE!
DIGIKO!!
USADA!!!
OH, SO I SUPPOSE YOU'VE COME TO MAKE FUN OF ME FOR BEING ALL **ALONE**!!! WELL, I'LL HAVE YOU KNOW---
?
WHAT ARE YOU TALKING ABOUT?
HERE.

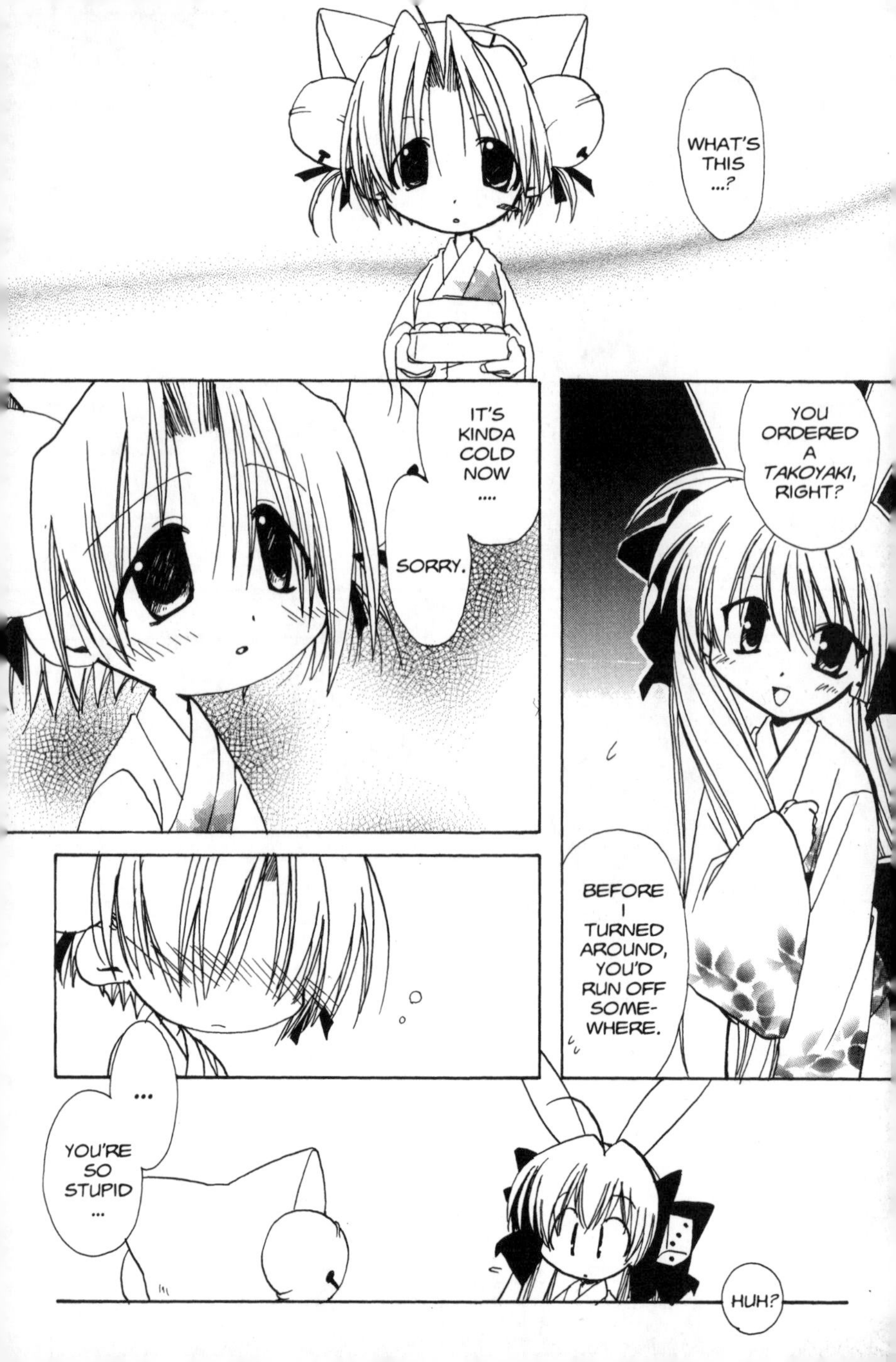
WHAT'S THIS ...?
YOU ORDERED A TAKOYAKI, RIGHT?
BEFORE I TURNED AROUND, YOU'D RUN OFF SOME-WHERE.
IT'S KINDA COLD NOW ....
SORRY.
... YOU'RE SO STUPID ...
HUH?

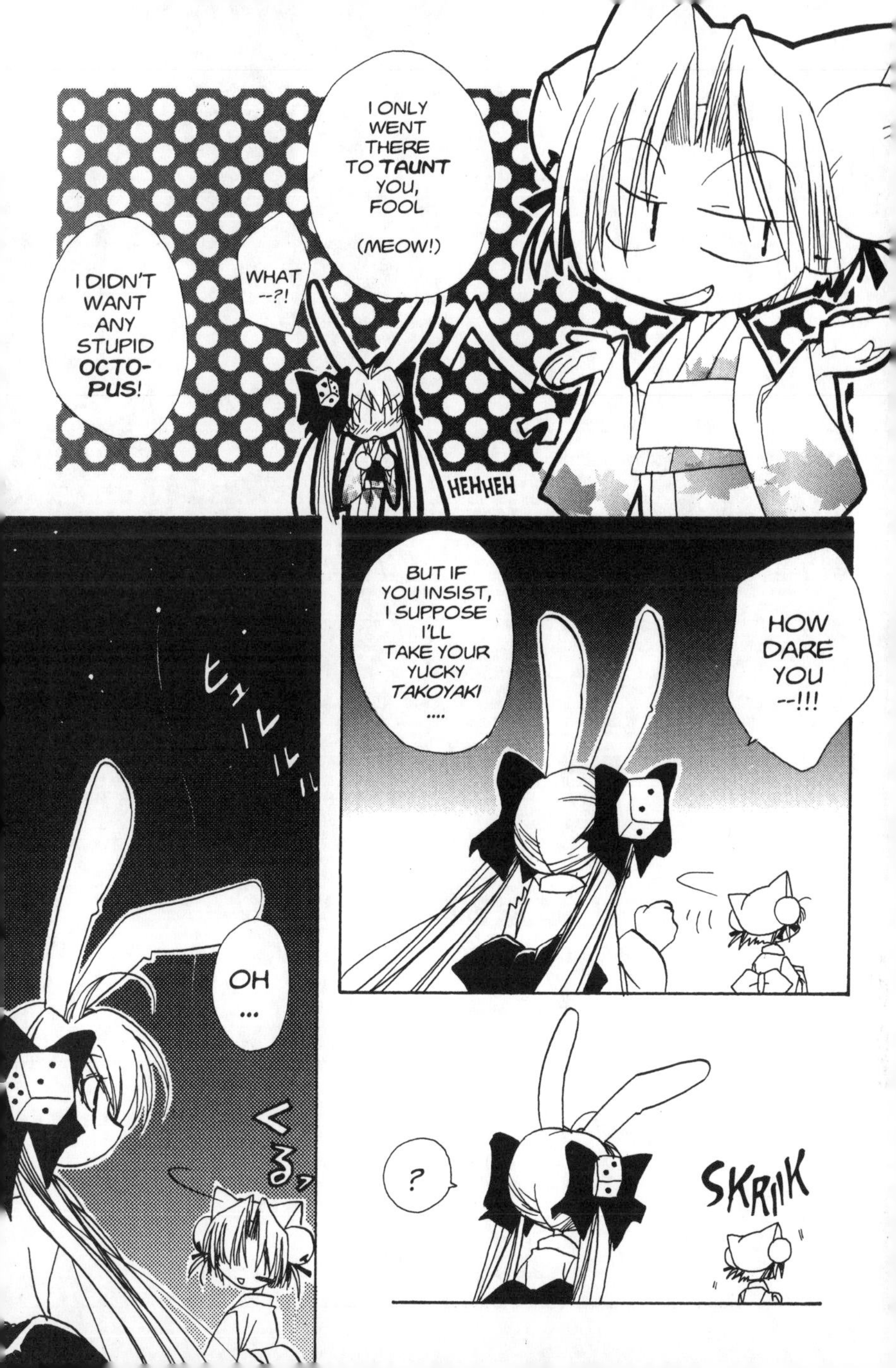
I ONLY WENT THERE TO **TAUNT** YOU, FOOL
(MEOW!)
WHAT --?!
I DIDN'T WANT ANY STUPID **OCTOPUS!**
HEHHEH
BUT IF YOU INSIST, I SUPPOSE I'LL TAKE YOUR YUCKY *TAKOYAKI* ....
HOW DARE YOU --!!!
?
SKRIIK
ヒュルルル
OH ...
くるっ

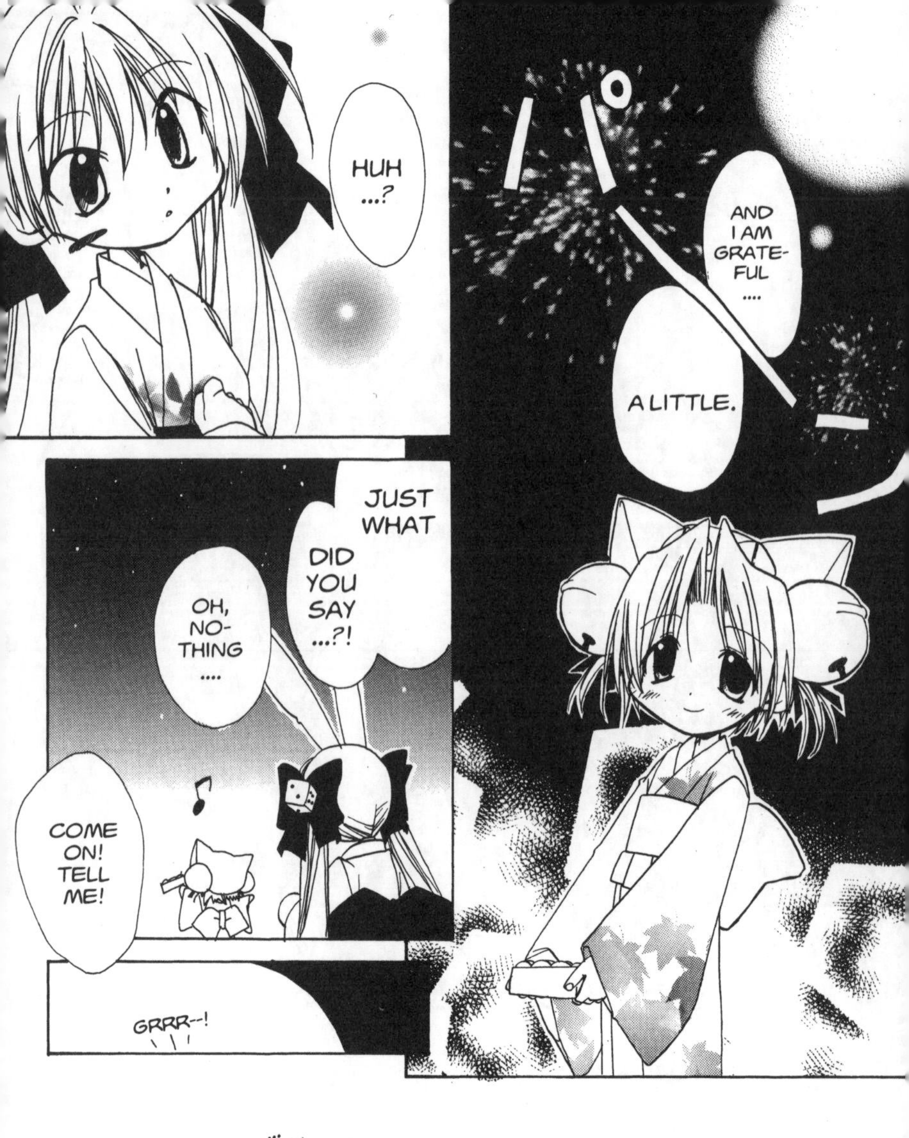
AND I AM GRATEFUL ....
A LITTLE.
HUH ...?
JUST WHAT DID YOU SAY ...?!
OH, NOTHING ....
COME ON! TELL ME!
GRRR--!
EWW. YOUR TAKOYAKI'S ALL **COLD**.
... FUNNY THAT YOU KEEP EATING IT...

END

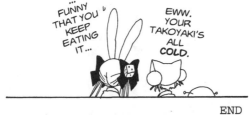

WHAT WOULD YOU LIKE TO SEE HAPPEN AT GAMERS?

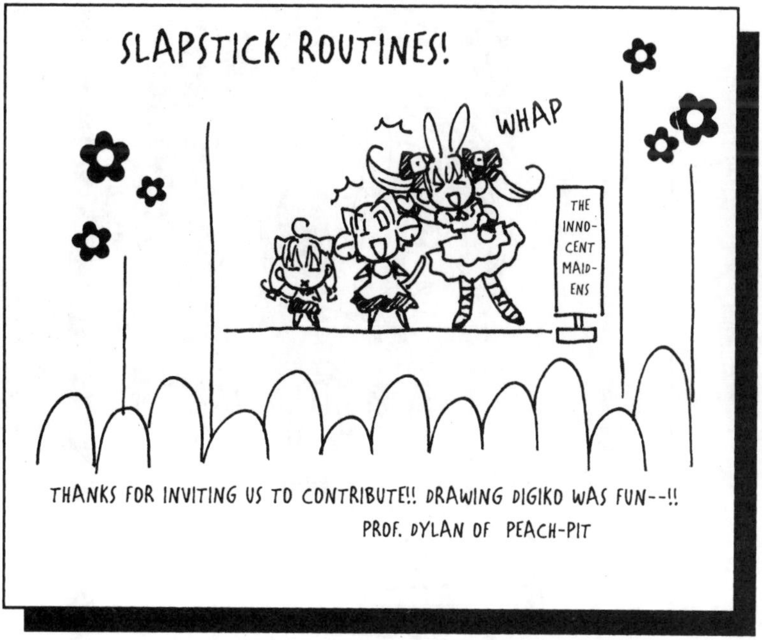
SLAPSTICK ROUTINES!
WHAP
THE INNO-CENT MAID-ENS
THANKS FOR INVITING US TO CONTRIBUTE!! DRAWING DIGIKO WAS FUN--!!
PROF. DYLAN OF PEACH-PIT

PEACH-PIT

WHAT WOULD YOU LIKE TO SEE HAPPEN AT GAMERS?

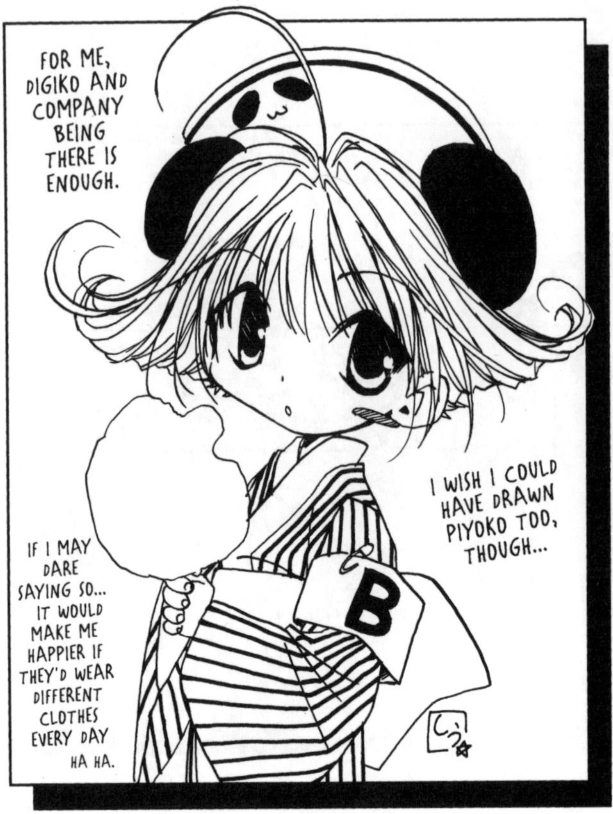
FOR ME, DIGIKO AND COMPANY BEING THERE IS ENOUGH.
I WISH I COULD HAVE DRAWN PIYOKO TOO, THOUGH...
IF I MAY DARE SAYING SO... IT WOULD MAKE ME HAPPIER IF THEY'D WEAR DIFFERENT CLOTHES EVERY DAY HA HA.
B

KAZUKI ☆ SHU

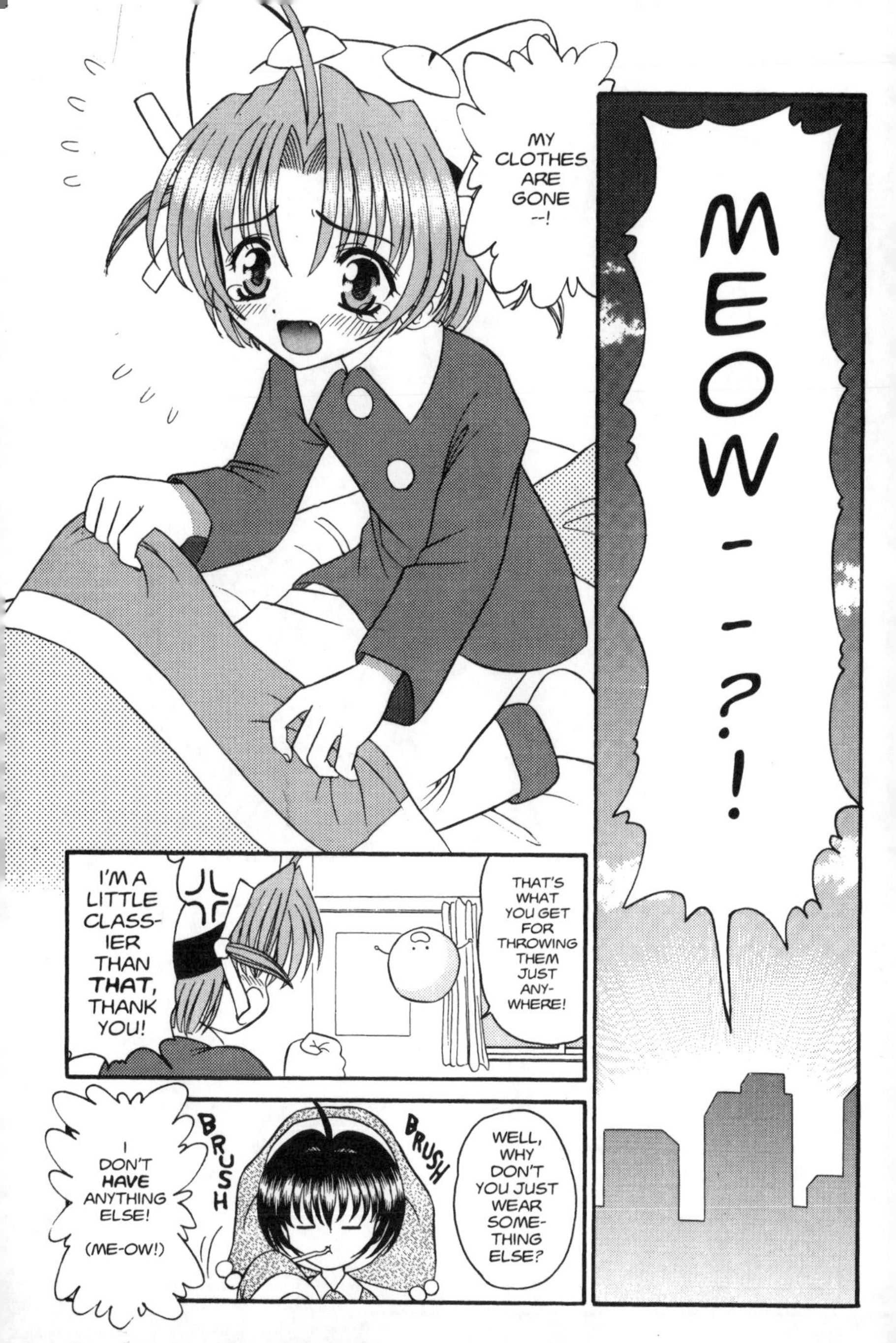
MEOW--?!
MY CLOTHES ARE GONE --!
THAT'S WHAT YOU GET FOR THROWING THEM JUST ANYWHERE!
I'M A LITTLE CLASSIER THAN THAT, THANK YOU!
WELL, WHY DON'T YOU JUST WEAR SOMETHING ELSE?
BRUSH
BRUSH
I DON'T HAVE ANYTHING ELSE!
(ME-OW!)

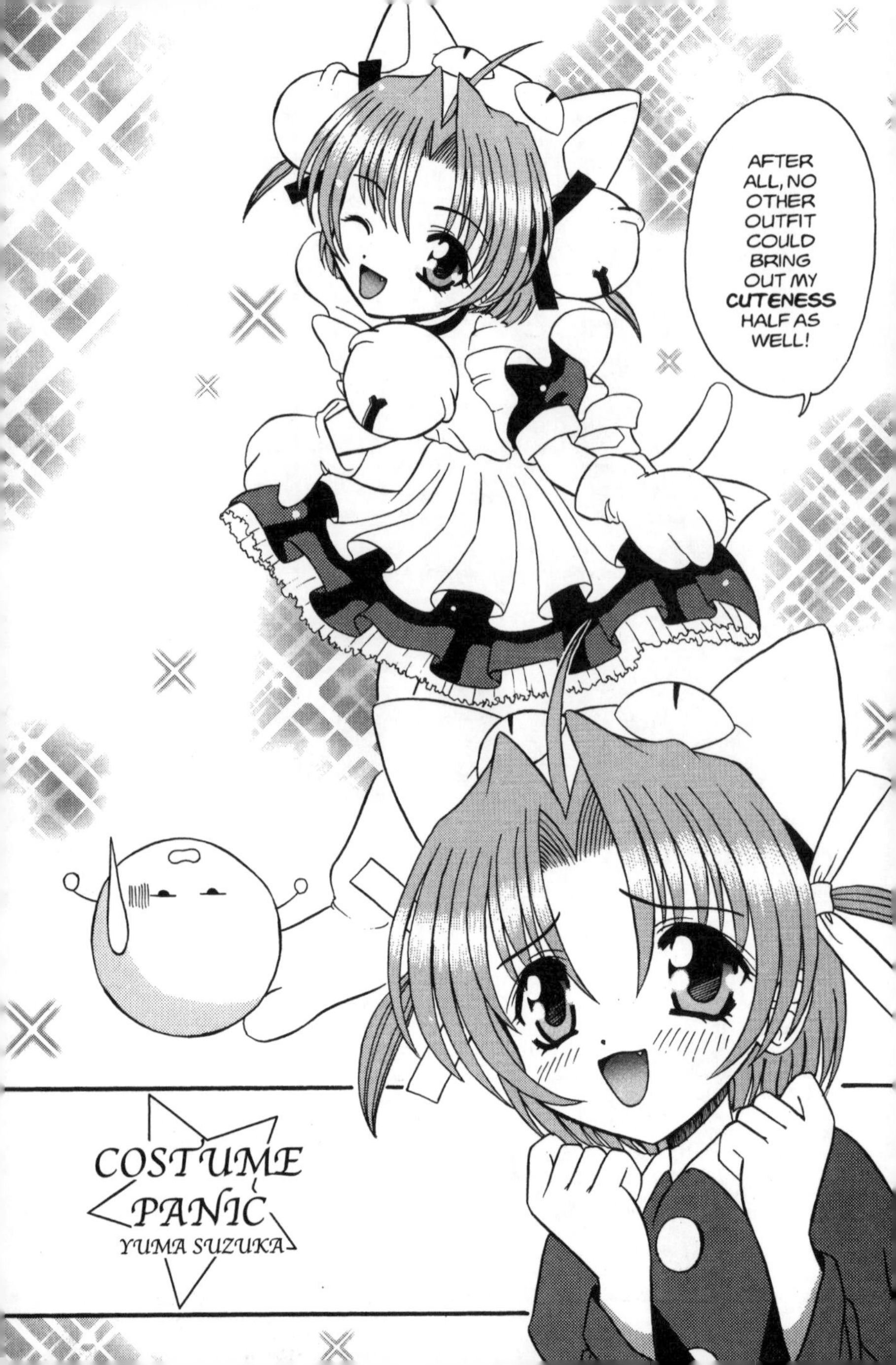
AFTER ALL, NO OTHER OUTFIT COULD BRING OUT MY CUTENESS HALF AS WELL!
COSTUME PANIC
YUMA SUZUKA

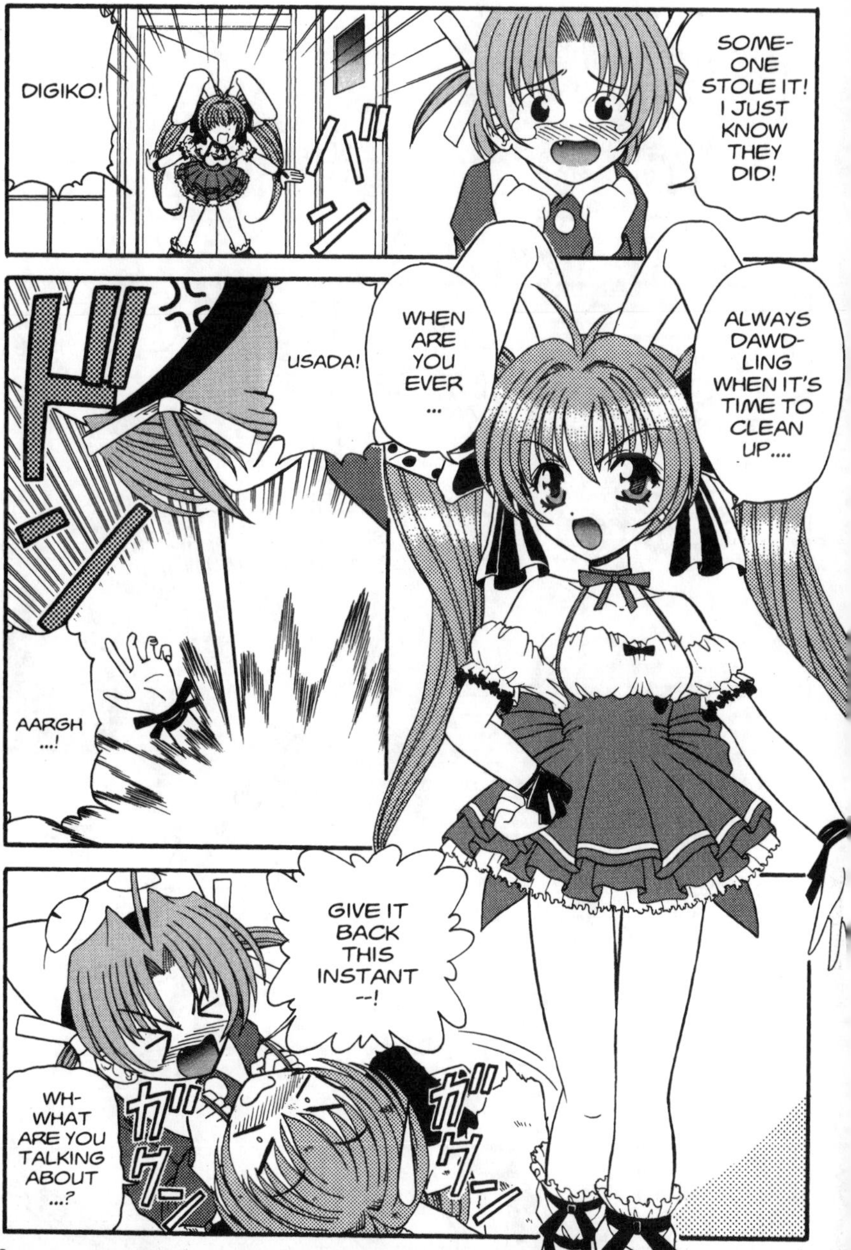
SOME-ONE STOLE IT! I JUST KNOW THEY DID!
DIGIKO!
ALWAYS DAWD-LING WHEN IT'S TIME TO CLEAN UP....
WHEN ARE YOU EVER ...
USADA!
ド
AARGH ...!
GIVE IT BACK THIS INSTANT --!
ガーン
ガーン
WH- WHAT ARE YOU TALKING ABOUT ...?

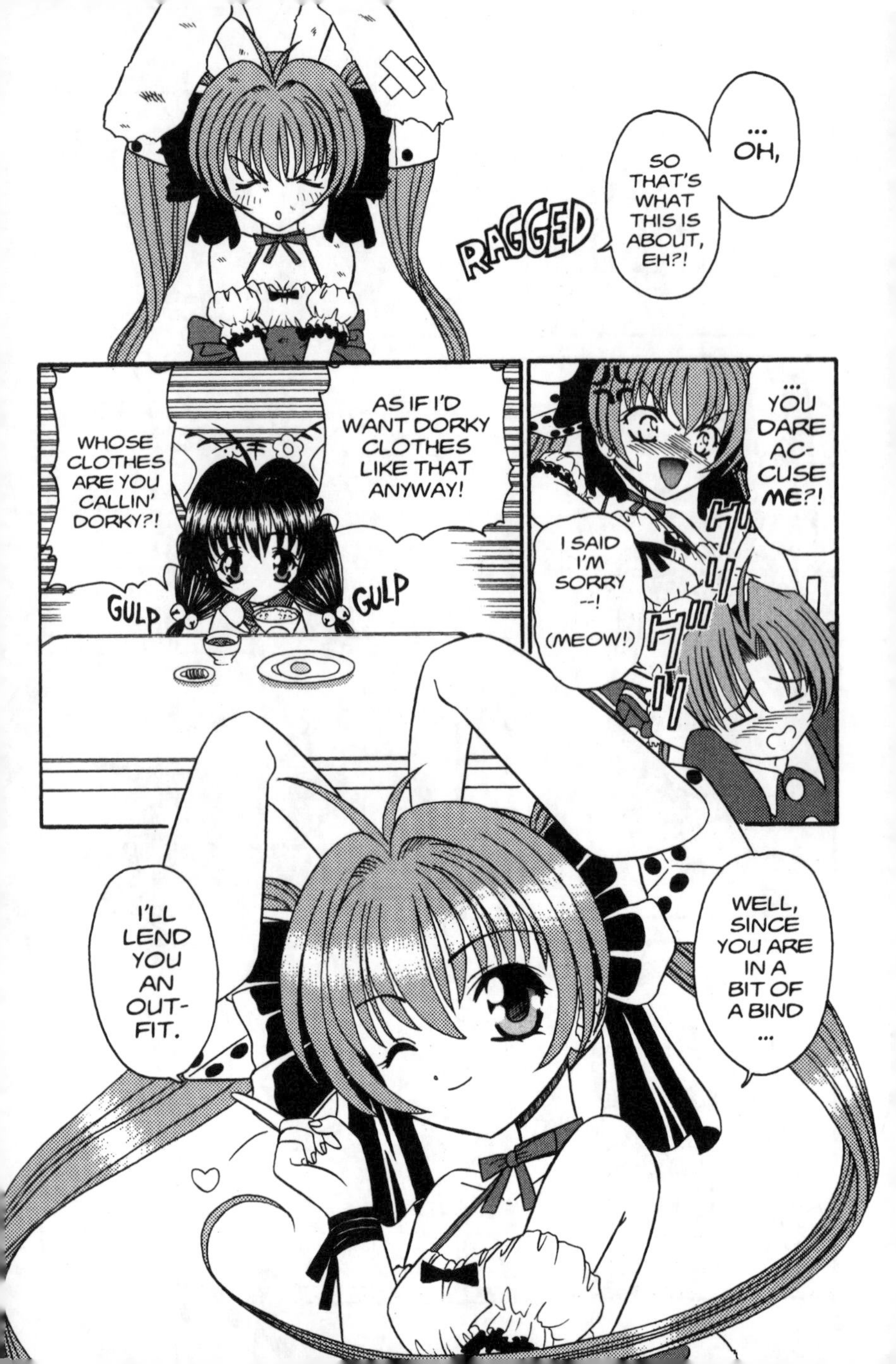
...OH,
SO THAT'S WHAT THIS IS ABOUT, EH?!
RAGGED
...YOU DARE ACCUSE ME?!
I SAID I'M SORRY --! (MEOW!)
AS IF I'D WANT DORKY CLOTHES LIKE THAT ANYWAY!
WHOSE CLOTHES ARE YOU CALLIN' DORKY?!
GULP
GULP
WELL, SINCE YOU ARE IN A BIT OF A BIND ...
I'LL LEND YOU AN OUTFIT.

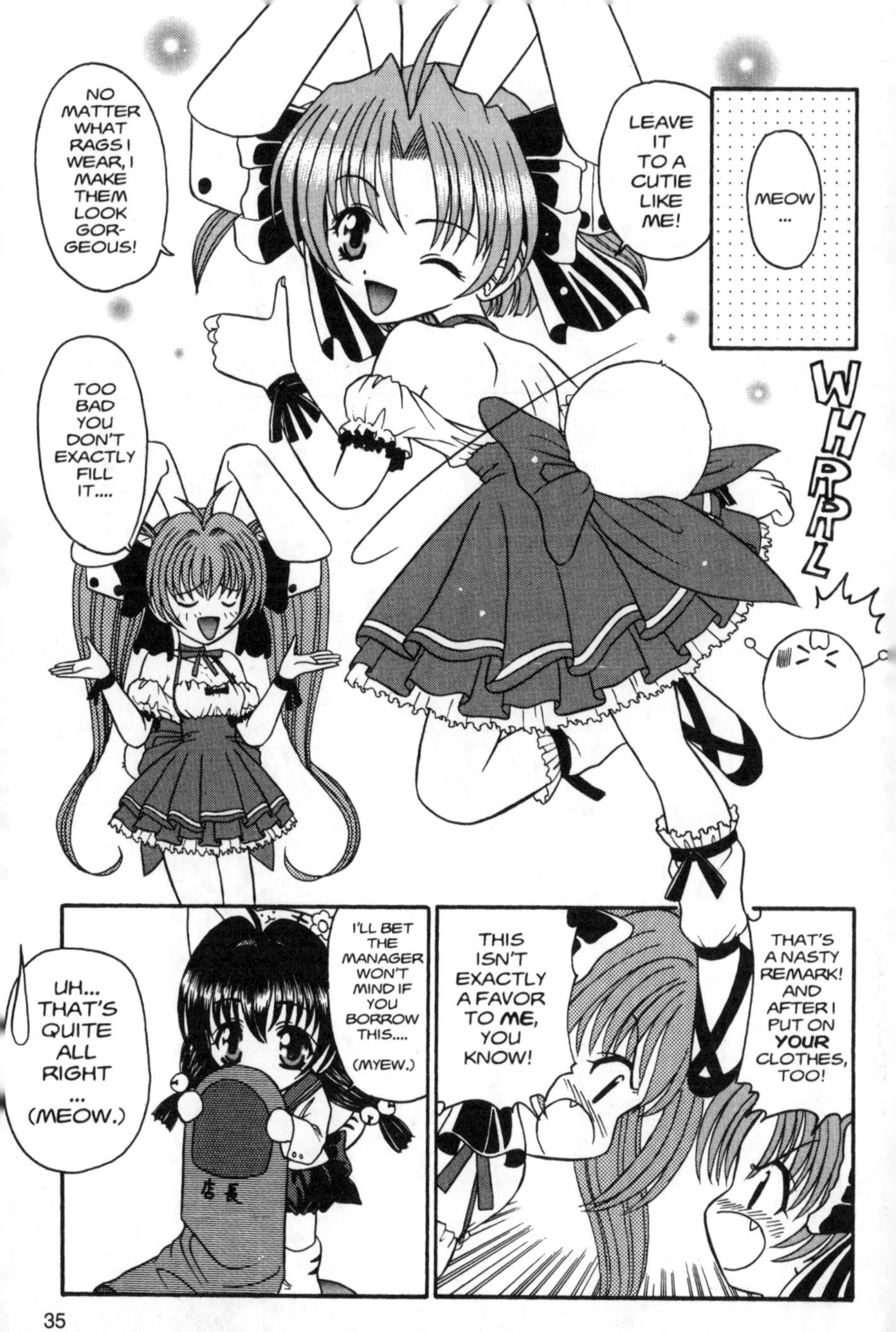
MEOW ...
LEAVE IT TO A CUTIE LIKE ME!
NO MATTER WHAT RAGS I WEAR, I MAKE THEM LOOK GOR-GEOUS!
WHRRL
TOO BAD YOU DON'T EXACTLY FILL IT....
THAT'S A NASTY REMARK! AND AFTER I PUT ON **YOUR** CLOTHES, TOO!
THIS ISN'T EXACTLY A FAVOR TO **ME**, YOU KNOW!
I'LL BET THE MANAGER WON'T MIND IF YOU BORROW THIS....
(MYEW.)
UH... THAT'S QUITE ALL RIGHT ... (MEOW.)

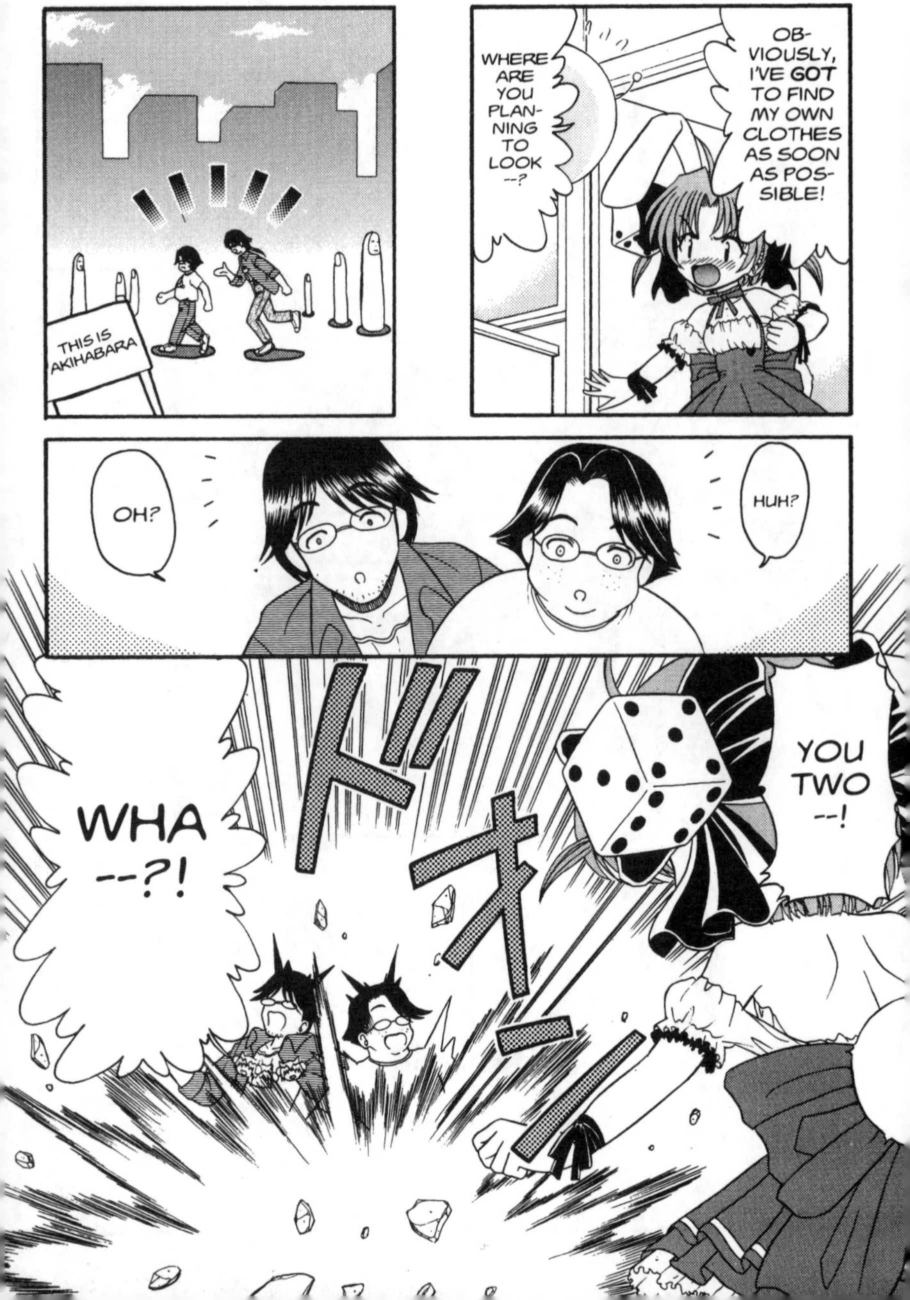
OBVIOUSLY, I'VE GOT TO FIND MY OWN CLOTHES AS SOON AS POSSIBLE!
WHERE ARE YOU PLANNING TO LOOK--?
THIS IS AKIHABARA
HUH?
OH?
YOU TWO--!
ドオー
WHA--?!

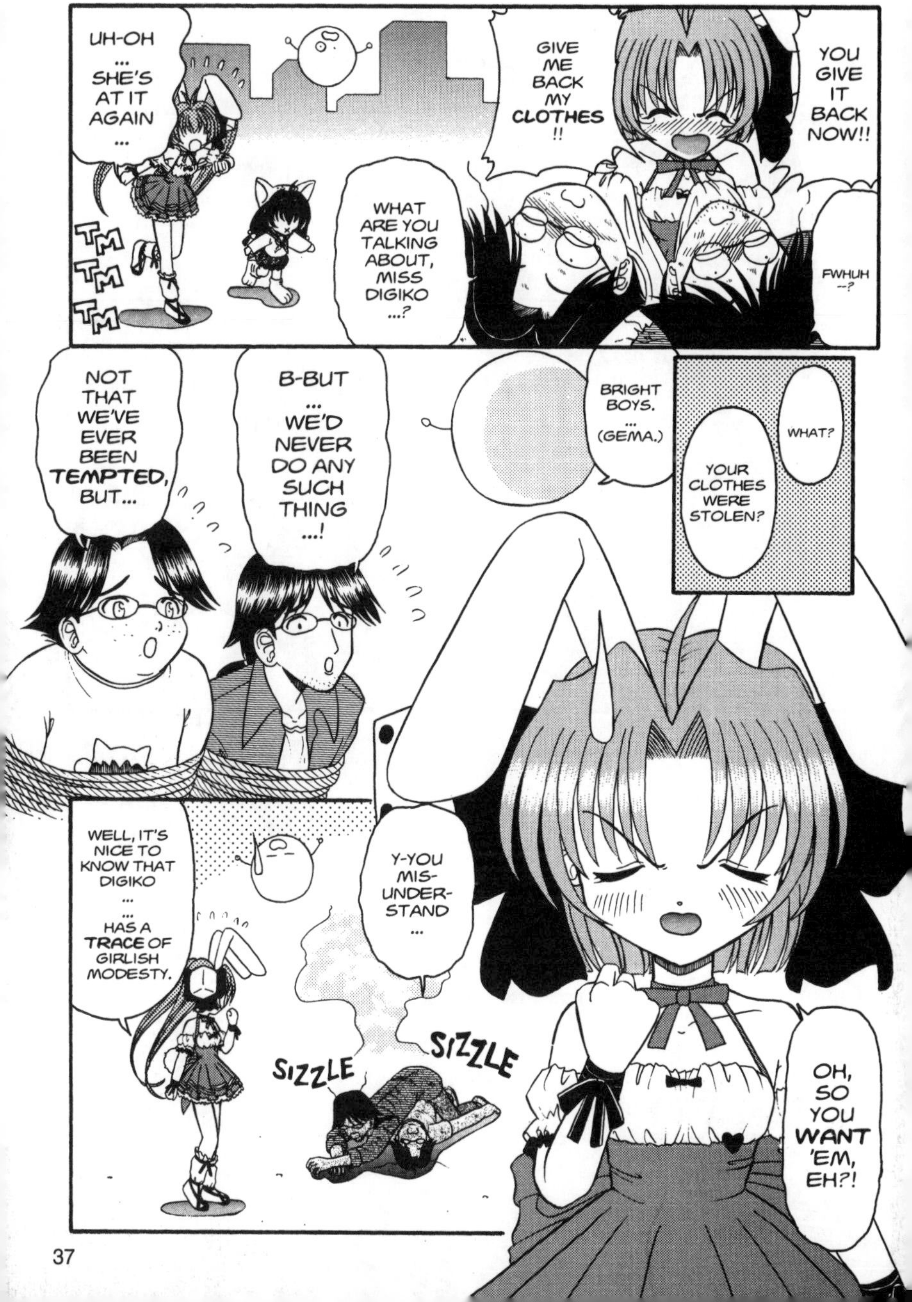
YOU GIVE IT BACK NOW!!
GIVE ME BACK MY CLOTHES!!
FWHUH--?
WHAT ARE YOU TALKING ABOUT, MISS DIGIKO...?
UH-OH... SHE'S AT IT AGAIN...
TM TM TM
WHAT?
YOUR CLOTHES WERE STOLEN?
BRIGHT BOYS. ... (GEMA.)
OH, SO YOU WANT 'EM, EH?!
B-BUT... WE'D NEVER DO ANY SUCH THING...!
NOT THAT WE'VE EVER BEEN TEMPTED, BUT...
Y-YOU MIS-UNDERSTAND...
SIZZLE
SIZZLE
WELL, IT'S NICE TO KNOW THAT DIGIKO... ... HAS A TRACE OF GIRLISH MODESTY.

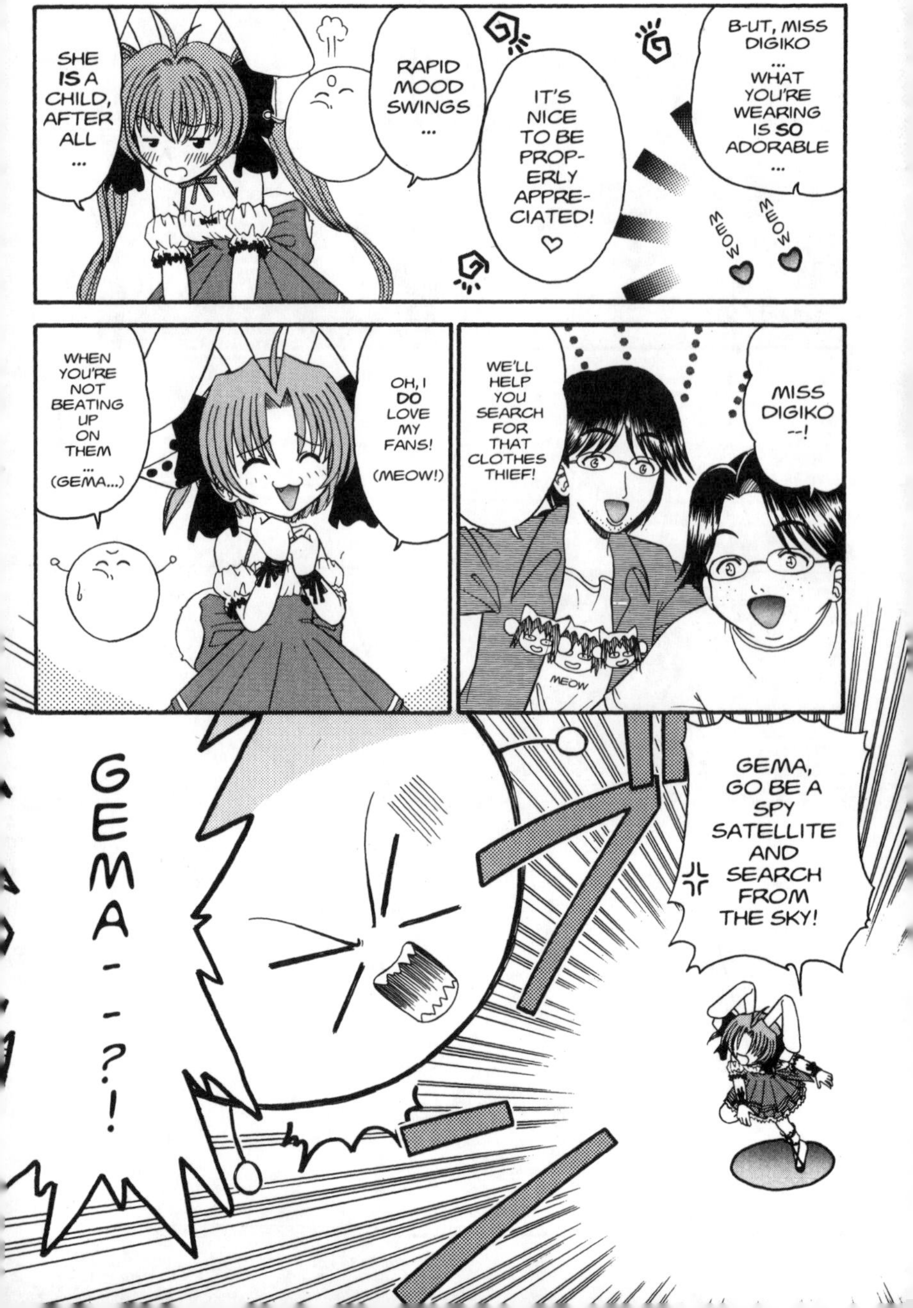
B-UT, MISS DIGIKO ... WHAT YOU'RE WEARING IS SO ADORABLE ...
MEOW ♥
MEOW ♥
IT'S NICE TO BE PROPERLY APPRECIATED! ♥
RAPID MOOD SWINGS ...
SHE IS A CHILD, AFTER ALL ...
MISS DIGIKO --!
WE'LL HELP YOU SEARCH FOR THAT CLOTHES THIEF!
MEOW
OH, I DO LOVE MY FANS! (MEOW!)
WHEN YOU'RE NOT BEATING UP ON THEM ... (GEMA...)
GEMA, GO BE A SPY SATELLITE AND SEARCH FROM THE SKY!
GEMA--?!

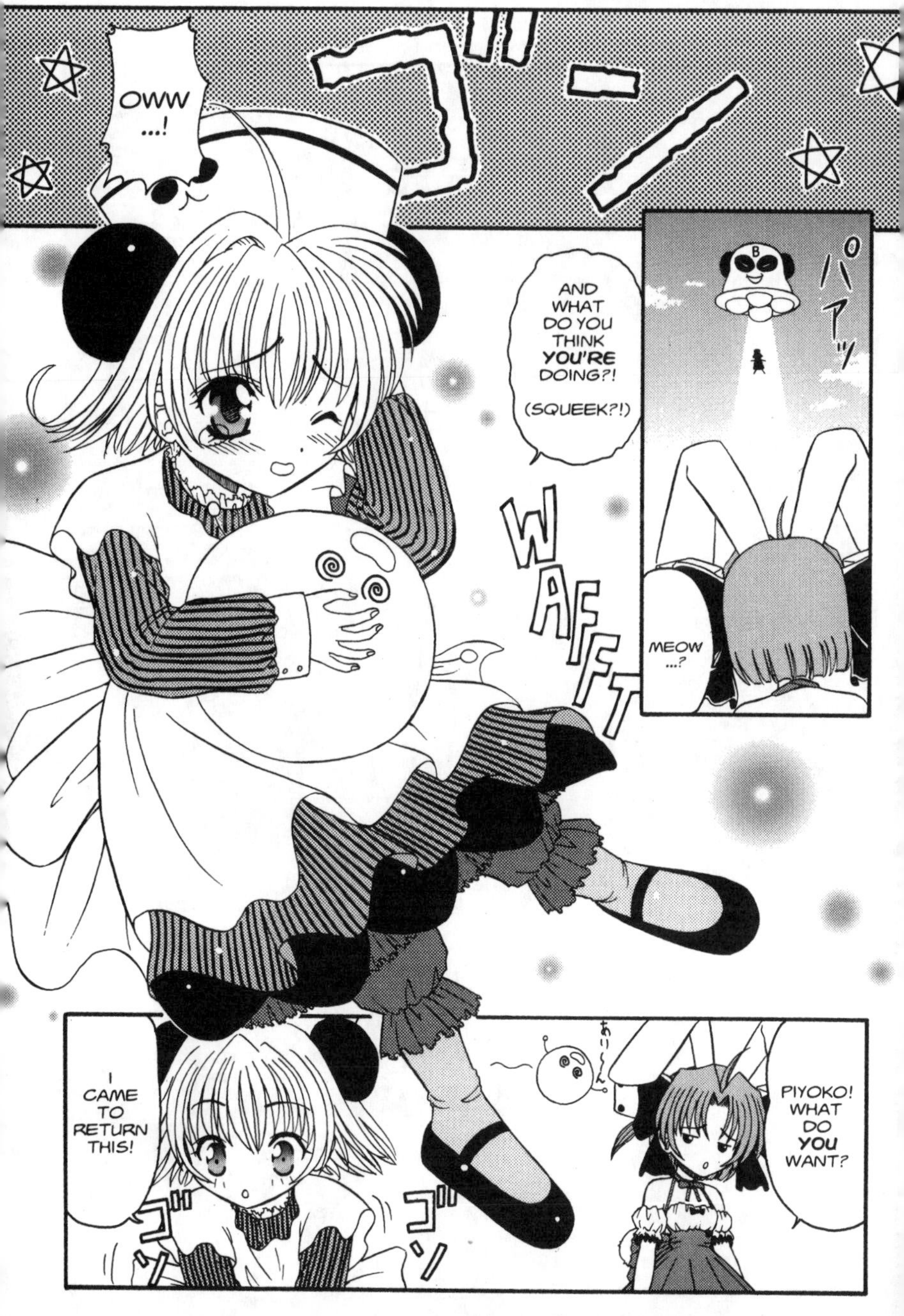

OWW ...!
ゴーン
パアッ
MEOW ...?
AND WHAT DO YOU THINK **YOU'RE** DOING?! (SQUEEK?!)
WAFFT
PIYOKO! WHAT DO **YOU** WANT?
あい～ん
I CAME TO RETURN THIS!
ゴン
ゴン

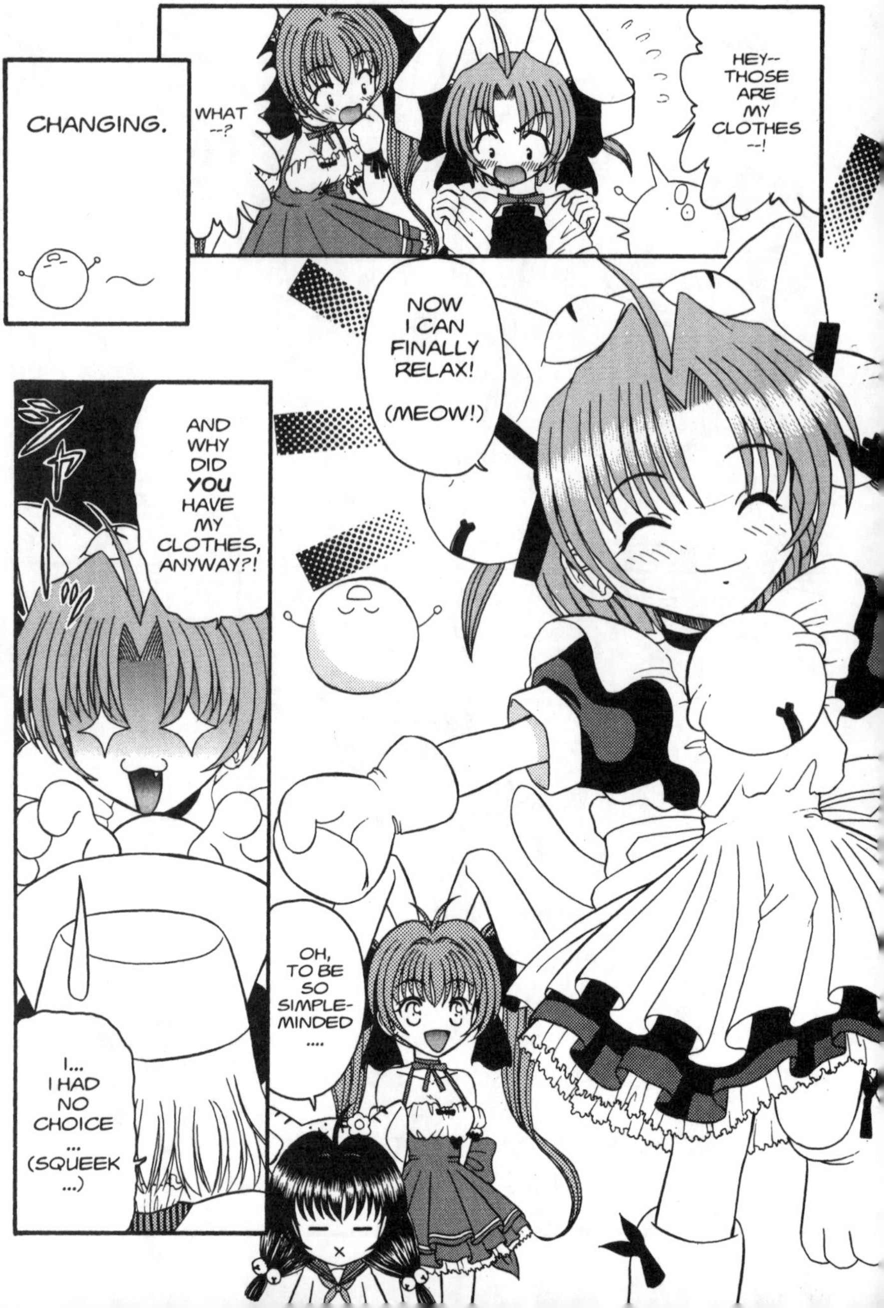
HEY-- THOSE ARE MY CLOTHES --!
WHAT --?
CHANGING.
NOW I CAN FINALLY RELAX!
(MEOW!)
OH, TO BE SO SIMPLE-MINDED ....
AND WHY DID **YOU** HAVE MY CLOTHES, ANYWAY?!
I... I HAD NO CHOICE ... (SQUEEK ...)

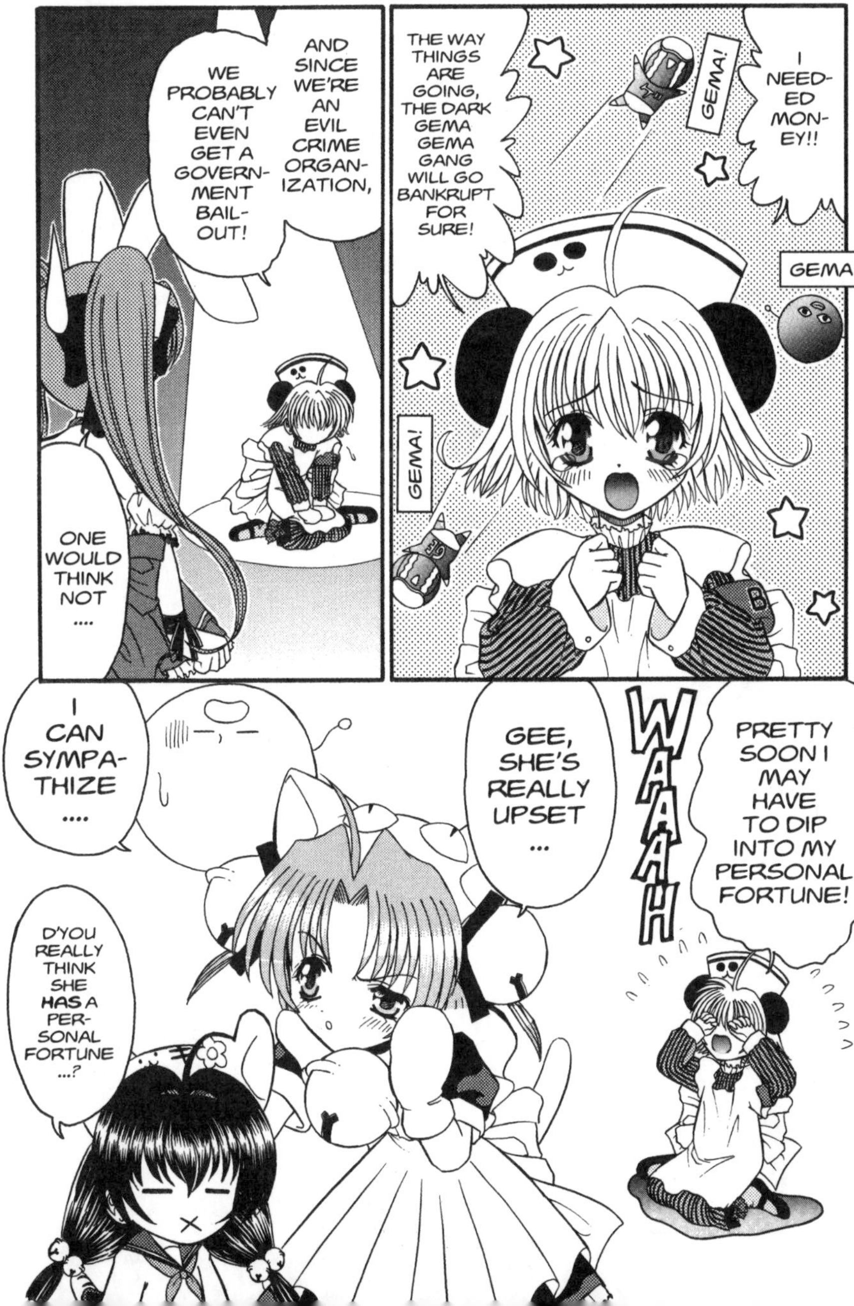
I NEEDED MONEY!!
GEMA!
THE WAY THINGS ARE GOING, THE DARK GEMA GEMA GANG WILL GO BANKRUPT FOR SURE!
GEMA?
GEMA!
AND SINCE WE'RE AN EVIL CRIME ORGANIZATION,
WE PROBABLY CAN'T EVEN GET A GOVERNMENT BAIL-OUT!
ONE WOULD THINK NOT ....
PRETTY SOON I MAY HAVE TO DIP INTO MY PERSONAL FORTUNE!
WAAAAH
GEE, SHE'S REALLY UPSET ...
I CAN SYMPATHIZE ....
D'YOU REALLY THINK SHE **HAS** A PERSONAL FORTUNE ...?

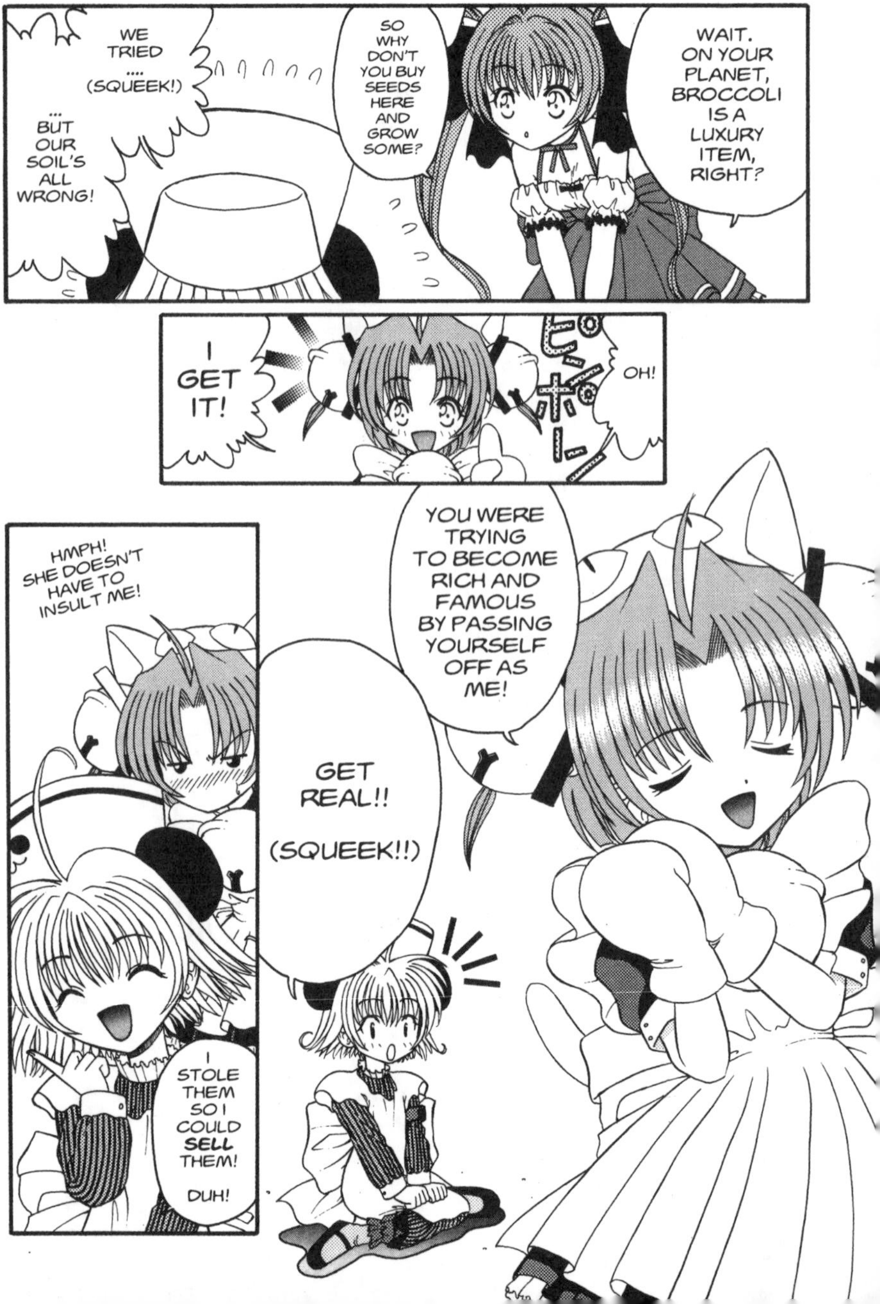
WAIT. ON YOUR PLANET, BROCCOLI IS A LUXURY ITEM, RIGHT?
SO WHY DON'T YOU BUY SEEDS HERE AND GROW SOME?
WE TRIED .... (SQUEEK!)
... BUT OUR SOIL'S ALL WRONG!
OH!
I GET IT!
YOU WERE TRYING TO BECOME RICH AND FAMOUS BY PASSING YOURSELF OFF AS ME!
GET REAL!! (SQUEEK!!)
HMPH! SHE DOESN'T HAVE TO INSULT ME!
I STOLE THEM SO I COULD **SELL** THEM!
DUH!

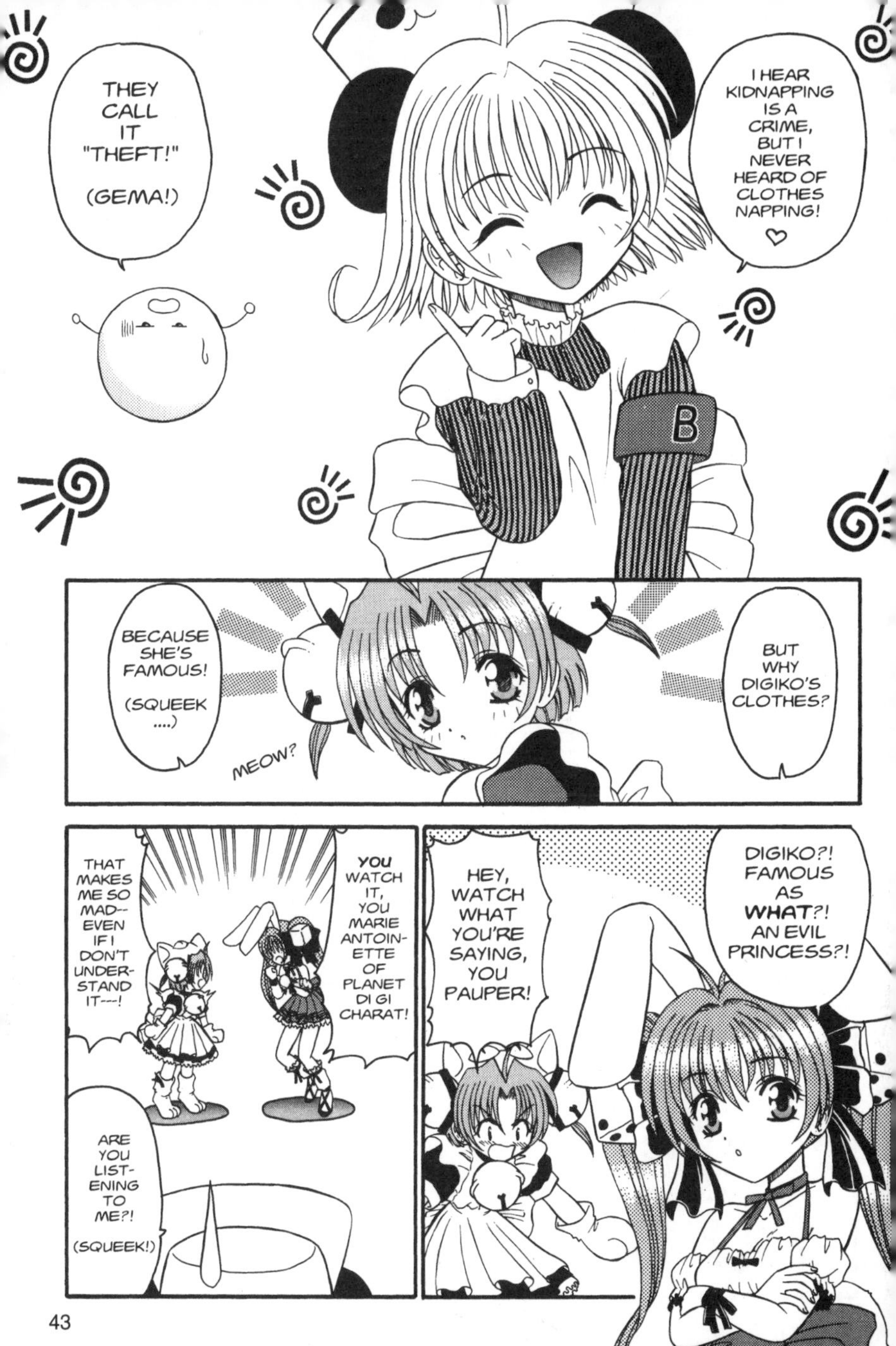
I HEAR KIDNAPPING IS A CRIME, BUT I NEVER HEARD OF CLOTHES NAPPING! ♡
THEY CALL IT "THEFT!" (GEMA!)
BUT WHY DIGIKO'S CLOTHES?
BECAUSE SHE'S FAMOUS! (SQUEEK ....)
MEOW?
DIGIKO?! FAMOUS AS **WHAT**?! AN EVIL PRINCESS?!
HEY, WATCH WHAT YOU'RE SAYING, YOU PAUPER!
YOU WATCH IT, YOU MARIE ANTOIN-ETTE OF PLANET DI GI CHARAT!
THAT MAKES ME SO MAD-- EVEN IF I DON'T UNDER-STAND IT---!
ARE YOU LIST-ENING TO ME?!
(SQUEEK!)

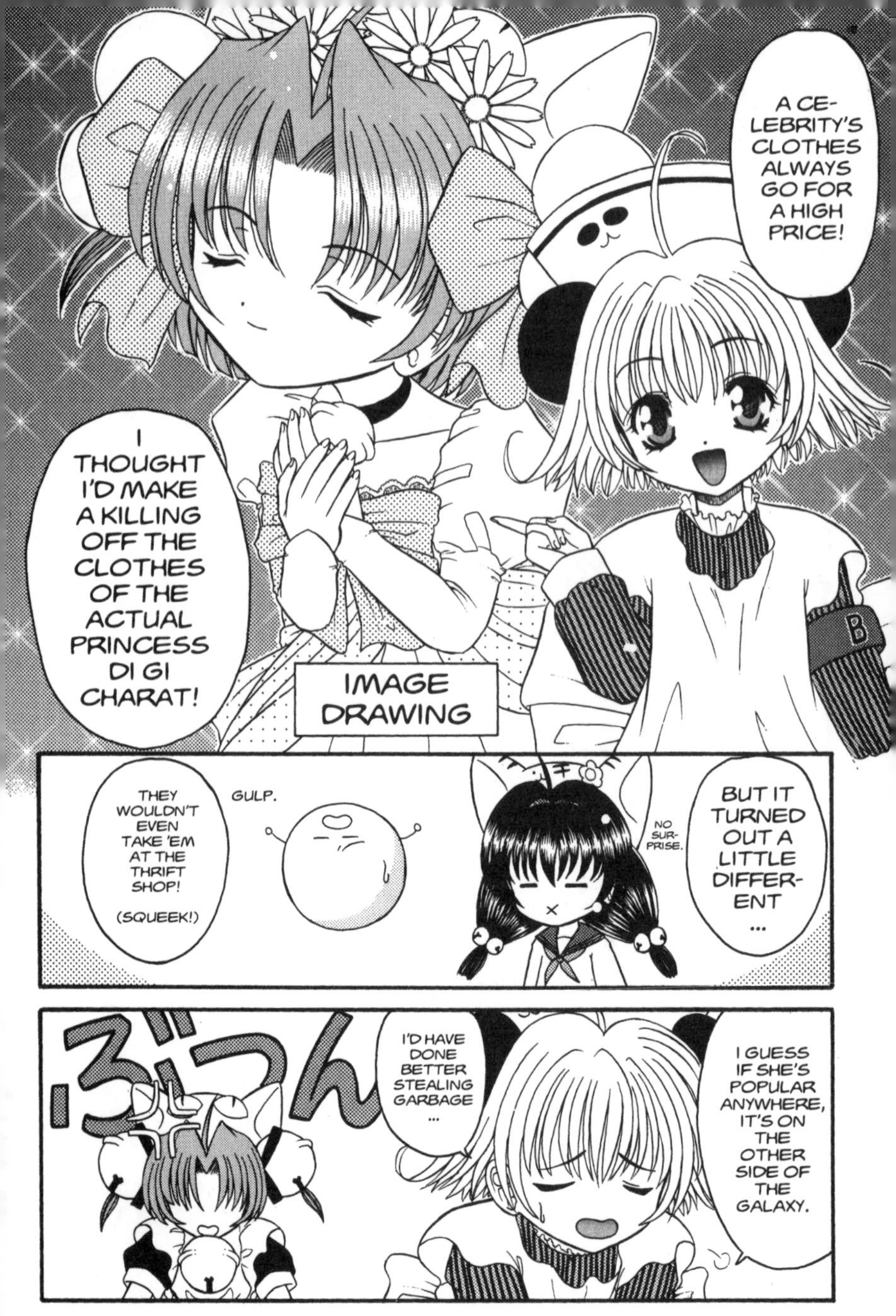
A CE-LEBRITY'S CLOTHES ALWAYS GO FOR A HIGH PRICE!
I THOUGHT I'D MAKE A KILLING OFF THE CLOTHES OF THE ACTUAL PRINCESS DI GI CHARAT!
IMAGE DRAWING
BUT IT TURNED OUT A LITTLE DIFFER-ENT ...
NO SUR-PRISE.
GULP.
THEY WOULDN'T EVEN TAKE 'EM AT THE THRIFT SHOP!
(SQUEEK!)
I GUESS IF SHE'S POPULAR ANYWHERE, IT'S ON THE OTHER SIDE OF THE GALAXY.
I'D HAVE DONE BETTER STEALING GARBAGE ...
ぶつん

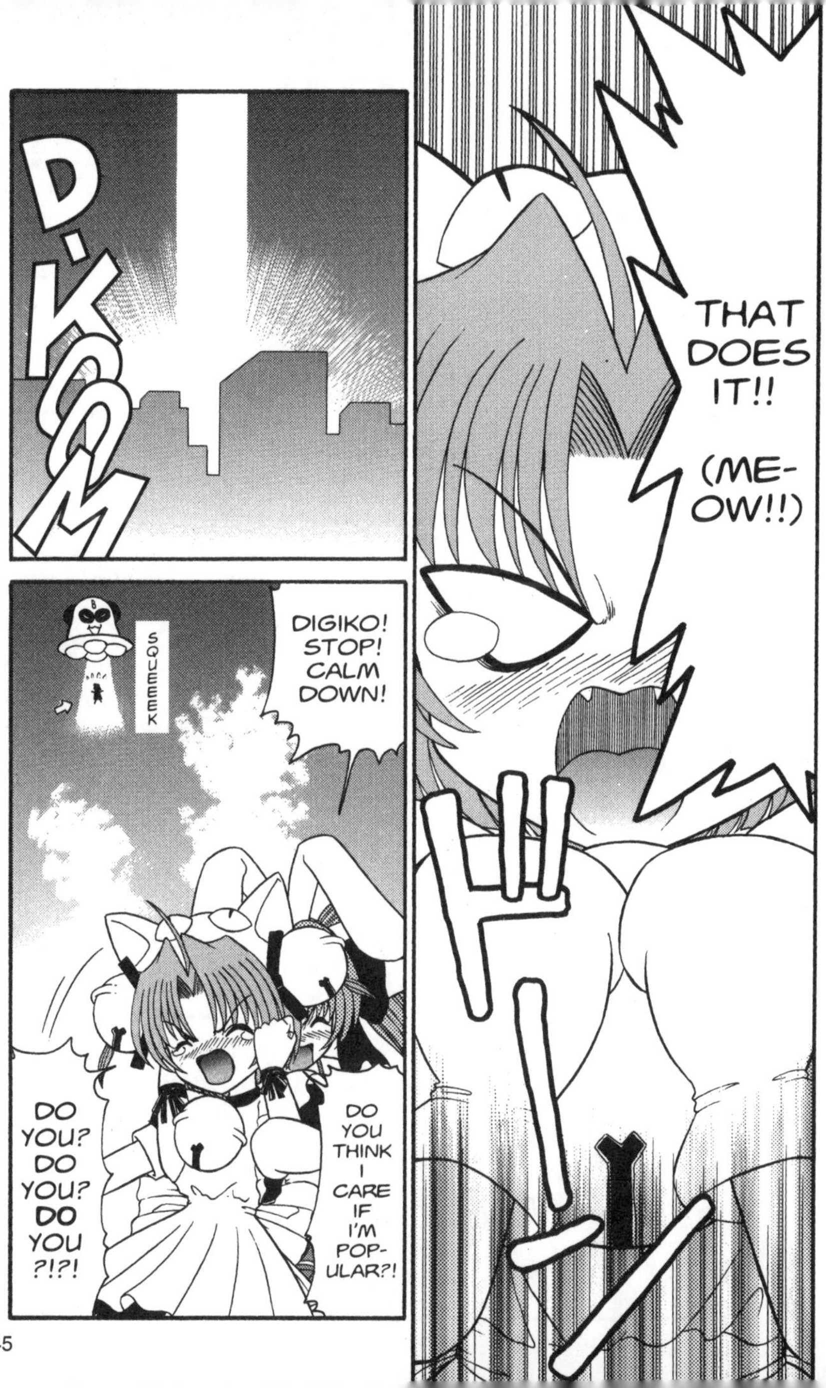
THAT DOES IT!!
(ME-OW!!)
D-KOOM
DIGIKO! STOP! CALM DOWN!
SQUEEEK
DO YOU THINK I CARE IF I'M POP-ULAR?!
DO YOU? DO YOU? DO YOU?!?!

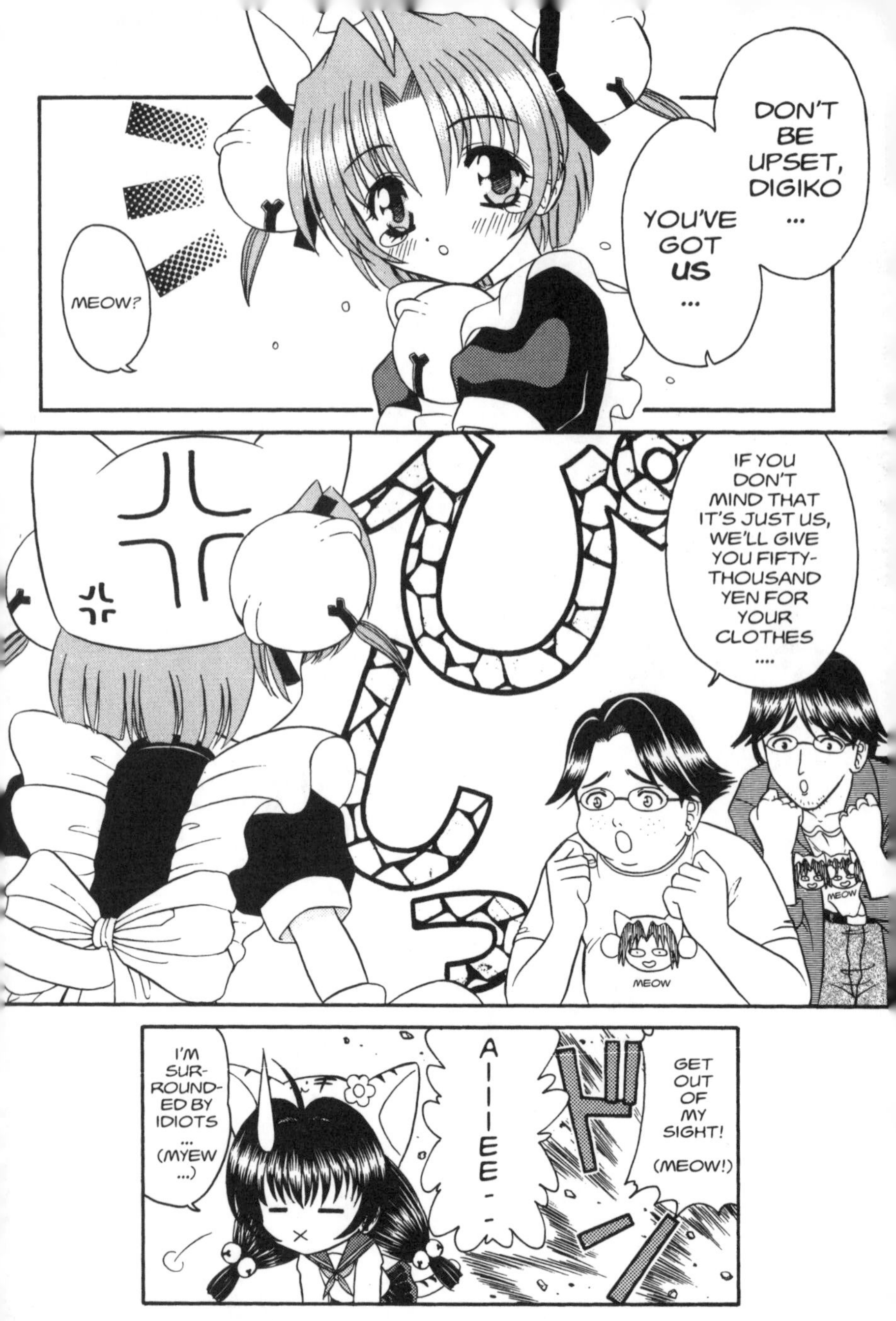
DON'T BE UPSET, DIGIKO ...
YOU'VE GOT US ...
MEOW?
IF YOU DON'T MIND THAT IT'S JUST US, WE'LL GIVE YOU FIFTY-THOUSAND YEN FOR YOUR CLOTHES ....
MEOW
MEOW
GET OUT OF MY SIGHT!
(MEOW!)
A-I-I-E-E--
I'M SUR-ROUND-ED BY IDIOTS ...
(MYEW ...)

WELCOME

SEARA

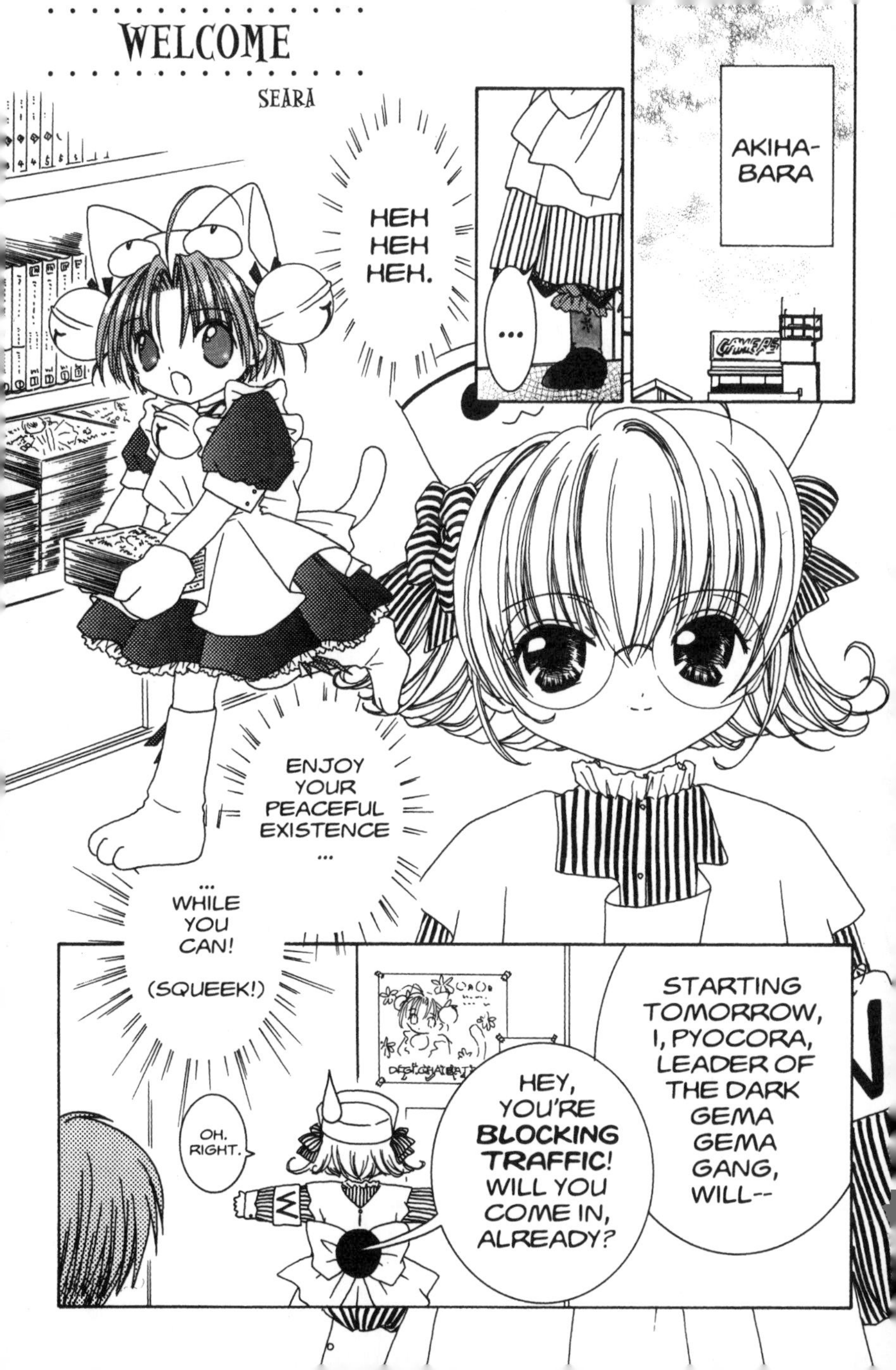
AKIHA-
BARA
...
HEH
HEH
HEH.
ENJOY YOUR PEACEFUL EXISTENCE ...
... WHILE YOU CAN!
(SQUEEK!)
STARTING TOMORROW, I, PYOCORA, LEADER OF THE DARK GEMA GEMA GANG, WILL--
HEY, YOU'RE **BLOCKING TRAFFIC!** WILL YOU COME IN, ALREADY?
OH. RIGHT.

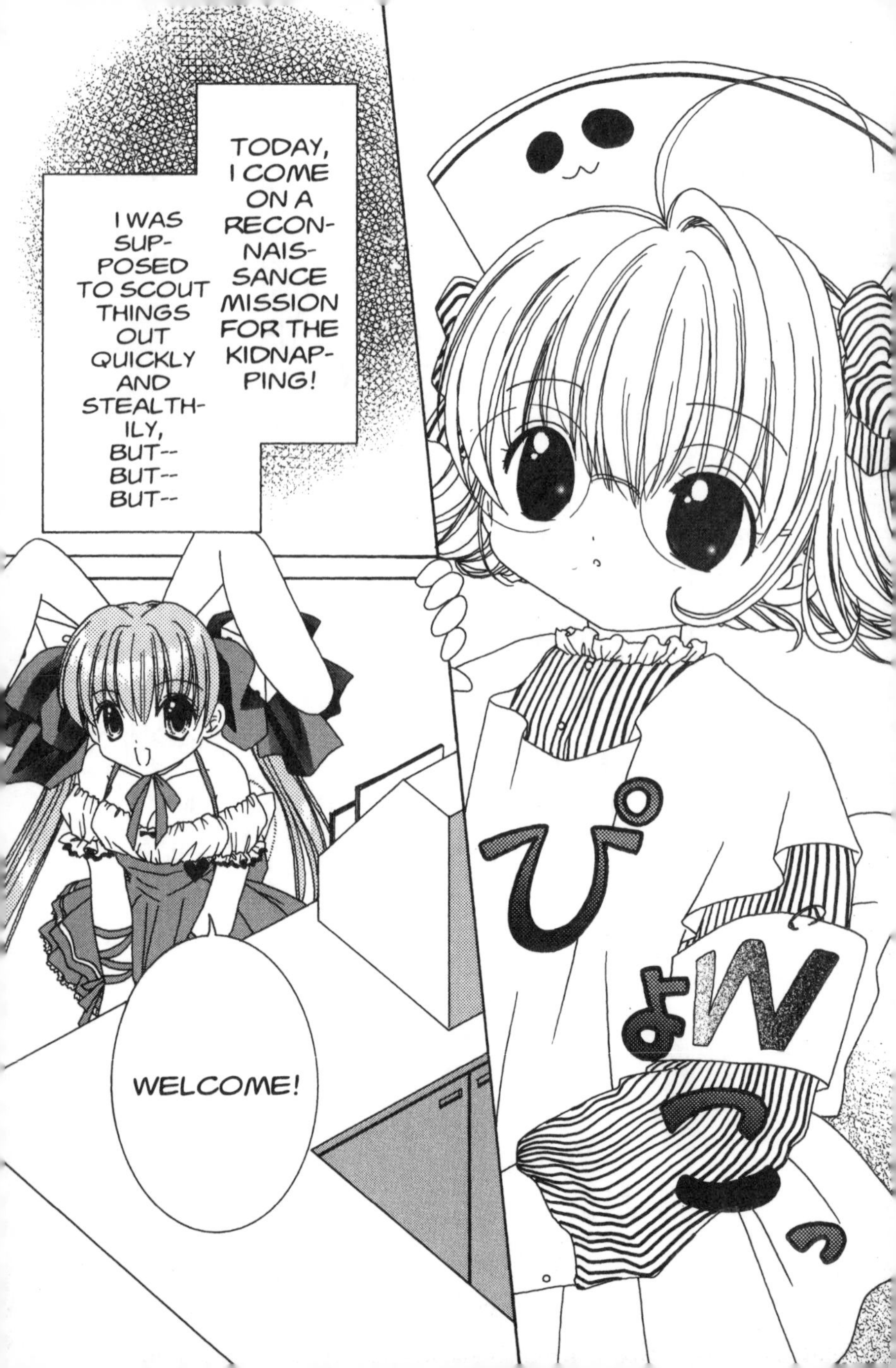

ぴょWっっ
TODAY, I COME ON A RECONNAISSANCE MISSION FOR THE KIDNAPPING!
I WAS SUPPOSED TO SCOUT THINGS OUT QUICKLY AND STEALTHILY, BUT-- BUT-- BUT--
WELCOME!

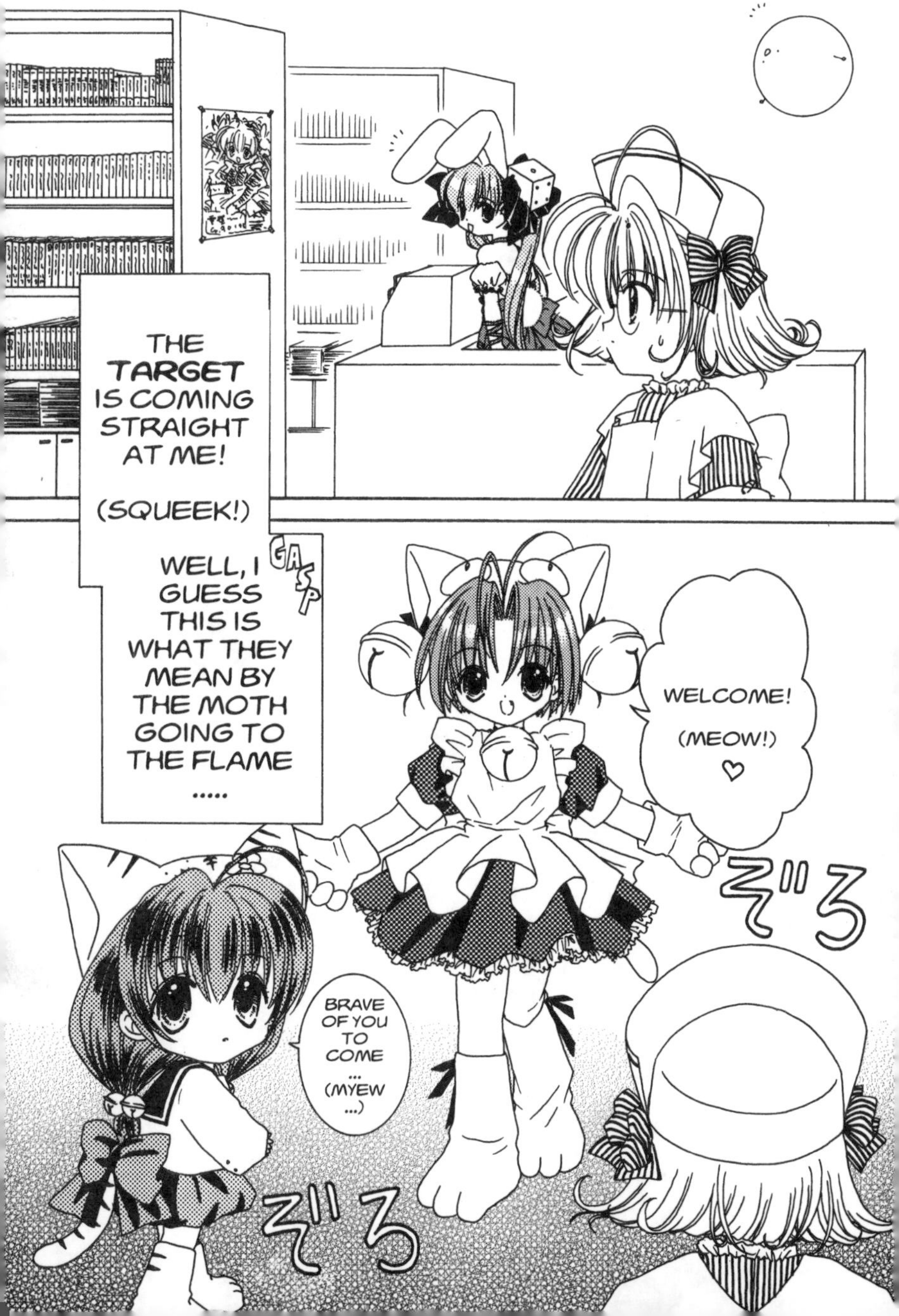
THE TARGET IS COMING STRAIGHT AT ME!
(SQUEEK!)
WELL, I GUESS THIS IS WHAT THEY MEAN BY THE MOTH GOING TO THE FLAME .....
GASP
WELCOME! (MEOW!) ♡
ぞろ
BRAVE OF YOU TO COME ... (MYEW ...)
ぞろ

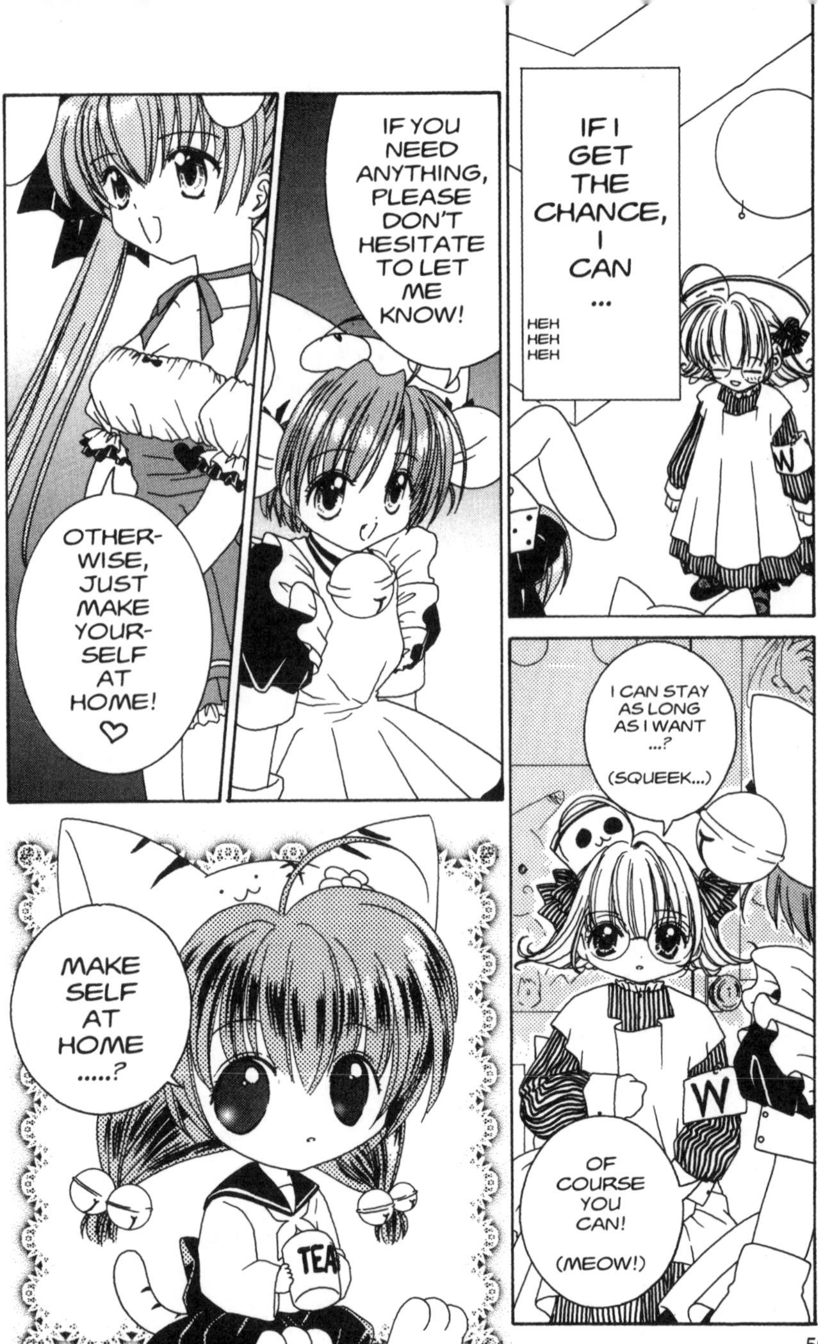
IF I GET THE CHANCE, I CAN ...
HEH HEH HEH
IF YOU NEED ANYTHING, PLEASE DON'T HESITATE TO LET ME KNOW!
OTHER-WISE, JUST MAKE YOUR-SELF AT HOME! ♡
I CAN STAY AS LONG AS I WANT ...?
(SQUEEK...)
OF COURSE YOU CAN!
(MEOW!)
MAKE SELF AT HOME .....?
TEA
W

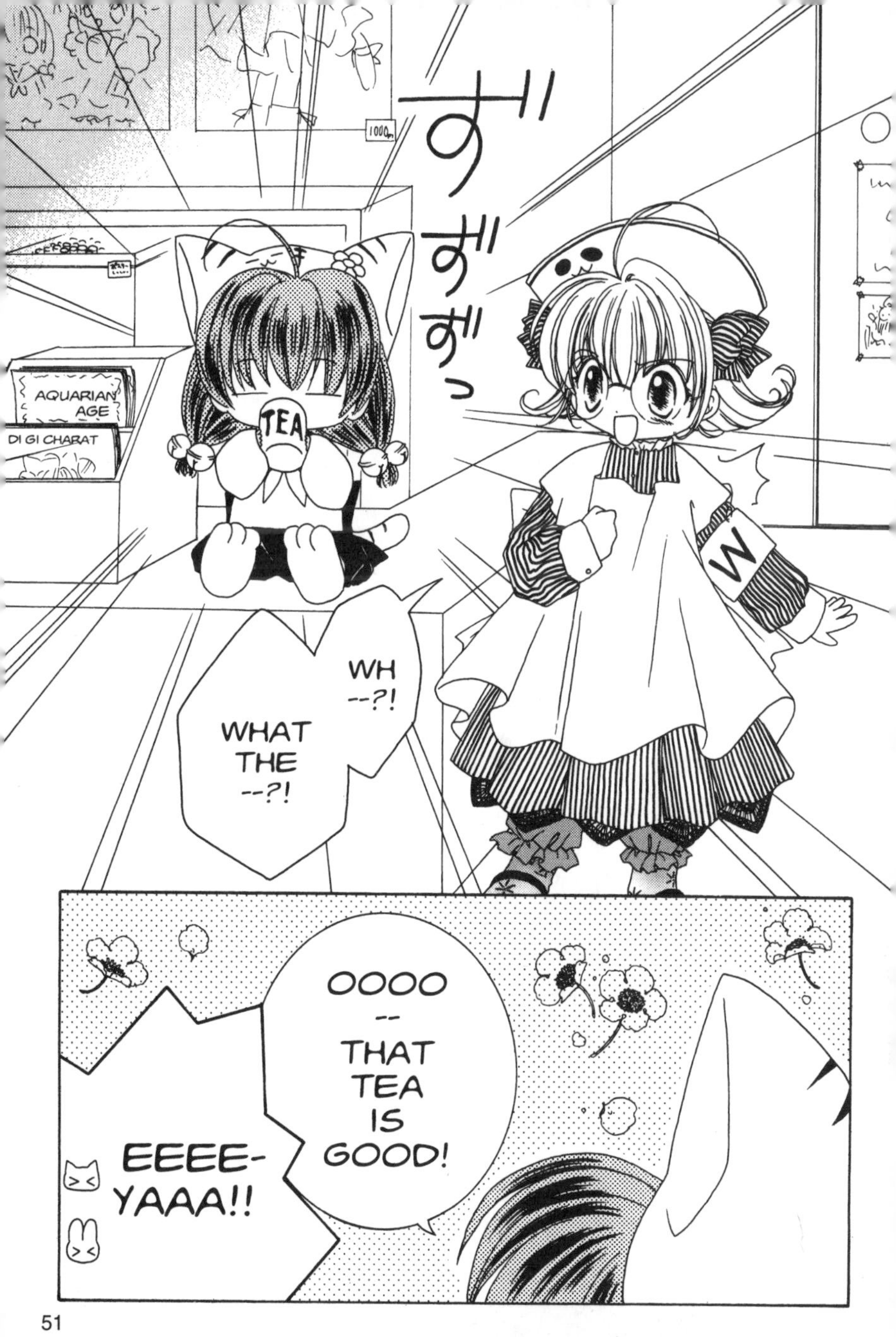
ずずずっ
TEA
AQUARIAN AGE
DI GI CHARAT
WH --?!
WHAT THE --?!
OOOO -- THAT TEA IS GOOD!
EEEE-YAAA!!

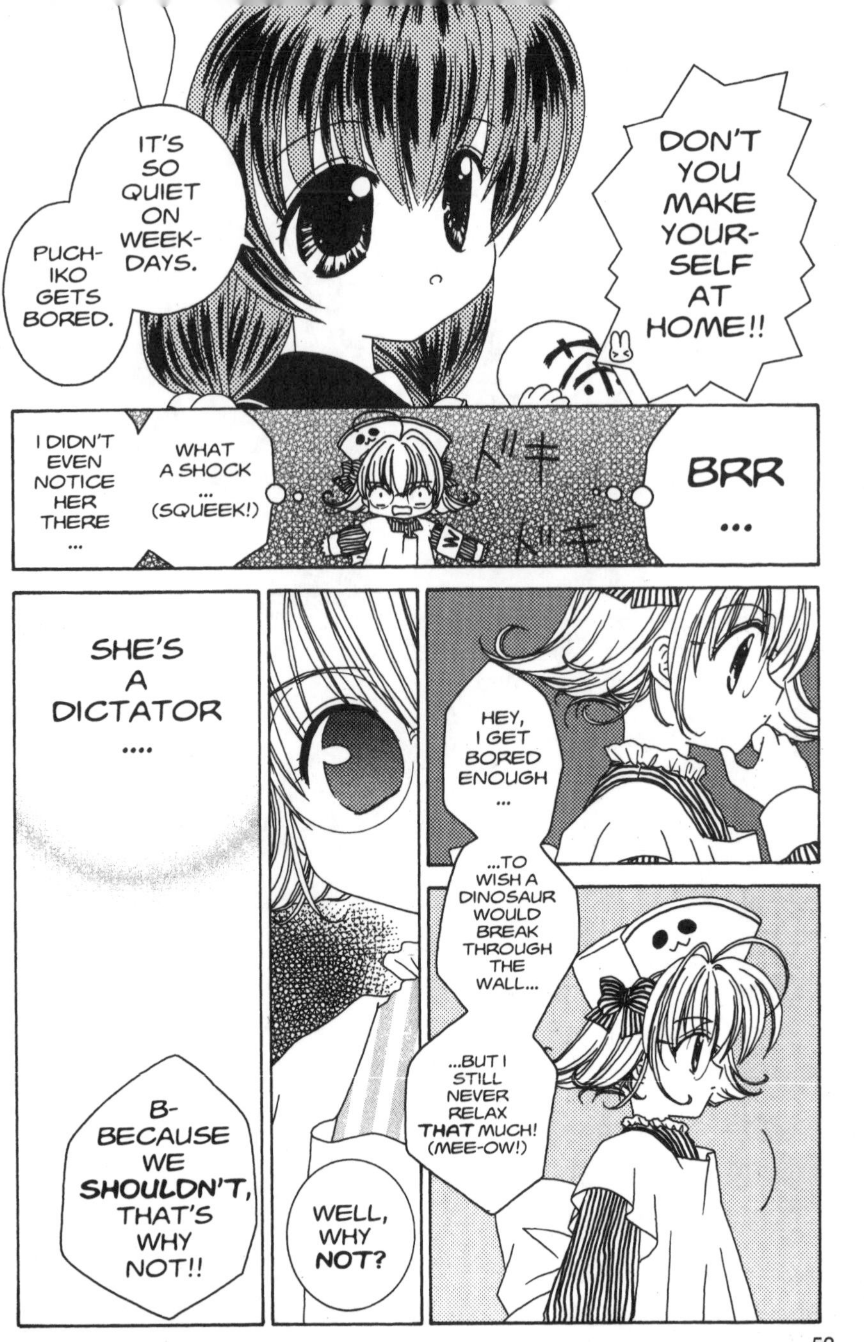
DON'T YOU MAKE YOURSELF AT HOME!!
IT'S SO QUIET ON WEEKDAYS.
PUCHIKO GETS BORED.
BRR ...
ドキ ドキ
WHAT A SHOCK ... (SQUEEK!)
I DIDN'T EVEN NOTICE HER THERE ...
HEY, I GET BORED ENOUGH ...
...TO WISH A DINOSAUR WOULD BREAK THROUGH THE WALL...
...BUT I STILL NEVER RELAX **THAT** MUCH! (MEE-OW!)
WELL, WHY **NOT?**
SHE'S A DICTATOR ....
B-BECAUSE WE **SHOULDN'T**, THAT'S WHY NOT!!

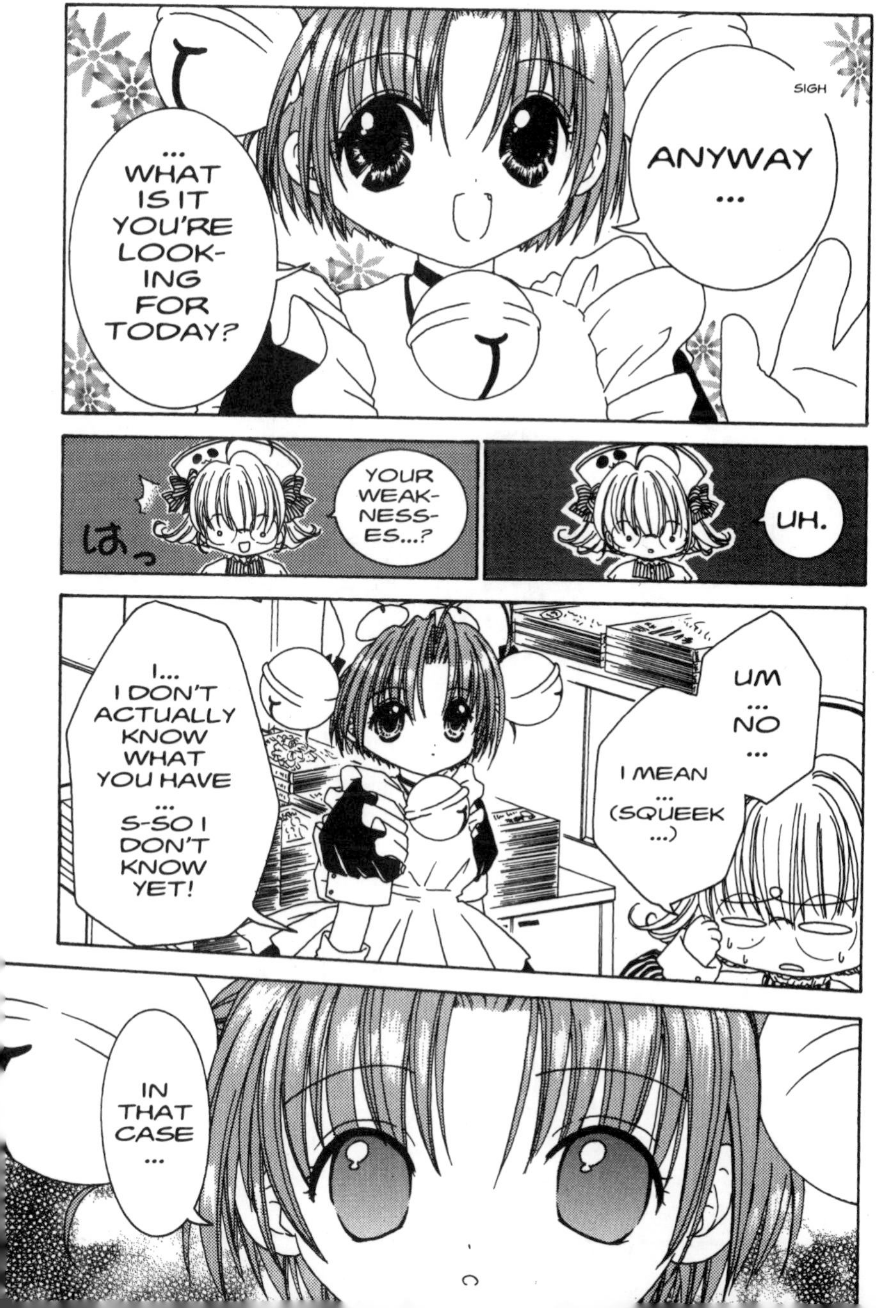
SIGH
ANYWAY ...
... WHAT IS IT YOU'RE LOOKING FOR TODAY?
UH.
YOUR WEAKNESSES...?
はっ
UM ... NO ... I MEAN ... (SQUEEK ...)
I... I DON'T ACTUALLY KNOW WHAT YOU HAVE ... S-SO I DON'T KNOW YET!
IN THAT CASE ...

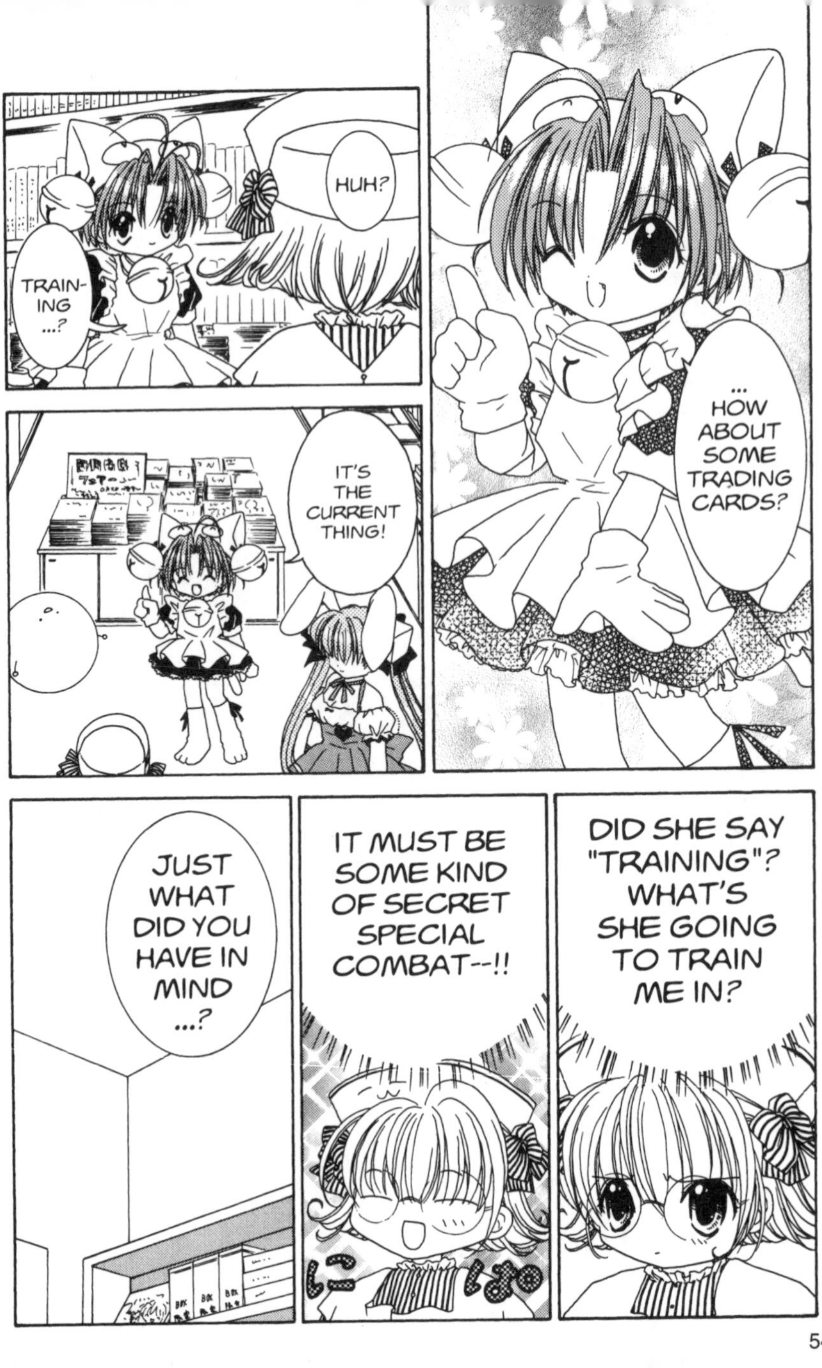
... HOW ABOUT SOME TRADING CARDS?
HUH?
TRAIN-ING ...?
IT'S THE CURRENT THING!
DID SHE SAY "TRAINING"? WHAT'S SHE GOING TO TRAIN ME IN?
IT MUST BE SOME KIND OF SECRET SPECIAL COMBAT--!!
JUST WHAT DID YOU HAVE IN MIND ...?

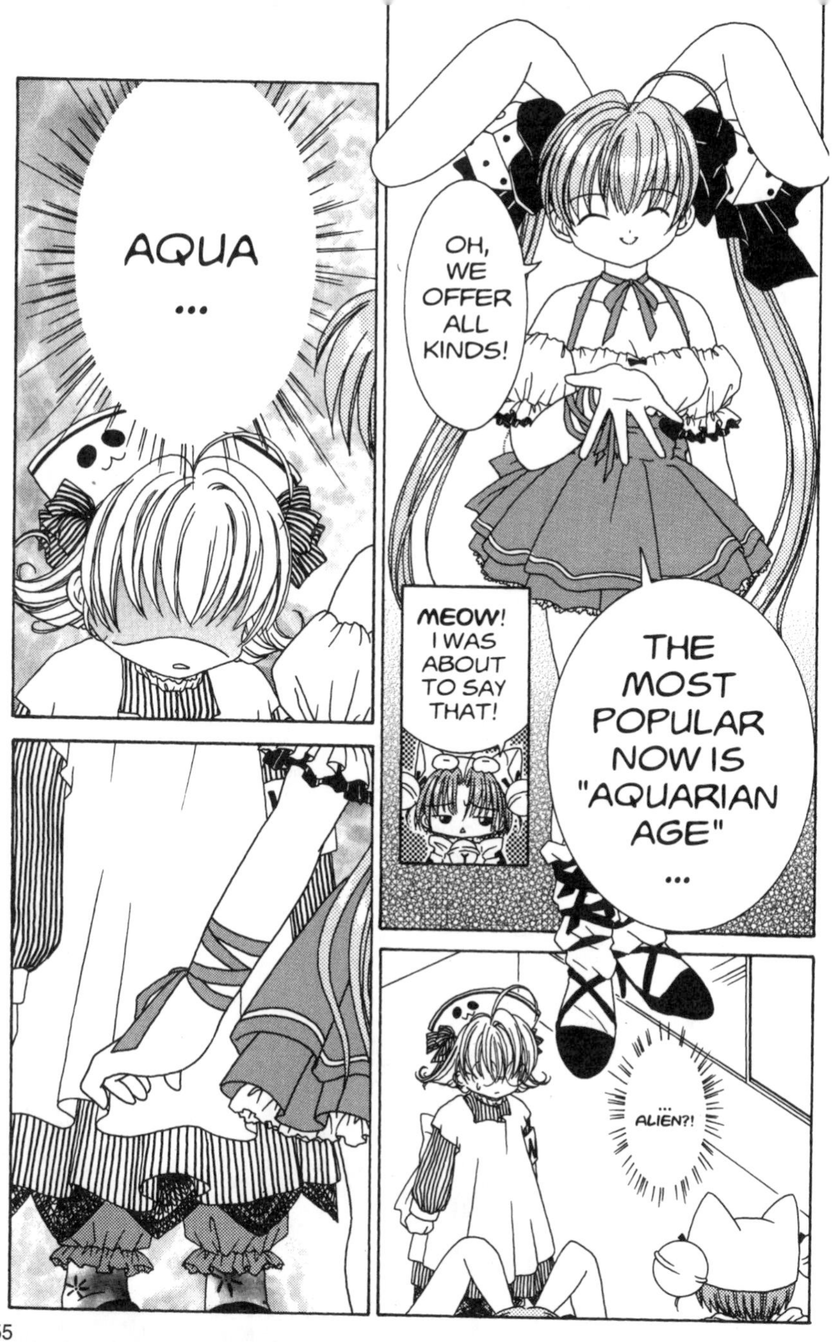
OH, WE OFFER ALL KINDS!
THE MOST POPULAR NOW IS "AQUARIAN AGE" ...
MEOW! I WAS ABOUT TO SAY THAT!
AQUA ...
... ALIEN?!

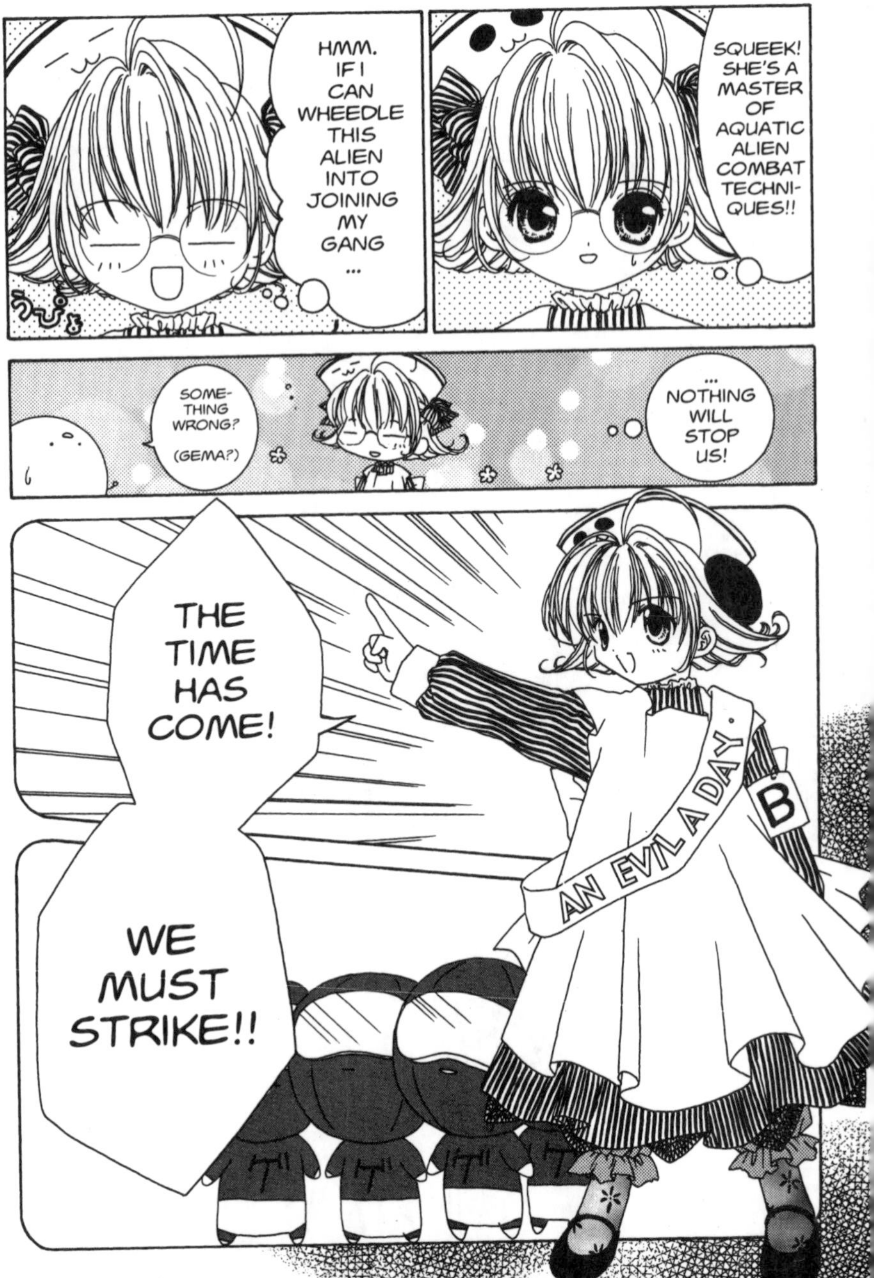
SQUEEK! SHE'S A MASTER OF AQUATIC ALIEN COMBAT TECHNI-QUES!!
HMM. IF I CAN WHEEDLE THIS ALIEN INTO JOINING MY GANG ...
... NOTHING WILL STOP US!
SOME-THING WRONG? (GEMA?)
THE TIME HAS COME!
WE MUST STRIKE!!
AN EVIL A DAY
B

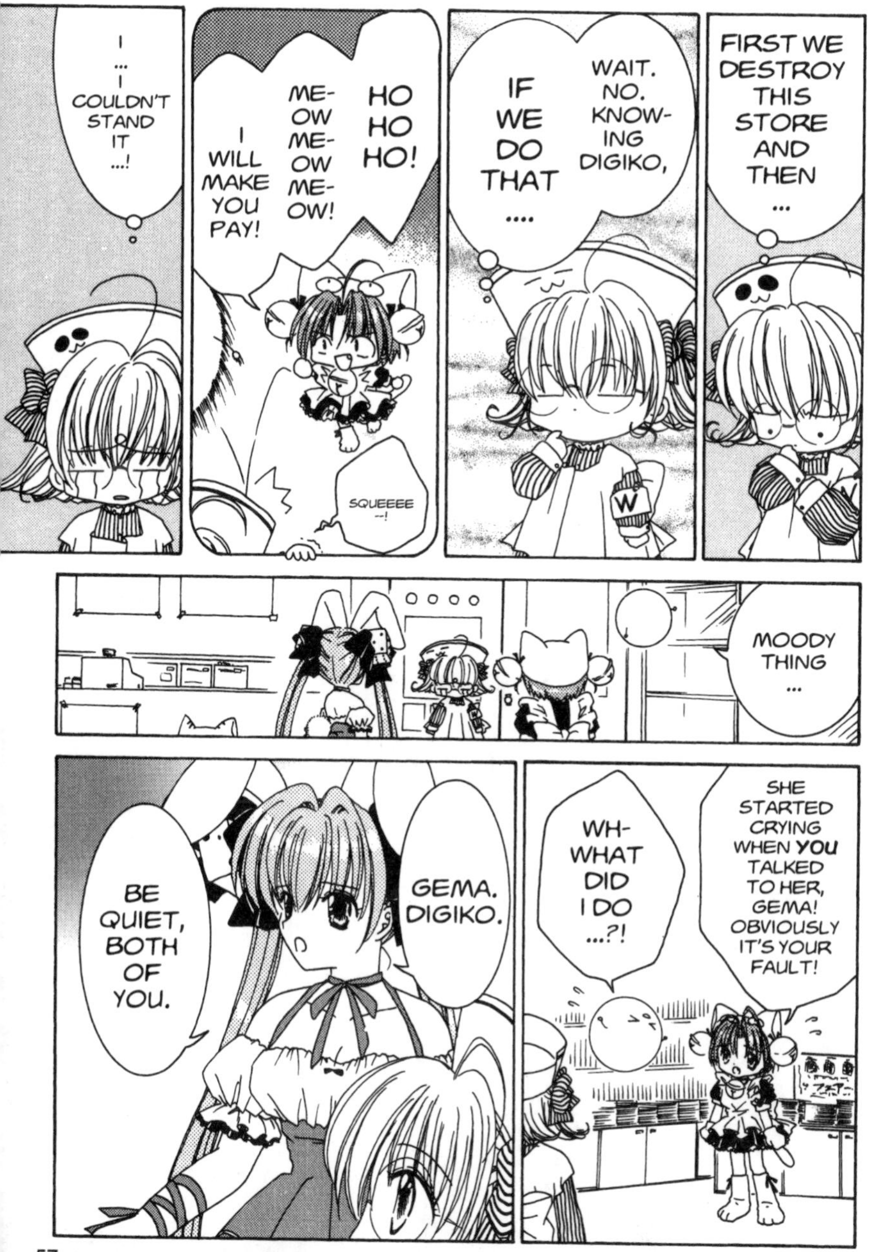
FIRST WE DESTROY THIS STORE AND THEN ...
WAIT. NO. KNOWING DIGIKO,
IF WE DO THAT ....
HO HO HO!
ME-OW ME-OW ME-OW!
I WILL MAKE YOU PAY!
SQUEEEE--!
I ... I COULDN'T STAND IT ...!
MOODY THING ...
SHE STARTED CRYING WHEN **YOU** TALKED TO HER, GEMA! OBVIOUSLY IT'S YOUR FAULT!
WH- WHAT DID I DO ...?!
GEMA. DIGIKO.
BE QUIET, BOTH OF YOU.

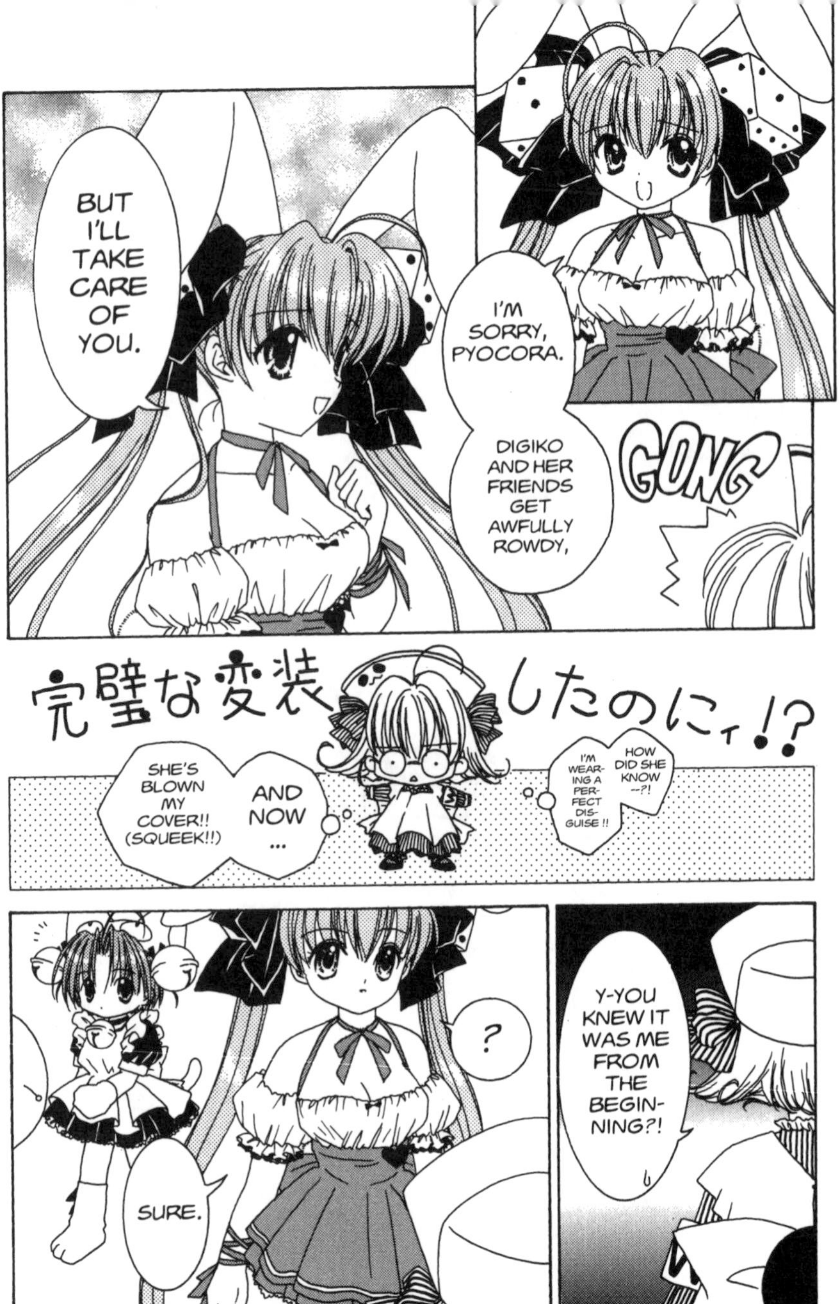
I'M SORRY, PYOCORA.
DIGIKO AND HER FRIENDS GET AWFULLY ROWDY,
GONG
BUT I'LL TAKE CARE OF YOU.
完璧な変装したのにィ!?
HOW DID SHE KNOW--?!
I'M WEARING A PERFECT DISGUISE!!
AND NOW...
SHE'S BLOWN MY COVER!! (SQUEEK!!)
Y-YOU KNEW IT WAS ME FROM THE BEGINNING?!
?
SURE.

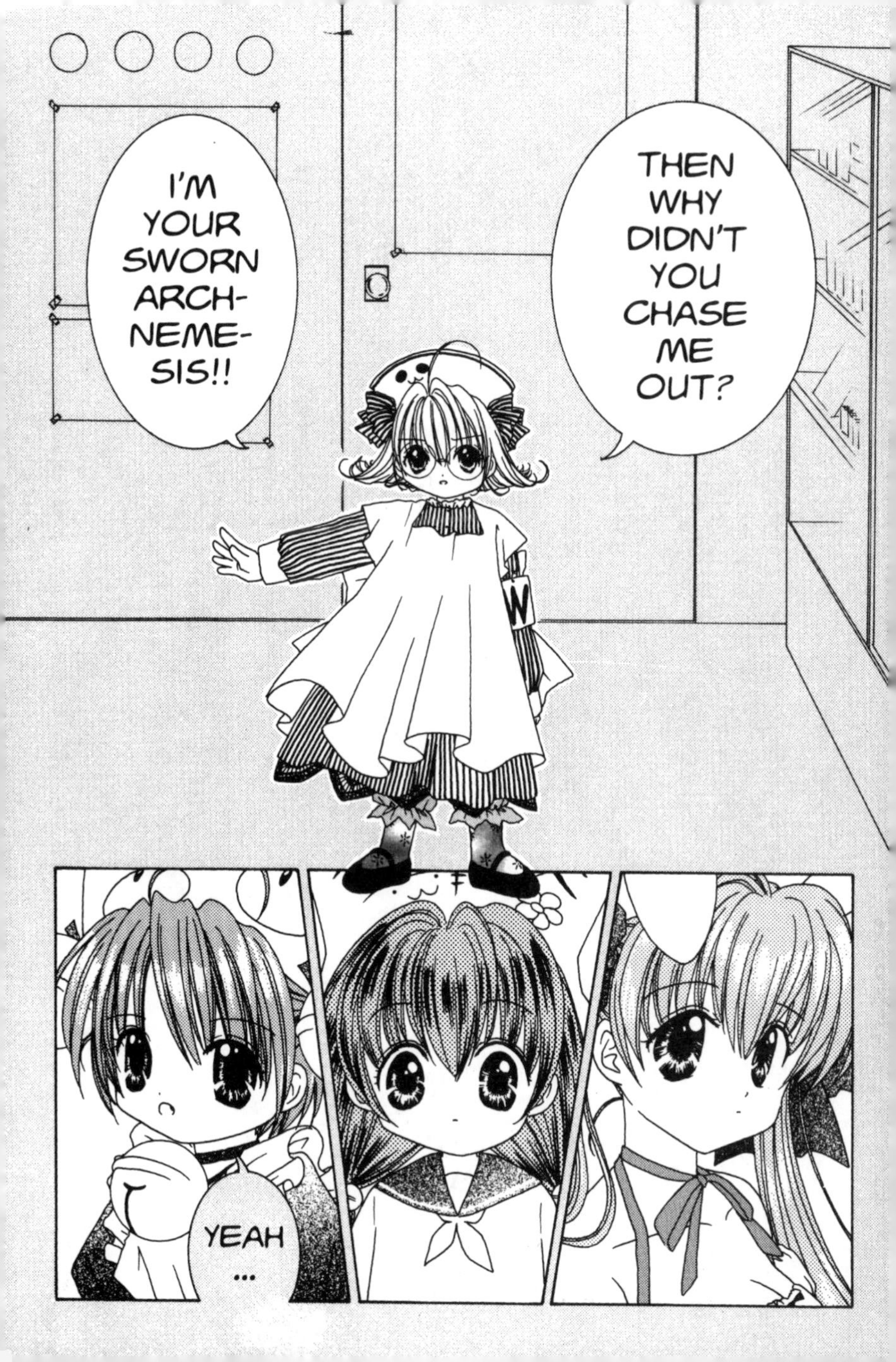
THEN WHY DIDN'T YOU CHASE ME OUT?
I'M YOUR SWORN ARCH-NEMESIS!!
YEAH ...

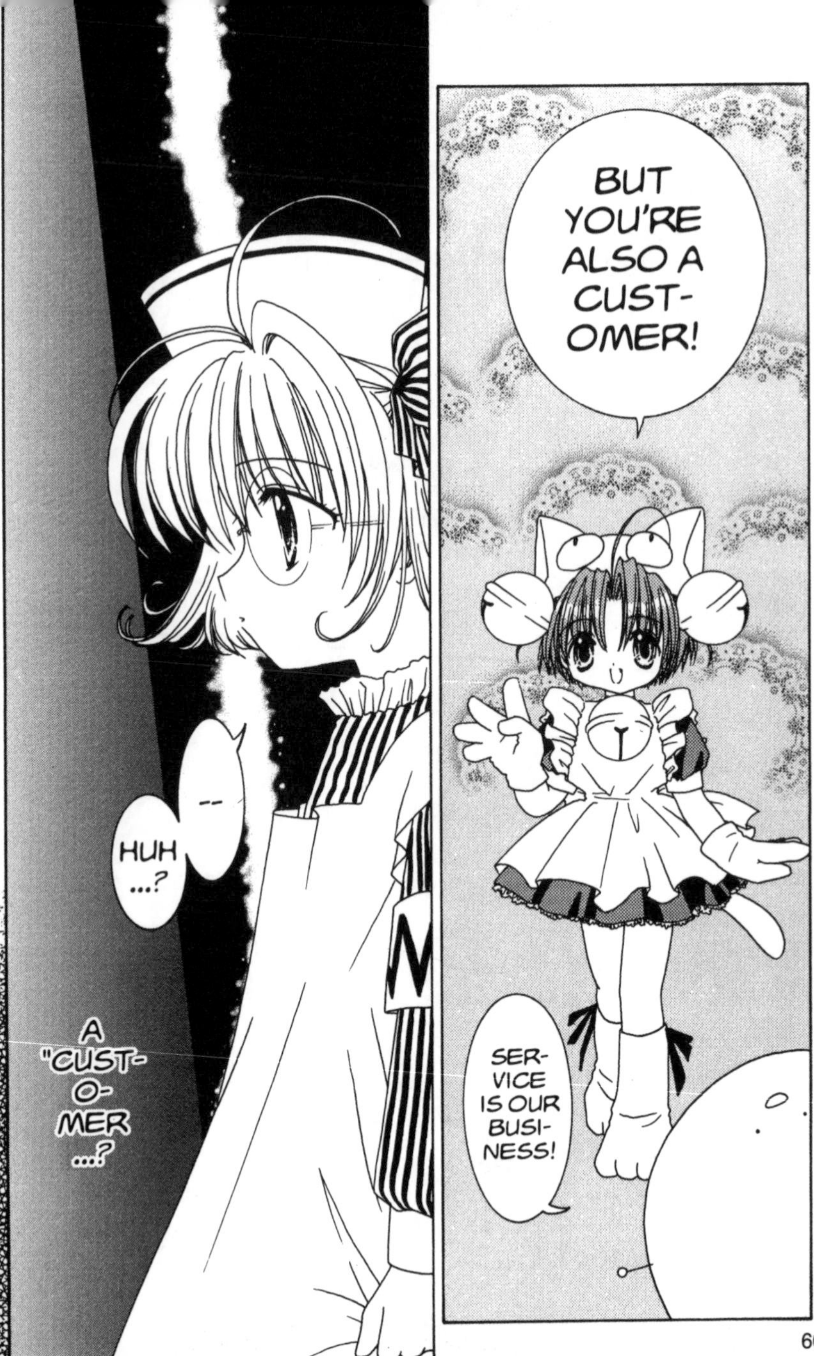
BUT YOU'RE ALSO A CUST-OMER!
SER-VICE IS OUR BUSI-NESS!
--
HUH ...?
A "CUST-O-MER ...?

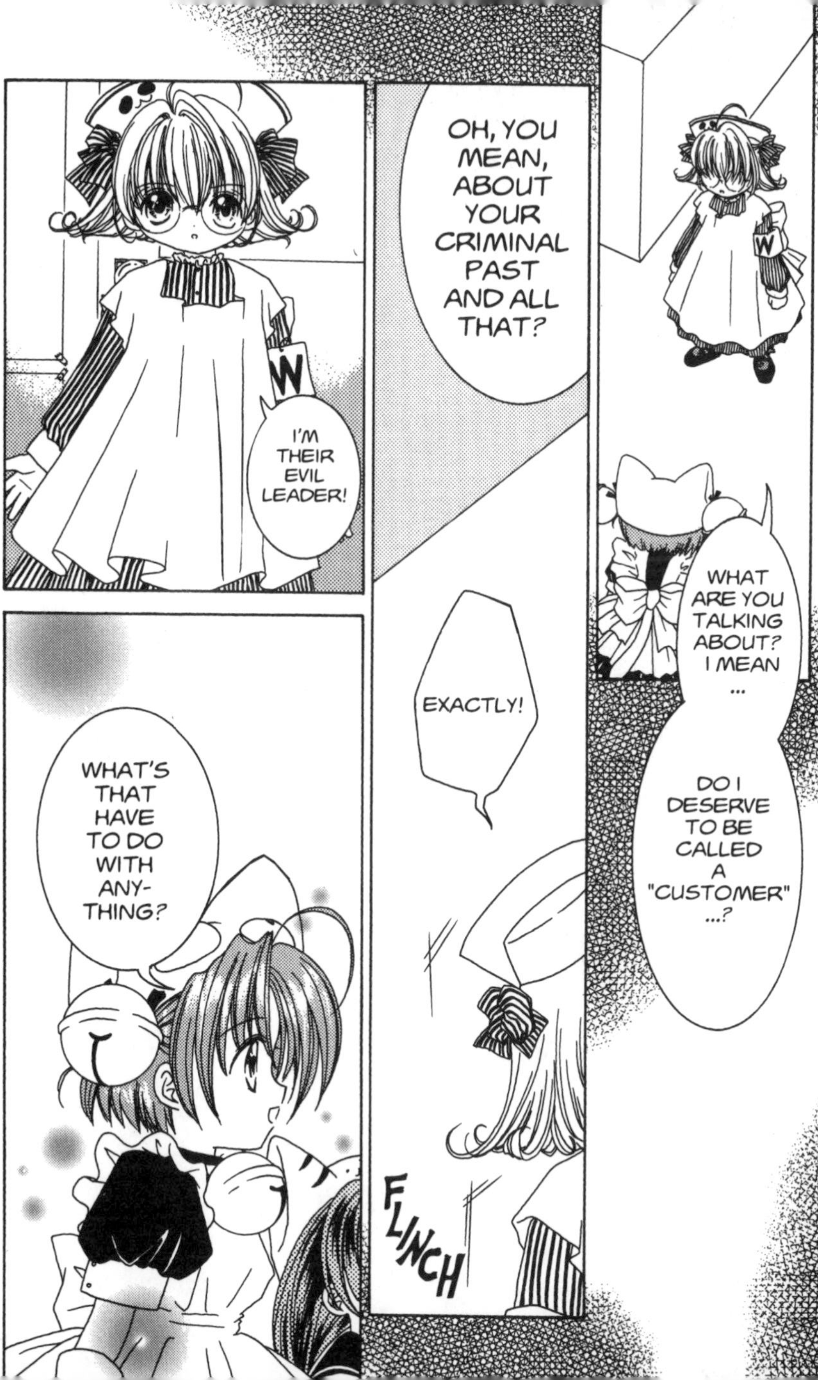
WHAT ARE YOU TALKING ABOUT? I MEAN ...
DO I DESERVE TO BE CALLED A "CUSTOMER" ...?
OH, YOU MEAN, ABOUT YOUR CRIMINAL PAST AND ALL THAT?
EXACTLY!
FLINCH
I'M THEIR EVIL LEADER!
WHAT'S THAT HAVE TO DO WITH ANY-THING?

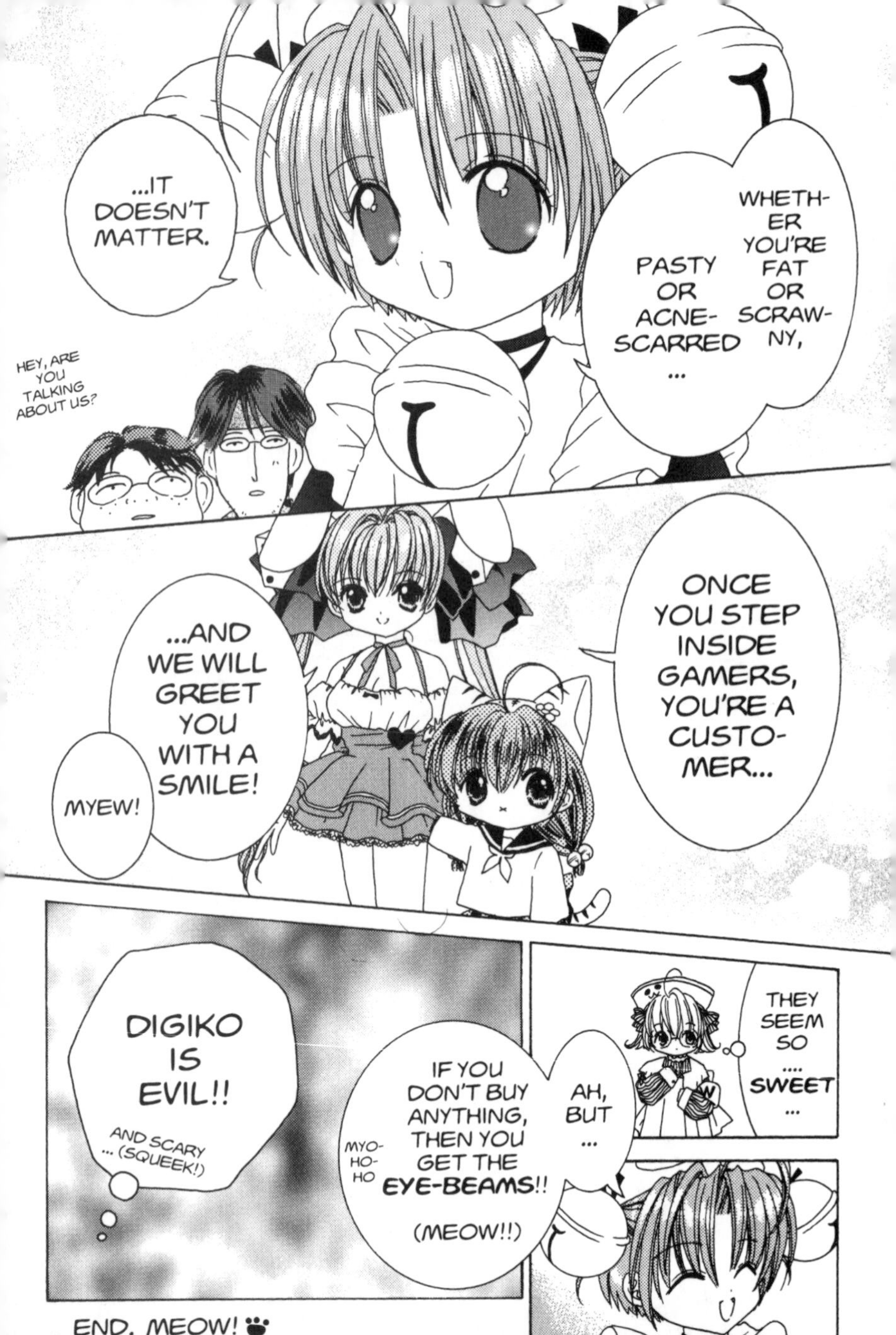
WHETHER YOU'RE FAT OR SCRAWNY, PASTY OR ACNE-SCARRED...
...IT DOESN'T MATTER.
HEY, ARE YOU TALKING ABOUT US?
ONCE YOU STEP INSIDE GAMERS, YOU'RE A CUSTOMER...
...AND WE WILL GREET YOU WITH A SMILE!
MYEW!
THEY SEEM SO .... SWEET ...
AH, BUT ...
IF YOU DON'T BUY ANYTHING, THEN YOU GET THE EYE-BEAMS!!
(MEOW!!)
MYO-HO-HO
DIGIKO IS EVIL!!
AND SCARY ... (SQUEEK!)

END. MEOW!

WHAT WOULD YOU LIKE TO SEE HAPPEN AT GAMERS?

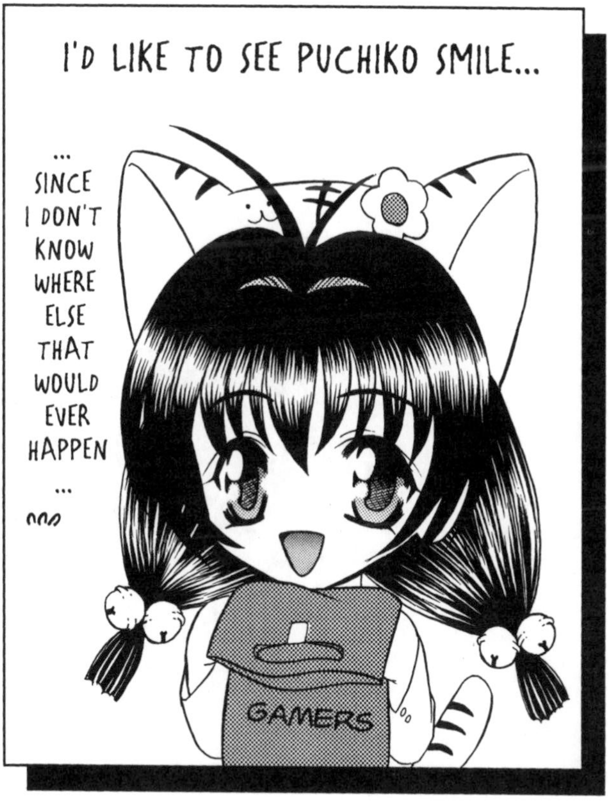

I'D LIKE TO SEE PUCHIKO SMILE...
... SINCE I DON'T KNOW WHERE ELSE THAT WOULD EVER HAPPEN ...
GAMERS

YUMA SUZUKA

WHAT WOULD YOU LIKE TO SEE HAPPEN AT GAMERS?

I'D BE SATISFIED JUST TO SEE DIGIKO AND HER FRIENDS HAPPY. (PUBLIC STATEMENT)

GEMA AS A TAKE-OUT ITEM. (THE TRUTH)

SEARA ♥ WITH PASTEL

THANKS TO: W. YUKIKO AND MIKAWA YUKI, YUMEKI

SEARA

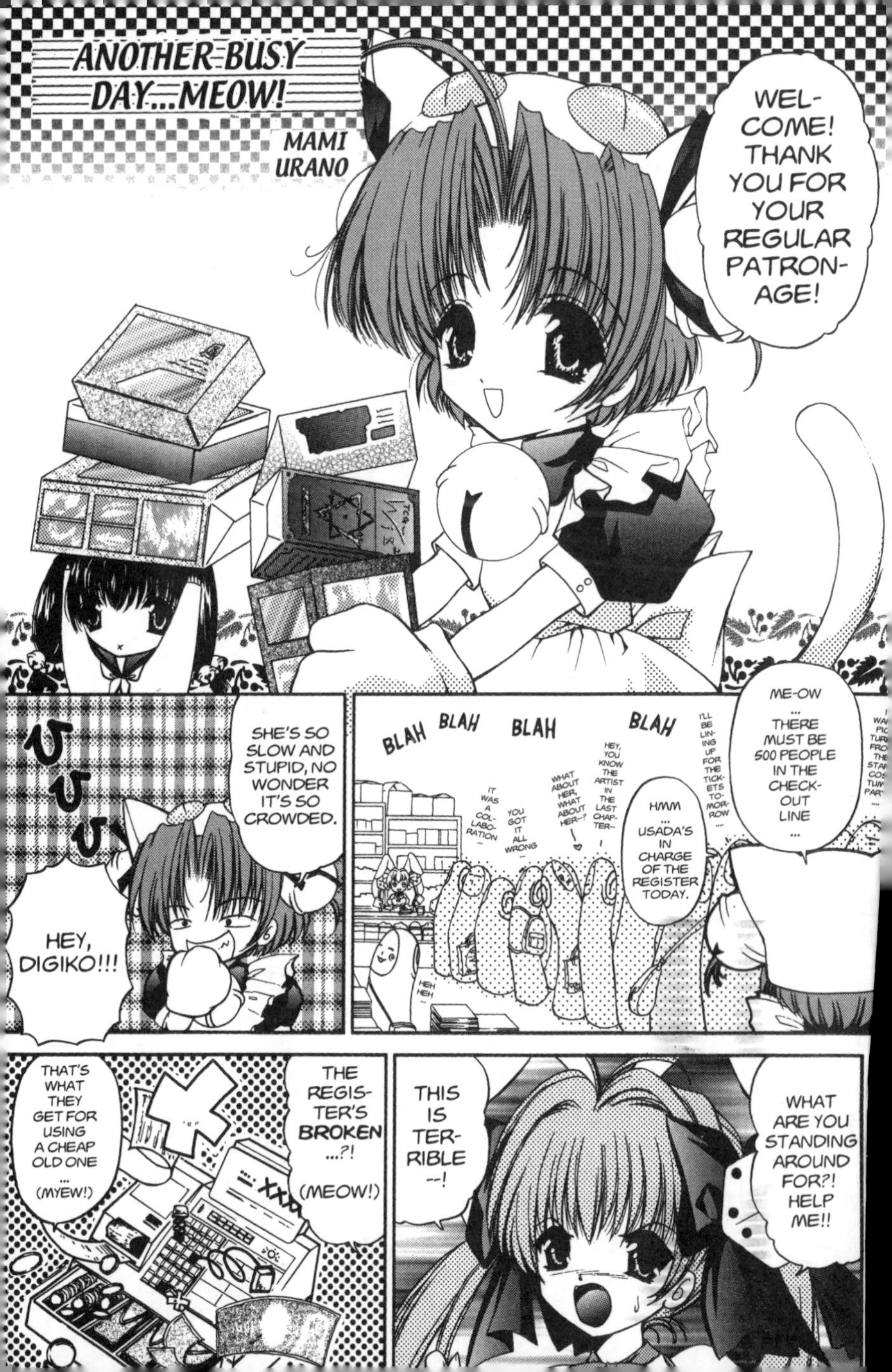
ANOTHER BUSY DAY...MEOW!
MAMI URANO
WEL-COME! THANK YOU FOR YOUR REGULAR PATRON-AGE!
ME-OW ... THERE MUST BE 500 PEOPLE IN THE CHECK-OUT LINE ...
I'LL BE LINING UP FOR THE TICK-ETS TO-MOR-ROW ...
BLAH
HEY, YOU KNOW THE ARTIST IN THE LAST CHAP-TER--
HMM ... USADA'S IN CHARGE OF THE REGISTER TODAY.
BLAH
WHAT ABOUT HER, WHAT ABOUT HER--?
BLAH
YOU GOT IT ALL WRONG --
IT WAS A COL-LABO-RATION --
BLAH
HEH HEH --
SHE'S SO SLOW AND STUPID, NO WONDER IT'S SO CROWDED.
HEY, DIGIKO!!!
WHAT ARE YOU STANDING AROUND FOR?! HELP ME!!
THIS IS TER-RIBLE --!
THE REGIS-TER'S **BROKEN** ...?! (MEOW!)
THAT'S WHAT THEY GET FOR USING A CHEAP OLD ONE ... (MYEW!)

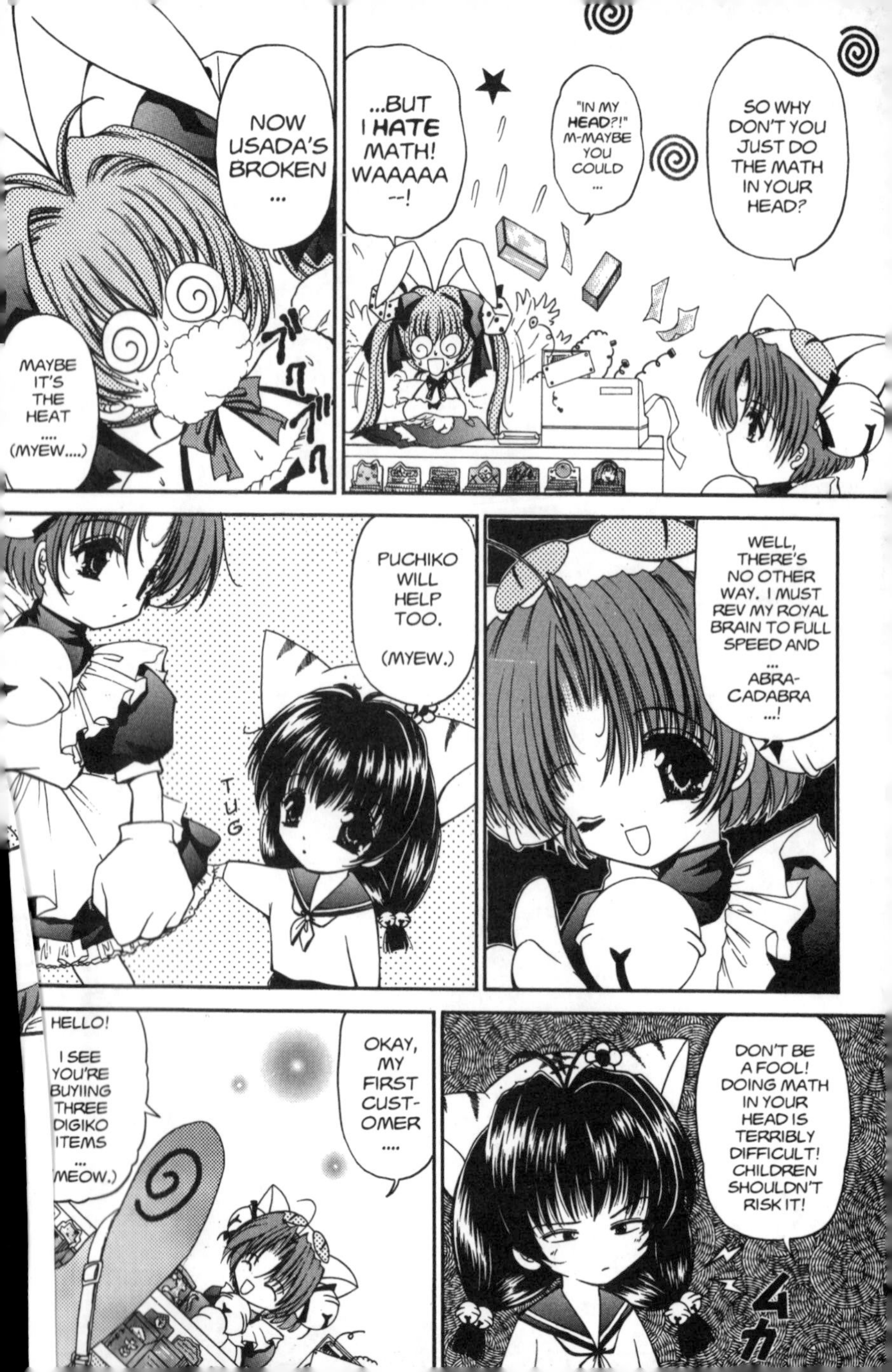
SO WHY DON'T YOU JUST DO THE MATH IN YOUR HEAD?
"IN MY HEAD?!" M-MAYBE YOU COULD ...
...BUT I HATE MATH! WAAAAA--!
NOW USADA'S BROKEN ...
MAYBE IT'S THE HEAT .... (MYEW....)
WELL, THERE'S NO OTHER WAY. I MUST REV MY ROYAL BRAIN TO FULL SPEED AND ... ABRA-CADABRA ...!
PUCHIKO WILL HELP TOO. (MYEW.)
TUG
DON'T BE A FOOL! DOING MATH IN YOUR HEAD IS TERRIBLY DIFFICULT! CHILDREN SHOULDN'T RISK IT!
ムカ
OKAY, MY FIRST CUST-OMER ....
HELLO! I SEE YOU'RE BUYIING THREE DIGIKO ITEMS ... MEOW.)

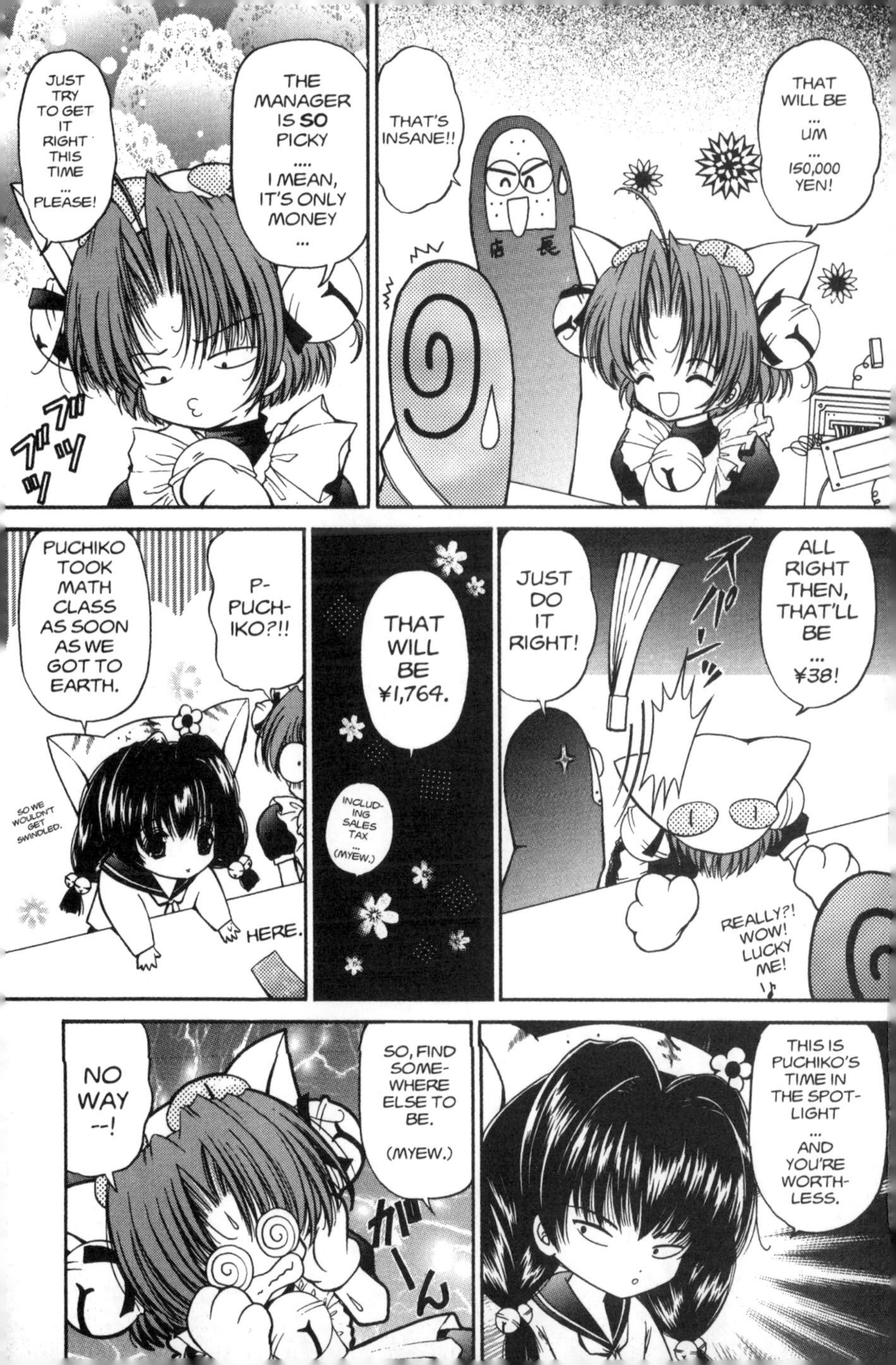
THAT WILL BE ... UM ... 150,000 YEN!
店長
THAT'S INSANE!!
THE MANAGER IS SO PICKY .... I MEAN, IT'S ONLY MONEY ...
JUST TRY TO GET IT RIGHT THIS TIME ... PLEASE!
ALL RIGHT THEN, THAT'LL BE ... ¥38!
JUST DO IT RIGHT!
REALLY?! WOW! LUCKY ME!
THAT WILL BE ¥1,764.
INCLUDING SALES TAX ... (MYEW.)
P-PUCHIKO?!!
PUCHIKO TOOK MATH CLASS AS SOON AS WE GOT TO EARTH.
SO WE WOULDN'T GET SWINDLED.
HERE.
THIS IS PUCHIKO'S TIME IN THE SPOTLIGHT ... AND YOU'RE WORTHLESS.
SO, FIND SOMEWHERE ELSE TO BE. (MYEW.)
NO WAY --!

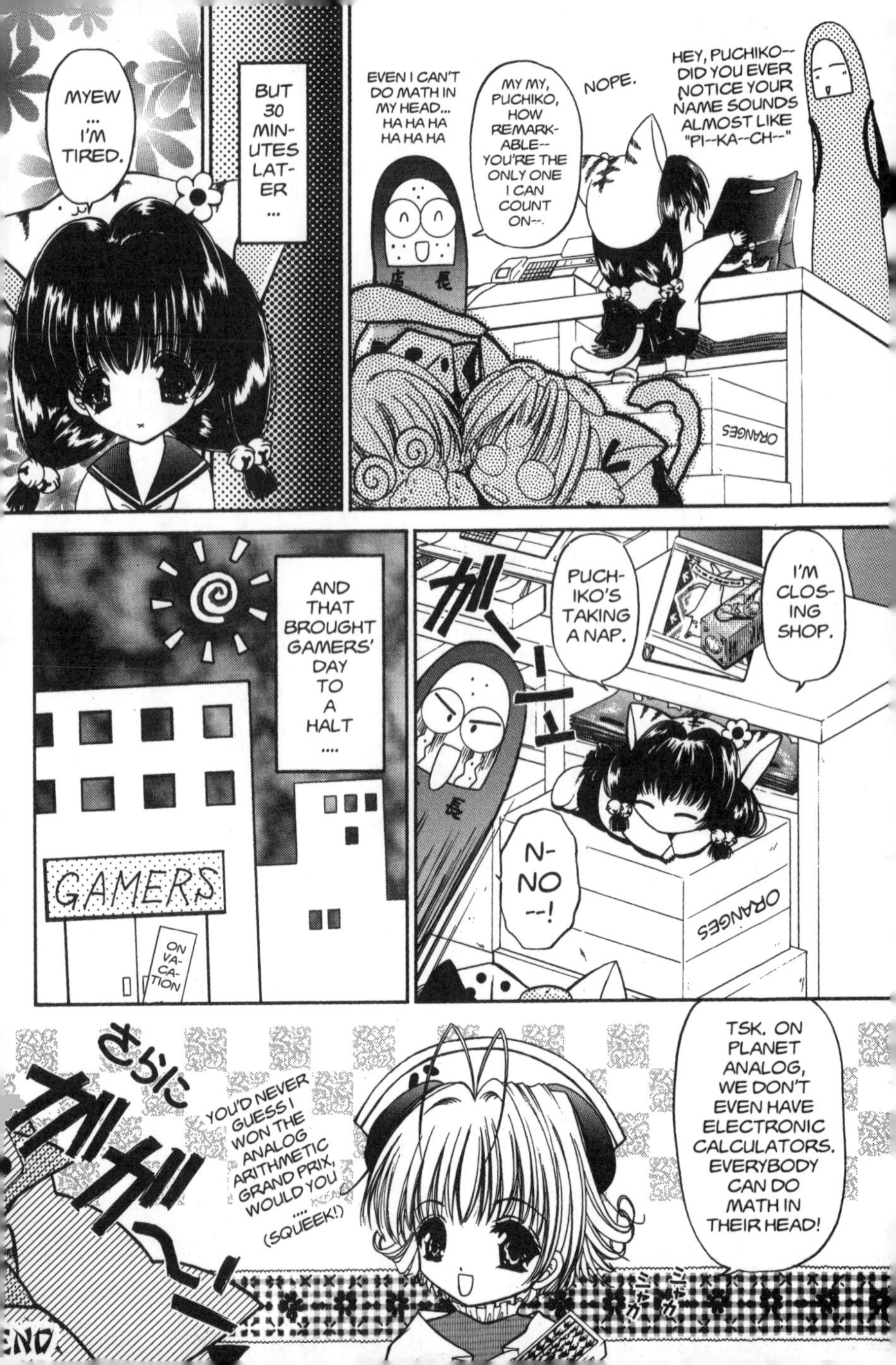

HEY, PUCHIKO-- DID YOU EVER NOTICE YOUR NAME SOUNDS ALMOST LIKE "PI--KA--CH--"
NOPE.
MY MY, PUCHIKO, HOW REMARKABLE-- YOU'RE THE ONLY ONE I CAN COUNT ON--.
EVEN I CAN'T DO MATH IN MY HEAD... HA HA HA HA HA HA
ORANGES
BUT 30 MINUTES LATER ...
MYEW ... I'M TIRED.
I'M CLOSING SHOP.
PUCHIKO'S TAKING A NAP.
ガーン
N-NO --!
ORANGES
AND THAT BROUGHT GAMERS' DAY TO A HALT ....
GAMERS
ON VACATION
TSK. ON PLANET ANALOG, WE DON'T EVEN HAVE ELECTRONIC CALCULATORS. EVERYBODY CAN DO MATH IN THEIR HEAD!
YOU'D NEVER GUESS I WON THE ANALOG ARITHMETIC GRAND PRIX, WOULD YOU .... (SQUEEK!)
さらに
ガガ〜ン
END

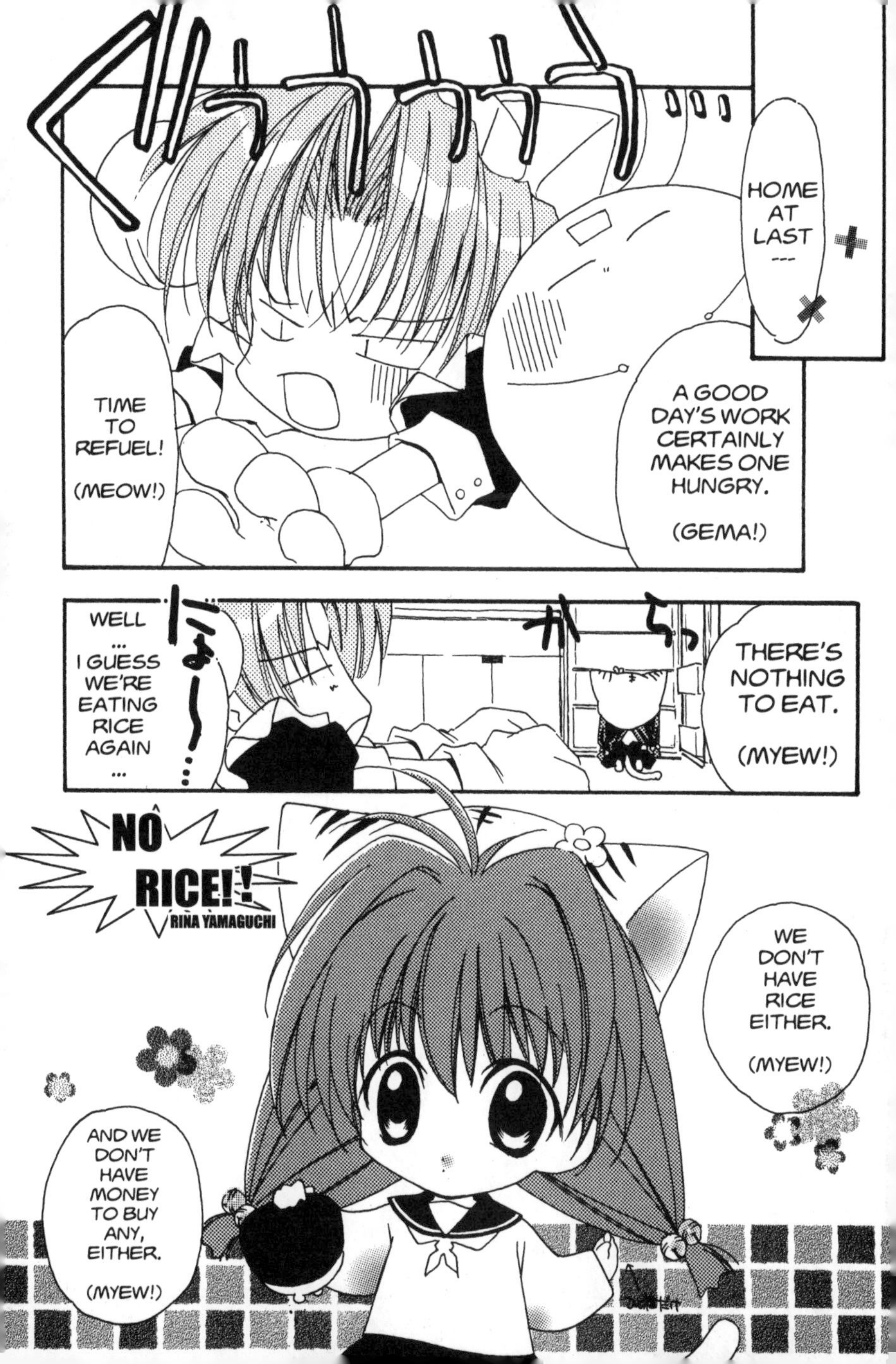
HOME AT LAST ---
A GOOD DAY'S WORK CERTAINLY MAKES ONE HUNGRY. (GEMA!)
TIME TO REFUEL! (MEOW!)
THERE'S NOTHING TO EAT. (MYEW!)
WELL ... I GUESS WE'RE EATING RICE AGAIN ...
NÔ RICE!!
RINA YAMAGUCHI
WE DON'T HAVE RICE EITHER. (MYEW!)
AND WE DON'T HAVE MONEY TO BUY ANY, EITHER. (MYEW!)

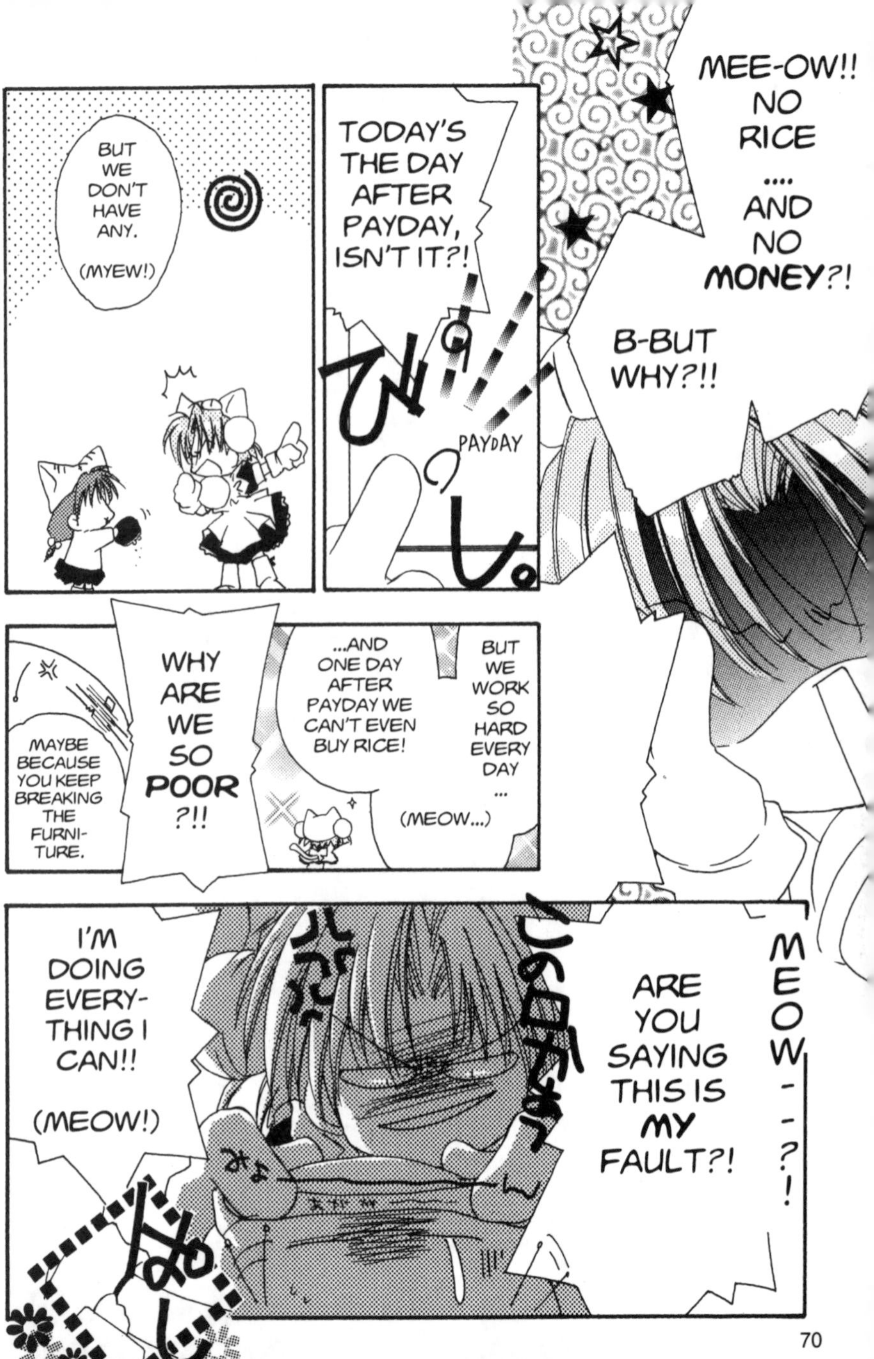
MEE-OW!! NO RICE .... AND NO MONEY?!
B-BUT WHY?!!
TODAY'S THE DAY AFTER PAYDAY, ISN'T IT?!
PAYDAY
BUT WE DON'T HAVE ANY.
(MYEW!)
BUT WE WORK SO HARD EVERY DAY ...
(MEOW...)
...AND ONE DAY AFTER PAYDAY WE CAN'T EVEN BUY RICE!
WHY ARE WE SO POOR?!!
MAYBE BECAUSE YOU KEEP BREAKING THE FURNITURE.
MEOW--?!
ARE YOU SAYING THIS IS MY FAULT?!
I'M DOING EVERYTHING I CAN!!
(MEOW!)

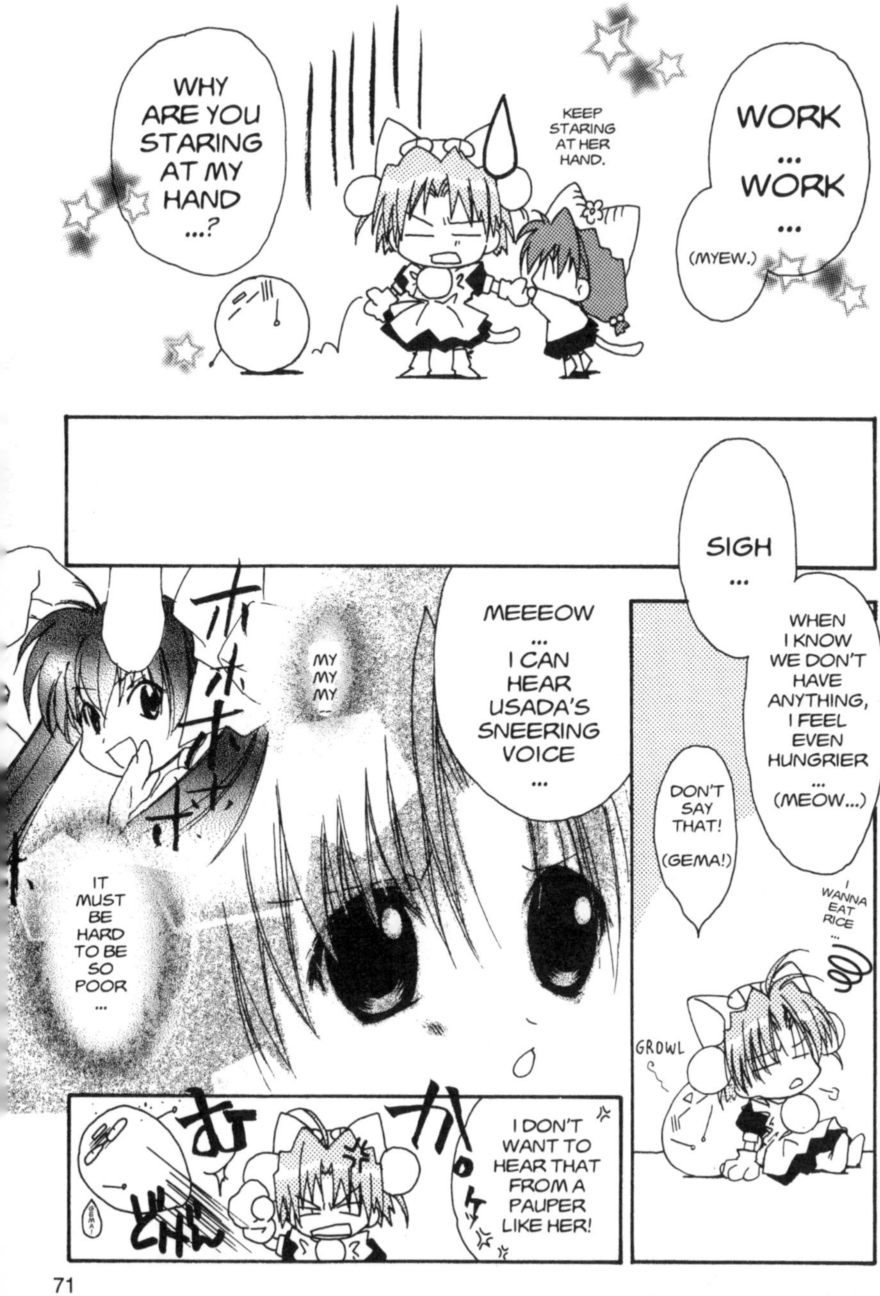
WORK ... WORK ...
(MYEW.)
KEEP STARING AT HER HAND.
WHY ARE YOU STARING AT MY HAND ...?
SIGH ...
WHEN I KNOW WE DON'T HAVE ANYTHING, I FEEL EVEN HUNGRIER ... (MEOW...)
DON'T SAY THAT!
(GEMA!)
I WANNA EAT RICE ...
GROWL
MEEEOW ... I CAN HEAR USADA'S SNEERING VOICE ...
MY MY MY ...
IT MUST BE HARD TO BE SO POOR ...
I DON'T WANT TO HEAR THAT FROM A PAUPER LIKE HER!
GEMA!

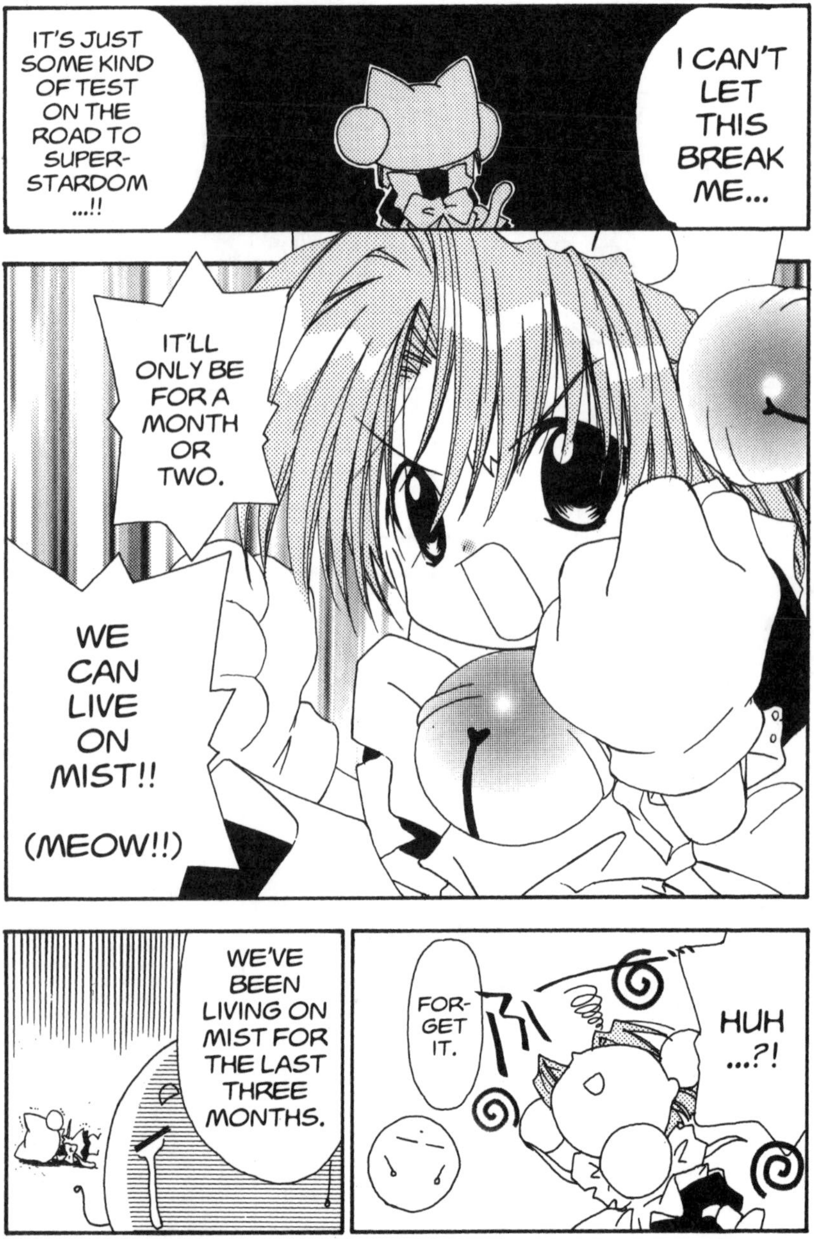

I CAN'T LET THIS BREAK ME...
IT'S JUST SOME KIND OF TEST ON THE ROAD TO SUPER-STARDOM ...!!
IT'LL ONLY BE FOR A MONTH OR TWO.
WE CAN LIVE ON MIST!! (MEOW!!)
HUH ...?!
FOR-GET IT.
WE'VE BEEN LIVING ON MIST FOR THE LAST THREE MONTHS.

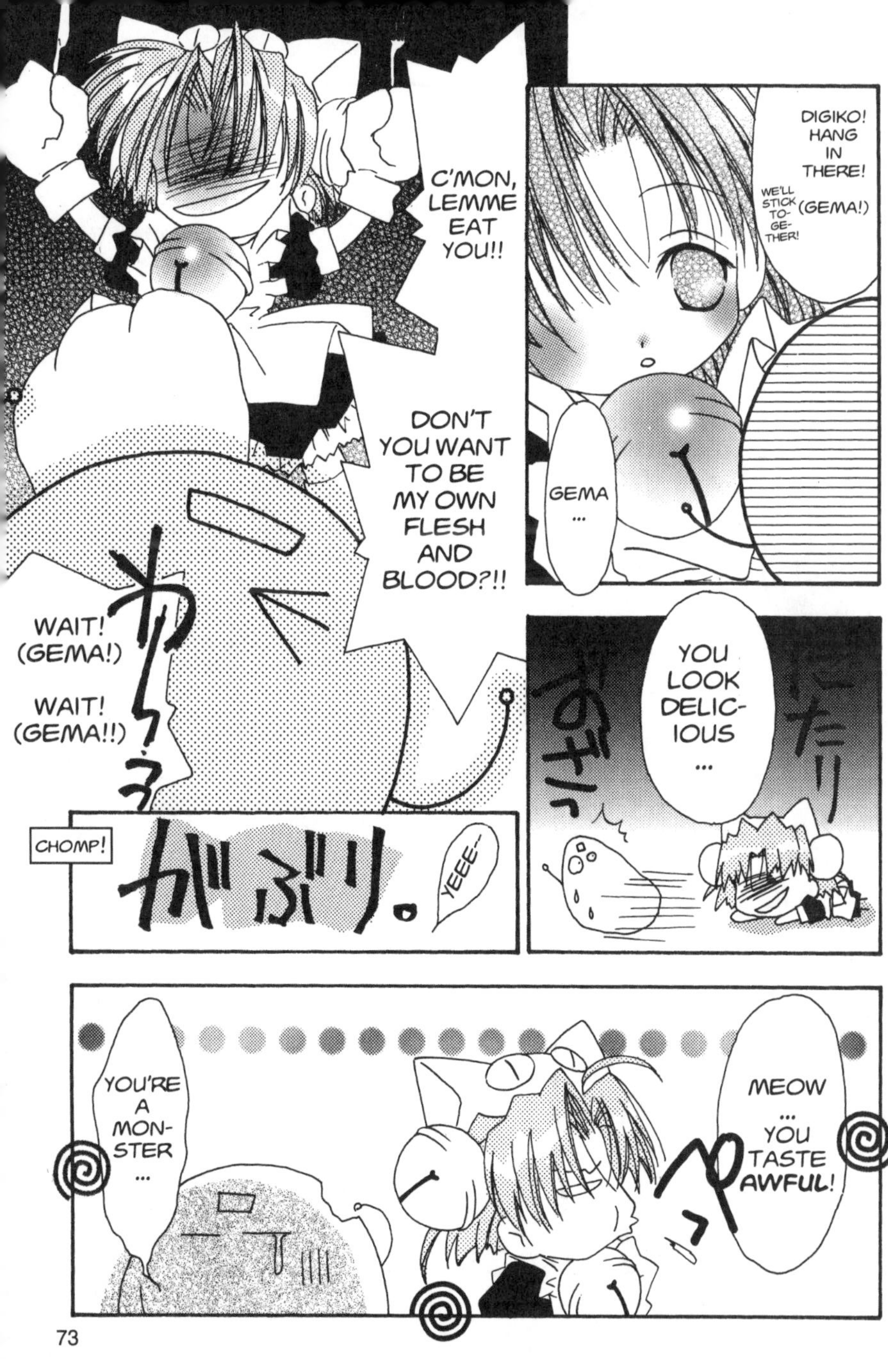

DIGIKO! HANG IN THERE! (GEMA!)
WE'LL STICK TO-GE-THER!
GEMA ...
YOU LOOK DELIC-IOUS ...
C'MON, LEMME EAT YOU!!
DON'T YOU WANT TO BE MY OWN FLESH AND BLOOD?!!
WAIT! (GEMA!)
WAIT! (GEMA!!)
CHOMP!
かぶり。
YEEE-
MEOW ... YOU TASTE AWFUL!
YOU'RE A MON-STER ...

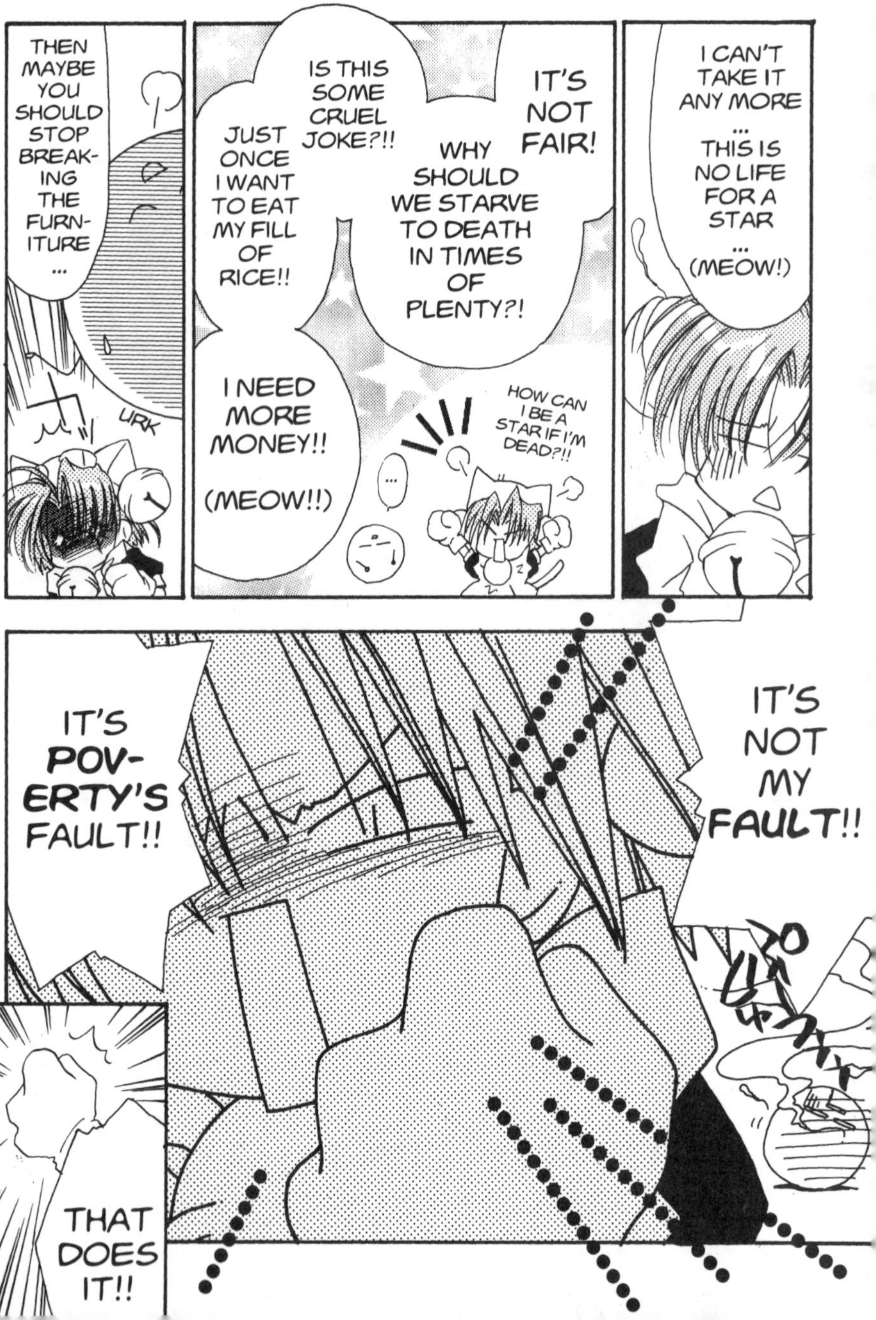
I CAN'T TAKE IT ANY MORE ... THIS IS NO LIFE FOR A STAR ... (MEOW!)
IT'S NOT FAIR!
WHY SHOULD WE STARVE TO DEATH IN TIMES OF PLENTY?!
IS THIS SOME CRUEL JOKE?!!
JUST ONCE I WANT TO EAT MY FILL OF RICE!!
HOW CAN I BE A STAR IF I'M DEAD?!!
I NEED MORE MONEY!! (MEOW!!)
...
THEN MAYBE YOU SHOULD STOP BREAKING THE FURNITURE ...
URK
IT'S NOT MY FAULT!!
IT'S POVERTY'S FAULT!!
THAT DOES IT!!

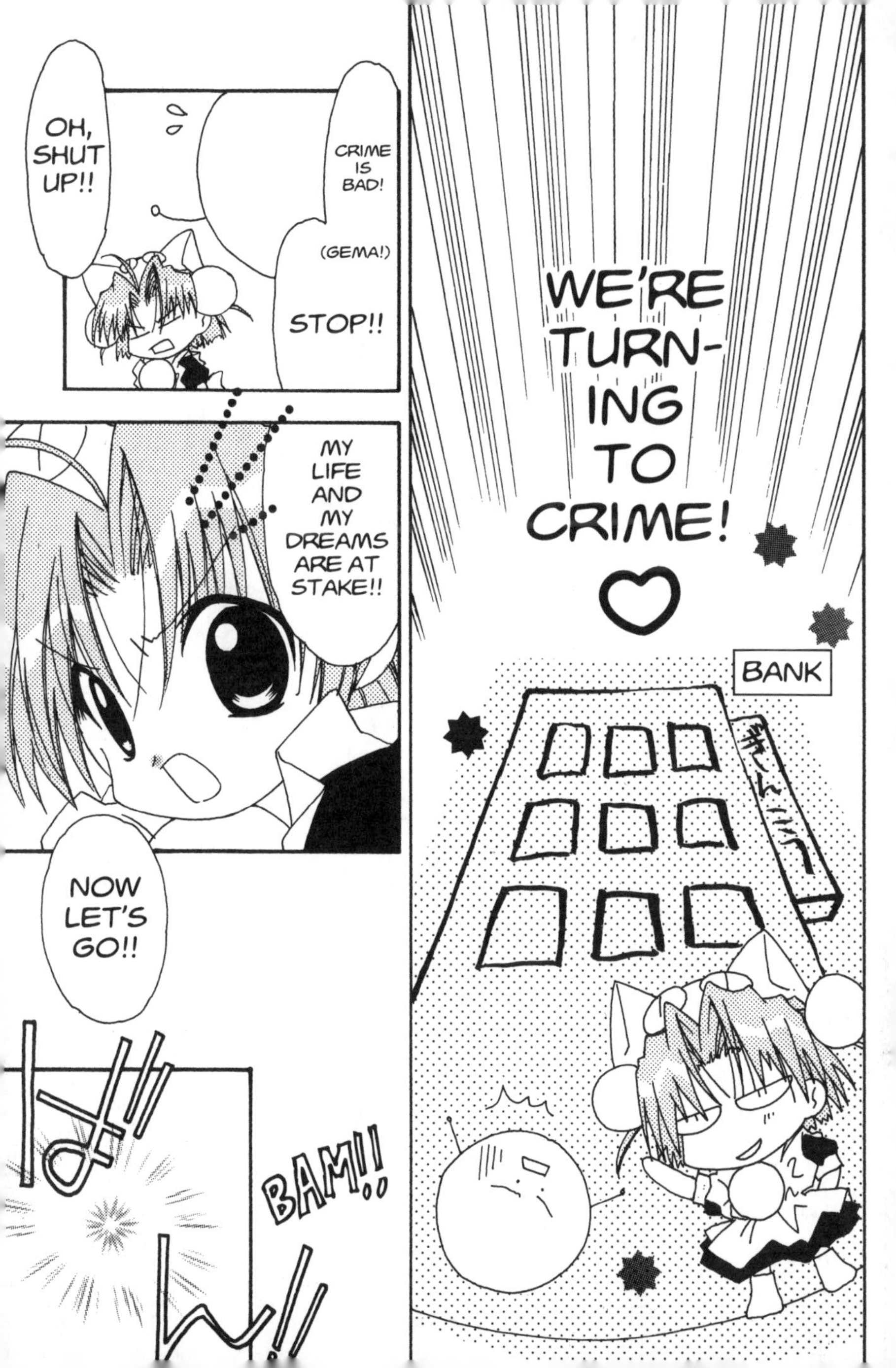
WE'RE TURNING-ING TO CRIME! ♡
BANK
CRIME IS BAD!
(GEMA!)
STOP!!
OH, SHUT UP!!
MY LIFE AND MY DREAMS ARE AT STAKE!!
NOW LET'S GO!!
BAM!!

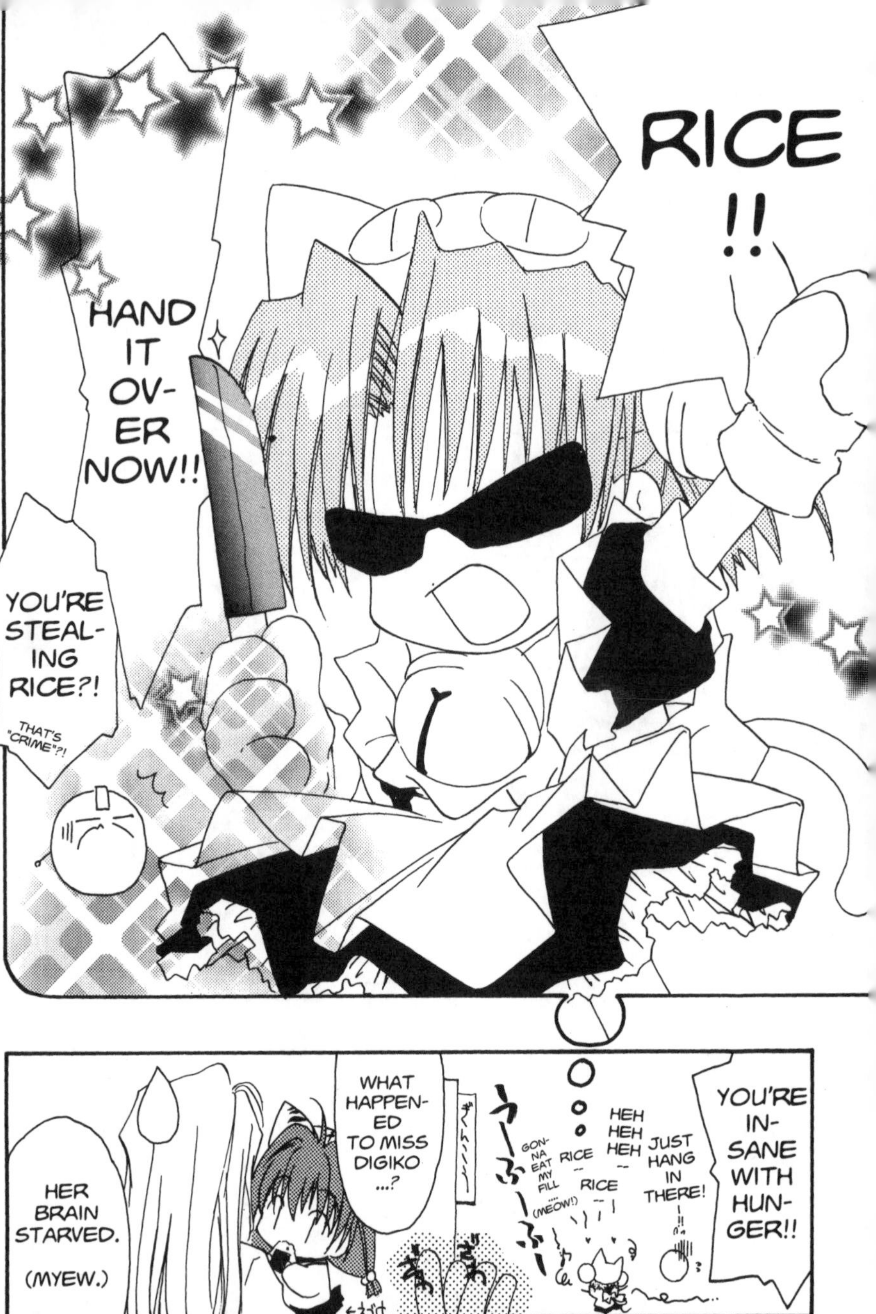
RICE!!
HAND IT OVER NOW!!
YOU'RE STEALING RICE?!
THAT'S "CRIME"?!
YOU'RE INSANE WITH HUNGER!!
JUST HANG IN THERE!
HEH HEH HEH
RICE RICE
GONNA EAT MY FILL.... (MEOW!)
WHAT HAPPENED TO MISS DIGIKO...?
HER BRAIN STARVED.
(MYEW.)

END

↑ BAITED BY FOOD

WHAT WOULD YOU LIKE TO SEE HAPPEN AT GAMERS?

A GAME OF TAG WITH DIGIKO... WITH THE FATE OF EARTH AT STAKE. WHOEVER GRABS HER CAT EARS WINS! SINCE DIGIKO BLASTS BEAMS FROM HER EYES...
THE EARTH WOULD GRADUALLY BE DESTROYED AS THE GAME PROGRESSES. YOU COULD TRY IT WITH USADA, TOO---

BUT SINCE SHE CAN FLY
WITH HER EARS,
IT'S A BIT TRICKIER...

HEE
HEE
HEE.

BYE!
MAMI URANO

MAMI URANO

WHAT WOULD YOU LIKE TO SEE HAPPEN AT GAMERS?

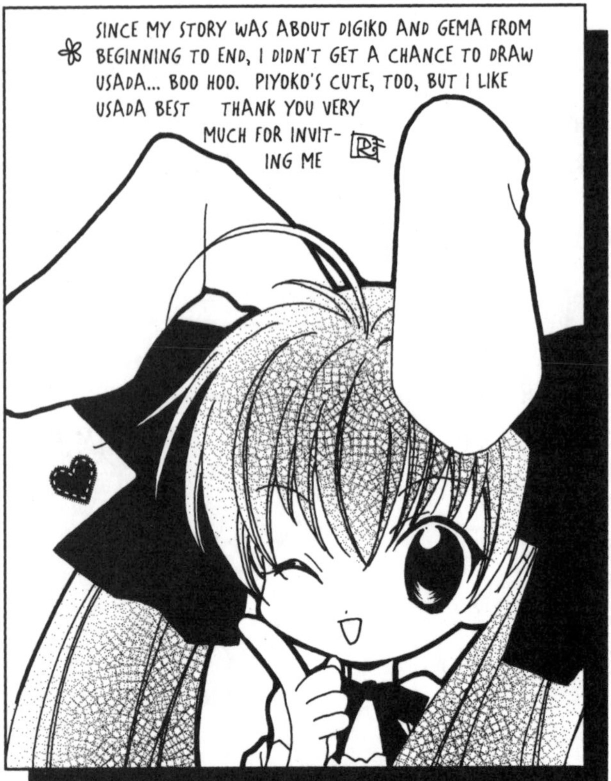
SINCE MY STORY WAS ABOUT DIGIKO AND GEMA FROM BEGINNING TO END, I DIDN'T GET A CHANCE TO DRAW USADA... BOO HOO. PIYOKO'S CUTE, TOO, BUT I LIKE USADA BEST THANK YOU VERY MUCH FOR INVITING ME

RINA YAMAGUCHI

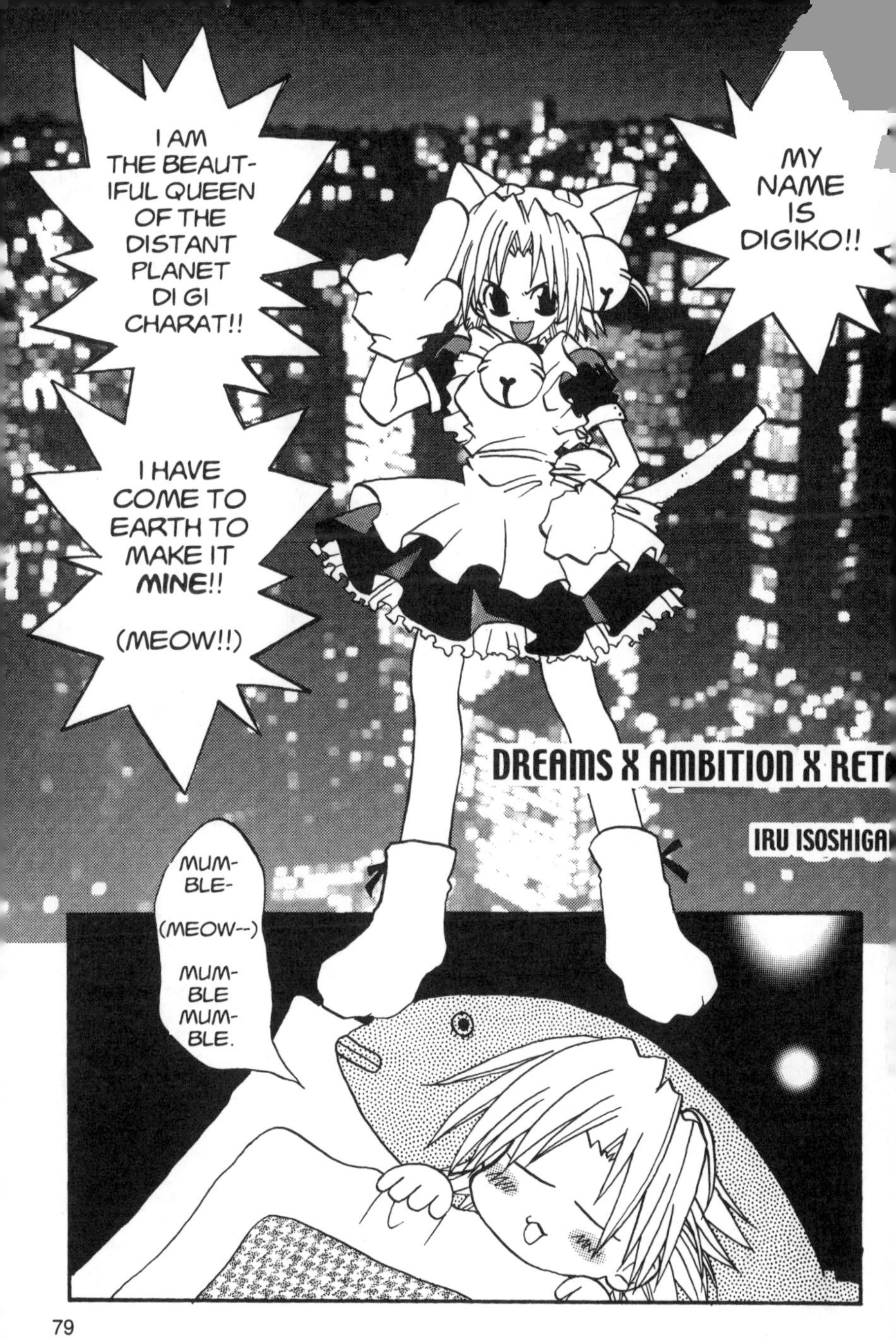
MY NAME IS DIGIKO!!
I AM THE BEAUT-IFUL QUEEN OF THE DISTANT PLANET DI GI CHARAT!!
I HAVE COME TO EARTH TO MAKE IT **MINE**!!
(MEOW!!)
DREAMS X AMBITION X RET
IRU ISOSHIGA
MUM-BLE-
(MEOW--)
MUM-BLE MUM-BLE.

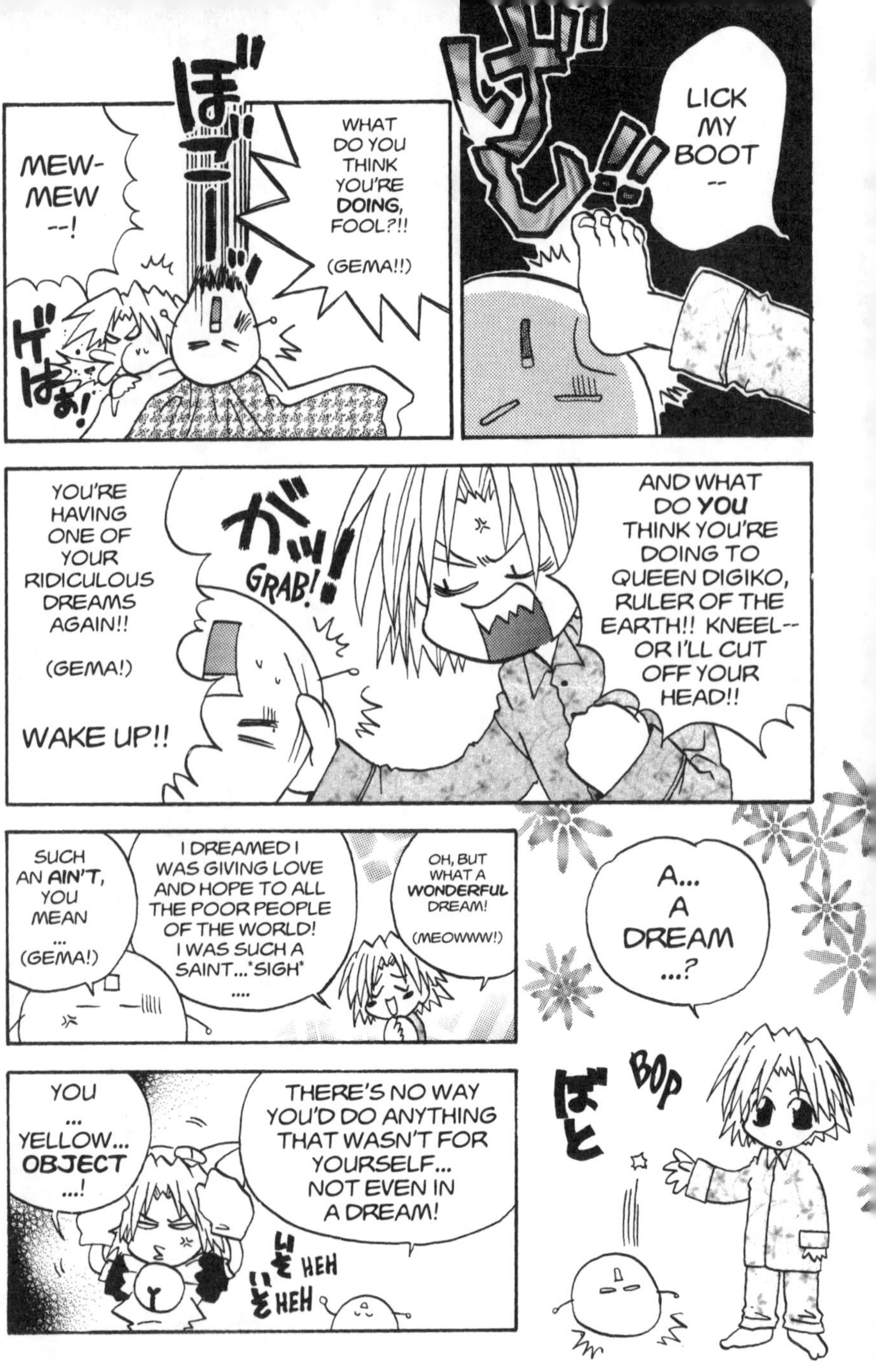
LICK MY BOOT --
WHAT DO YOU THINK YOU'RE **DOING**, FOOL?!!
(GEMA!!)
MEW-MEW --!
AND WHAT DO **YOU** THINK YOU'RE DOING TO QUEEN DIGIKO, RULER OF THE EARTH!! KNEEL-- OR I'LL CUT OFF YOUR HEAD!!
GRAB!!
YOU'RE HAVING ONE OF YOUR RIDICULOUS DREAMS AGAIN!!
(GEMA!)
WAKE UP!!
A... A DREAM ...?
OH, BUT WHAT A **WONDERFUL** DREAM!
(MEOWWW!)
I DREAMED I WAS GIVING LOVE AND HOPE TO ALL THE POOR PEOPLE OF THE WORLD! I WAS SUCH A SAINT...*SIGH* ....
SUCH AN **AIN'T**, YOU MEAN ... (GEMA!)
BOP
THERE'S NO WAY YOU'D DO ANYTHING THAT WASN'T FOR YOURSELF... NOT EVEN IN A DREAM!
YOU ... YELLOW... **OBJECT** ...!
HEH HEH

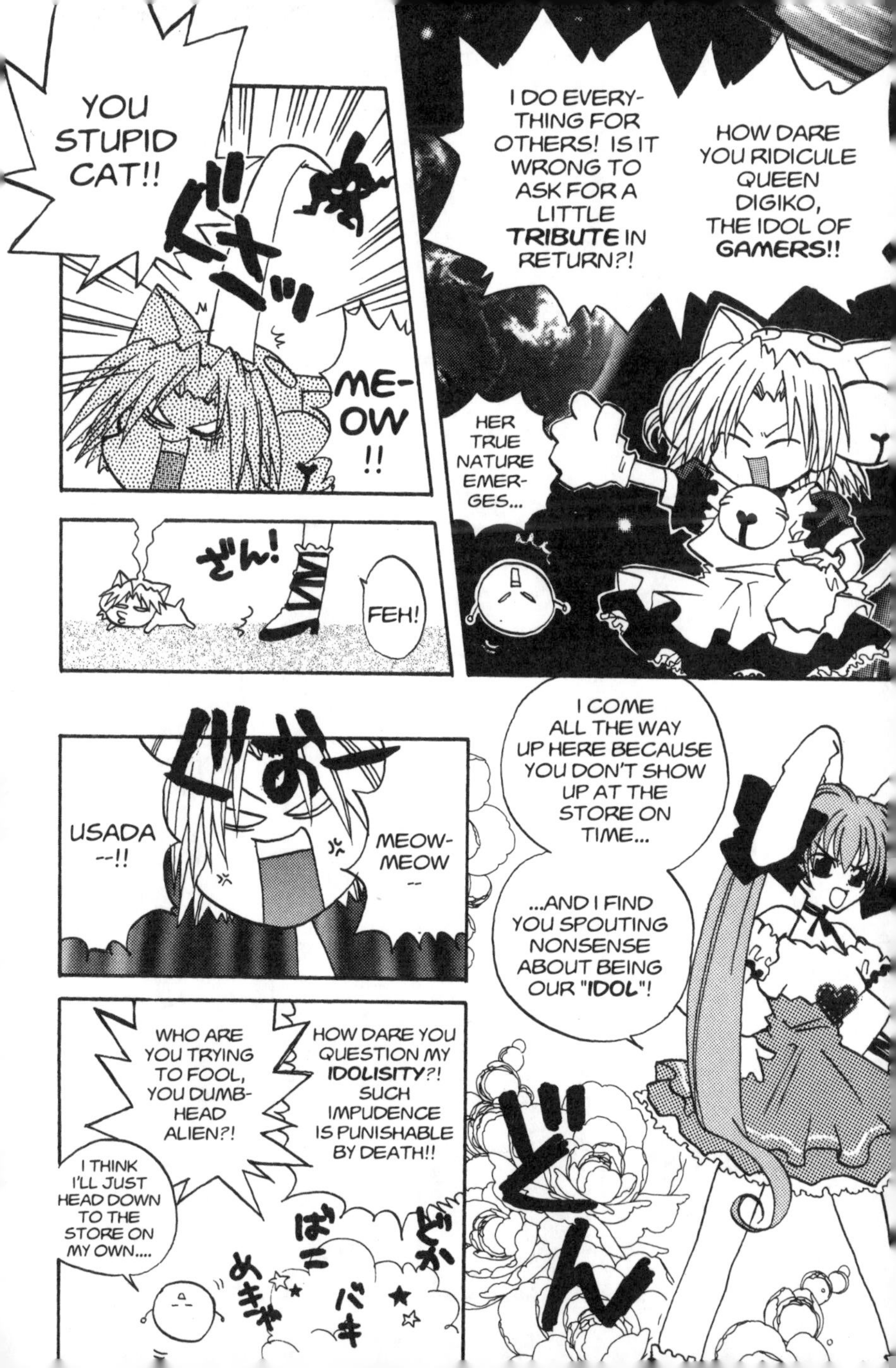
HOW DARE YOU RIDICULE QUEEN DIGIKO, THE IDOL OF GAMERS!!
I DO EVERY-THING FOR OTHERS! IS IT WRONG TO ASK FOR A LITTLE TRIBUTE IN RETURN?!
HER TRUE NATURE EMER-GES...
YOU STUPID CAT!!
ME-OW!!
ざん!
FEH!
I COME ALL THE WAY UP HERE BECAUSE YOU DON'T SHOW UP AT THE STORE ON TIME...
...AND I FIND YOU SPOUTING NONSENSE ABOUT BEING OUR "IDOL"!
どん
MEOW-MEOW --
USADA --!!
HOW DARE YOU QUESTION MY IDOLISITY?! SUCH IMPUDENCE IS PUNISHABLE BY DEATH!!
WHO ARE YOU TRYING TO FOOL, YOU DUMB-HEAD ALIEN?!
I THINK I'LL JUST HEAD DOWN TO THE STORE ON MY OWN....
どか
バキ
ばこ
めきゃ

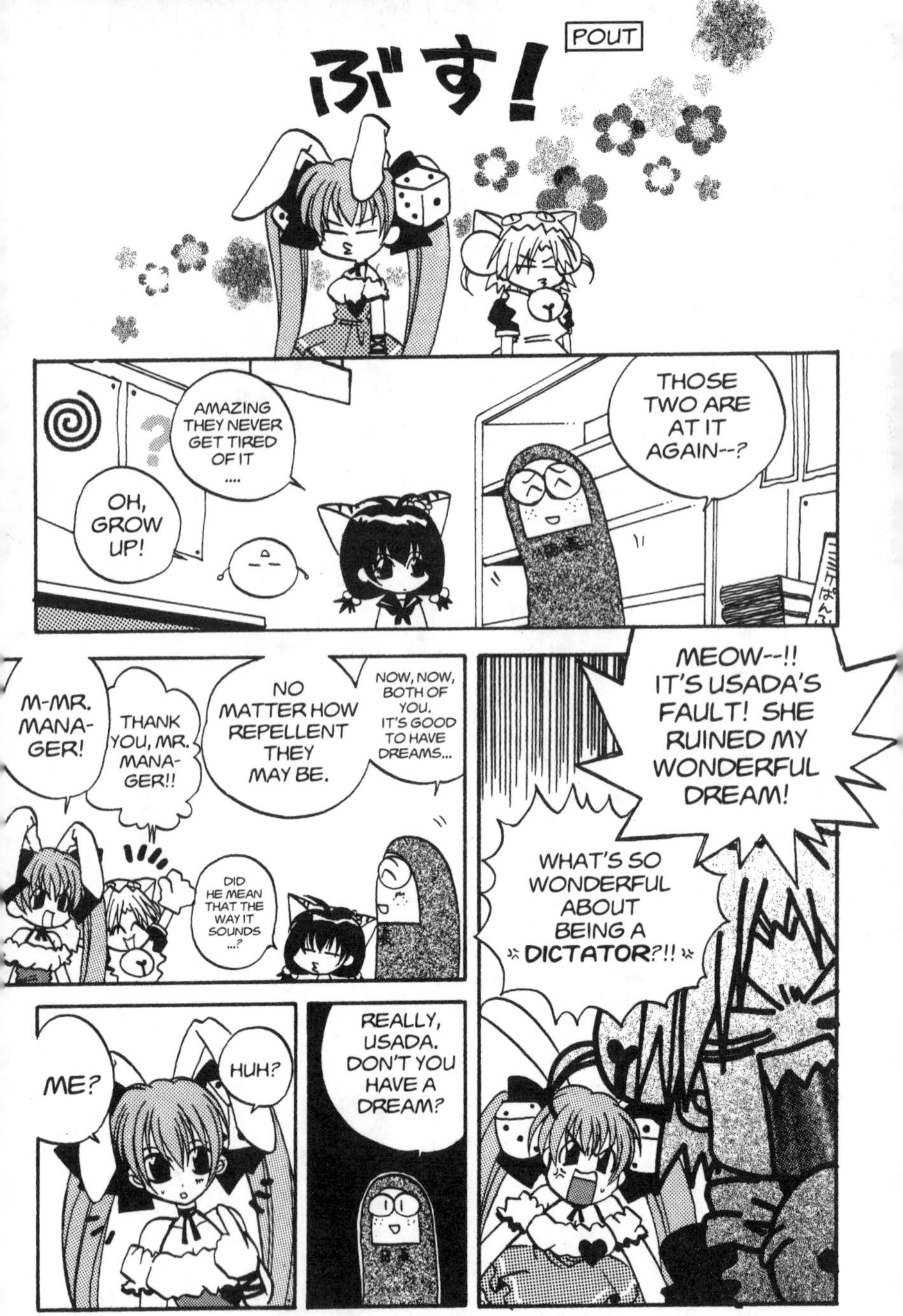
POUT
ぶす!
THOSE TWO ARE AT IT AGAIN--?
AMAZING THEY NEVER GET TIRED OF IT ....
OH, GROW UP!
MEOW--!! IT'S USADA'S FAULT! SHE RUINED MY WONDERFUL DREAM!
WHAT'S SO WONDERFUL ABOUT BEING A DICTATOR?!!
NOW, NOW, BOTH OF YOU. IT'S GOOD TO HAVE DREAMS...
NO MATTER HOW REPELLENT THEY MAY BE.
THANK YOU, MR. MANAGER!!
M-MR. MANAGER!
DID HE MEAN THAT THE WAY IT SOUNDS ...?
REALLY, USADA. DON'T YOU HAVE A DREAM?
HUH?
ME?

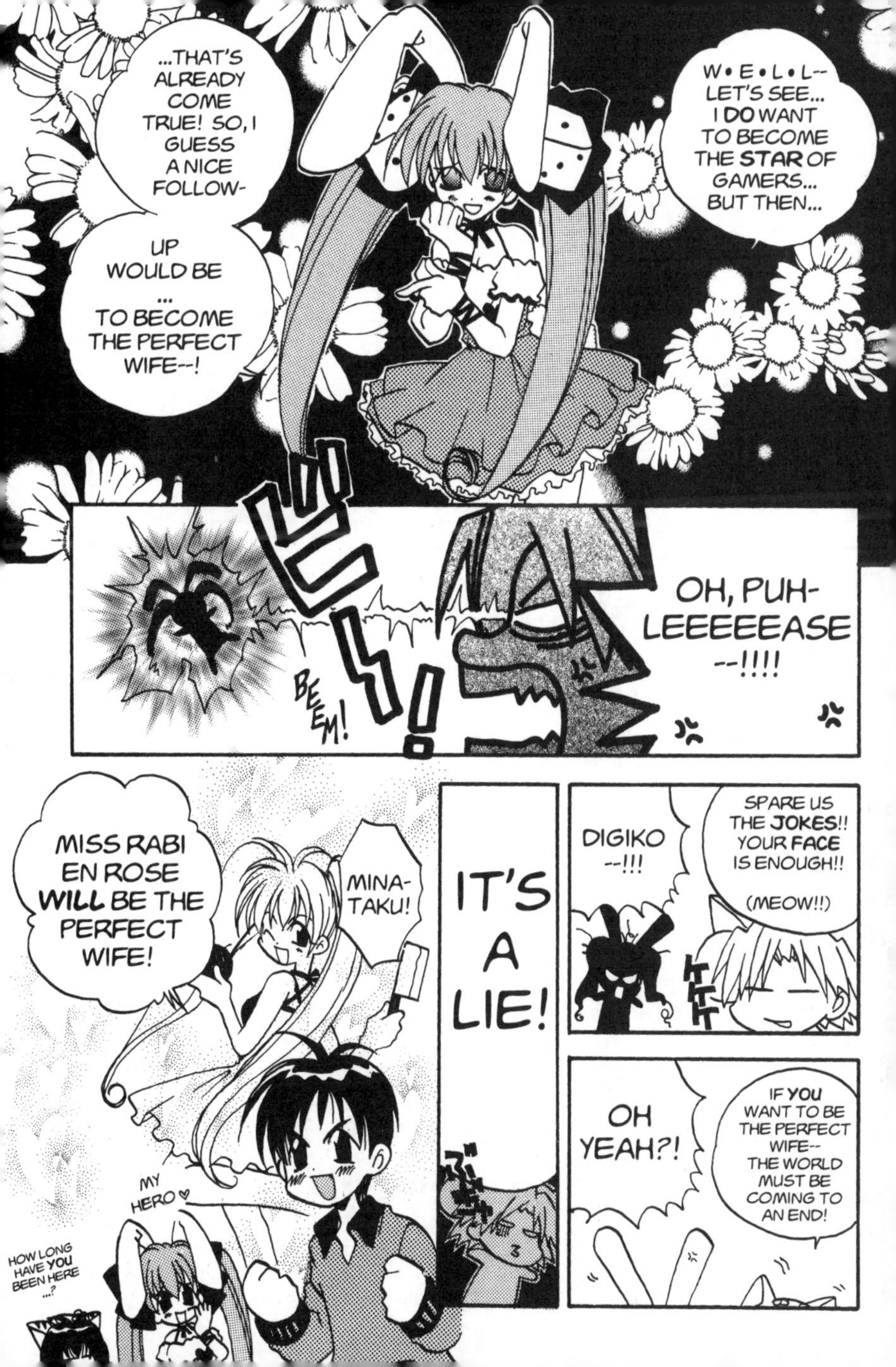
W•E•L•L-- LET'S SEE... I DO WANT TO BECOME THE STAR OF GAMERS... BUT THEN...
...THAT'S ALREADY COME TRUE! SO, I GUESS A NICE FOLLOW-
UP WOULD BE ... TO BECOME THE PERFECT WIFE--!
OH, PUH-LEEEEEEASE--!!!!
BEEM!
SPARE US THE JOKES!! YOUR FACE IS ENOUGH!!
(MEOW!!)
DIGIKO--!!!
IF YOU WANT TO BE THE PERFECT WIFE-- THE WORLD MUST BE COMING TO AN END!
OH YEAH?!
IT'S A LIE!
MINA-TAKU!
MISS RABI EN ROSE WILL BE THE PERFECT WIFE!
MY HERO♡
HOW LONG HAVE YOU BEEN HERE ...?

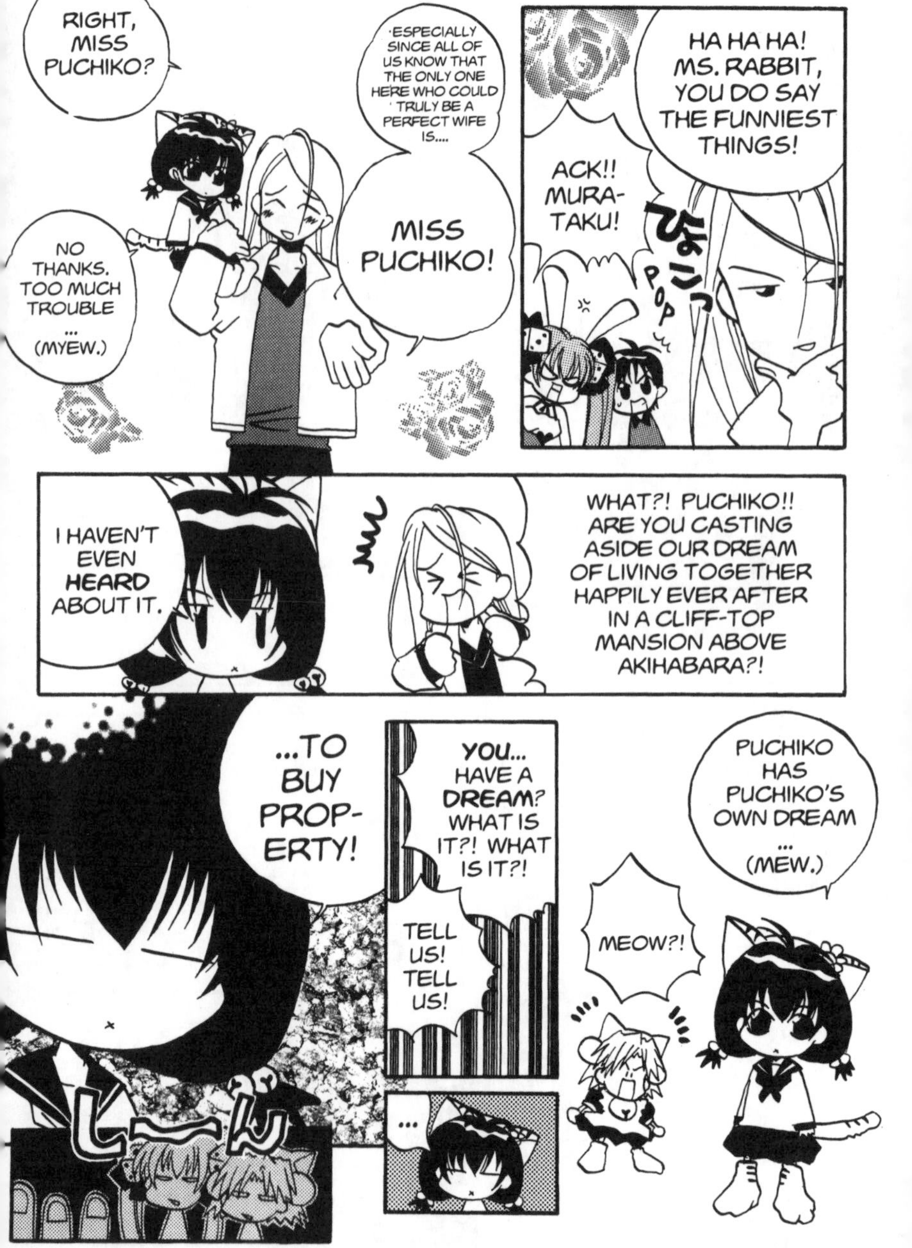
HA HA HA! MS. RABBIT, YOU DO SAY THE FUNNIEST THINGS!
ACK!! MURA-TAKU!
ぴょこっ
POP
·ESPECIALLY SINCE ALL OF US KNOW THAT THE ONLY ONE HERE WHO COULD TRULY BE A PERFECT WIFE IS....
MISS PUCHIKO!
RIGHT, MISS PUCHIKO?
NO THANKS. TOO MUCH TROUBLE ... (MYEW.)
WHAT?! PUCHIKO!! ARE YOU CASTING ASIDE OUR DREAM OF LIVING TOGETHER HAPPILY EVER AFTER IN A CLIFF-TOP MANSION ABOVE AKIHABARA?!
I HAVEN'T EVEN HEARD ABOUT IT.
PUCHIKO HAS PUCHIKO'S OWN DREAM ... (MEW.)
MEOW?!
YOU... HAVE A DREAM? WHAT IS IT?! WHAT IS IT?!
TELL US! TELL US!
...
...TO BUY PROPERTY!
しーん

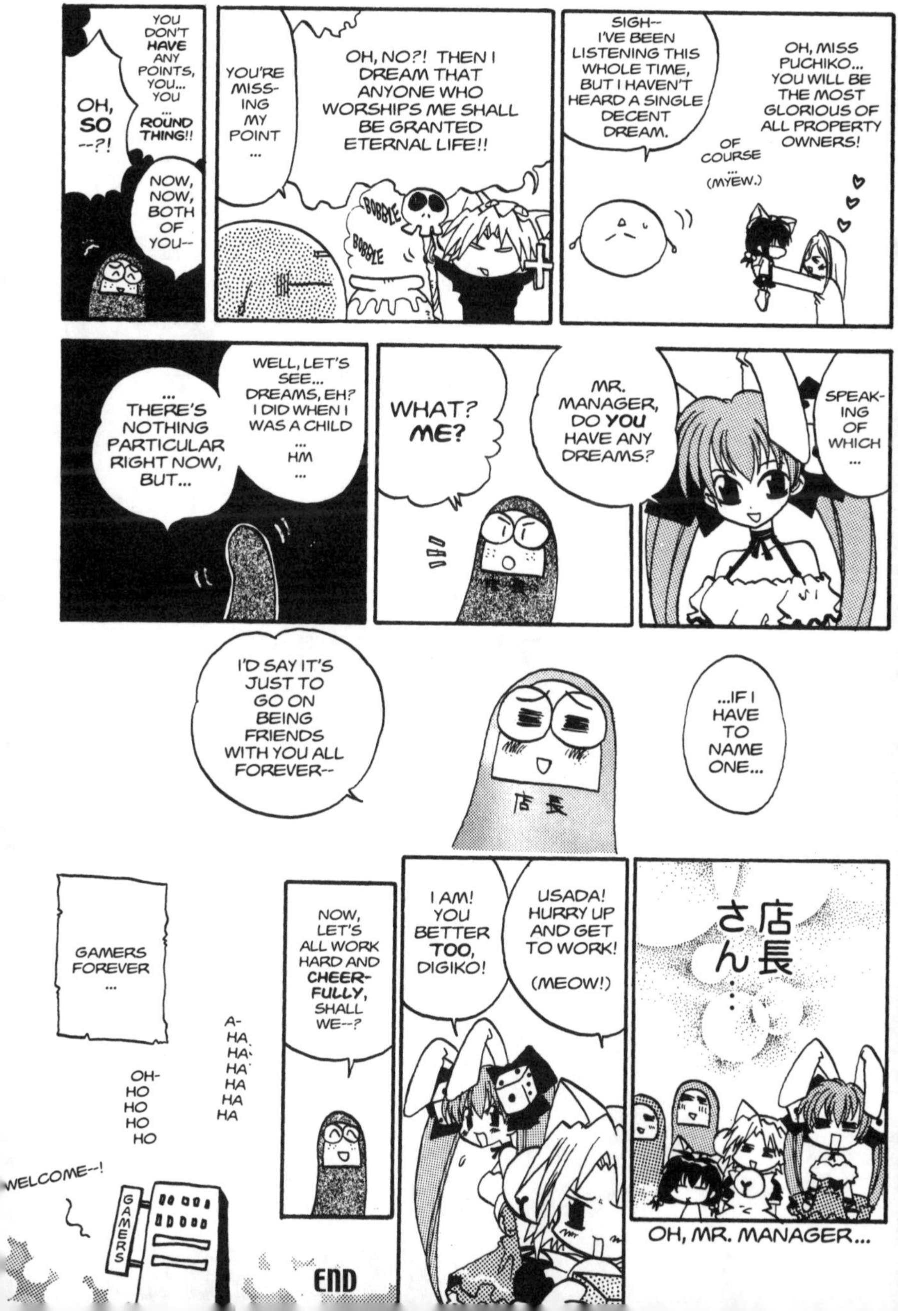

OH, MISS PUCHIKO... YOU WILL BE THE MOST GLORIOUS OF ALL PROPERTY OWNERS!
OF COURSE ... (MYEW.)
SIGH-- I'VE BEEN LISTENING THIS WHOLE TIME, BUT I HAVEN'T HEARD A SINGLE DECENT DREAM.
OH, NO?! THEN I DREAM THAT ANYONE WHO WORSHIPS ME SHALL BE GRANTED ETERNAL LIFE!!
YOU'RE MISSING MY POINT ...
BOBBLE
BOBBLE
YOU DON'T **HAVE** ANY POINTS, YOU... YOU ... **ROUND THING**!!
OH, **SO** --?!
NOW, NOW, BOTH OF YOU--
SPEAKING OF WHICH ...
MR. MANAGER, DO **YOU** HAVE ANY DREAMS?
WHAT? **ME?**
WELL, LET'S SEE... DREAMS, EH? I DID WHEN I WAS A CHILD ... HM ...
... THERE'S NOTHING PARTICULAR RIGHT NOW, BUT...
...IF I HAVE TO NAME ONE...
I'D SAY IT'S JUST TO GO ON BEING FRIENDS WITH YOU ALL FOREVER--
店長
店長さん…
OH, MR. MANAGER...
USADA! HURRY UP AND GET TO WORK! (MEOW!)
I AM! YOU BETTER **TOO**, DIGIKO!
NOW, LET'S ALL WORK HARD AND **CHEERFULLY**, SHALL WE--?
A-HA HA HA HA HA HA HA
OH-HO HO HO HO HO
GAMERS FOREVER ...
WELCOME--!
GAMERS
END

DARK GEMA GEMA GANG
NEW CHARACTERS

POWERFUL ALLIES OF PIYOKO,
SWORN ENEMY (AND CONSTANT
DUPE) OF DIGIKO! EVERY
ONE OF THEM
IS A DOCTOR!!
BUT THEIR
NAMES ARE
STILL TOP
SECRET!!

RANK: GENERAL
OCCUPATION:
VETERINARIAN

BLINDLY OBEDIENT TO PIYOKO,
BUT INCLINED TO AMPLIFY THE
EVIL DEEDS SHE COOKS UP.
SPEAKS CASUALLY OF THE
NEFARIOUS DEEDS HE'S
COMMITTED...BUT FOR SOME
REASON IS LOVED BY ANIMALS.

RANK: LIEUTENANT GENERAL
OCCUPATION: DENTIST

SUPERVISES PIYOKO'S FLOSSING
EVERY NIGHT. A POWERFUL
SENSE OF RESPONSIBILITY,
RAPIDLY CYCLES BETWEEN JOY
AND SORROW OVER PIYOKO'S
FORTUNES. BRISK AND EFFICIENT,
BUT PRONE TO FALL APART WHEN
PANICKING.

RANK: MAJOR
OCCUPATION: INTERNAL MEDICINE

MACHO, BOSSY AND SNOTTY.
GREW UP WITH PIYOKO. THINKS
OF HER AS A LITTLE SISTER. SEEMS
INCOMPETENT AT FIRST, BUT
VERY SKILLED AS A PHYSICIAN.

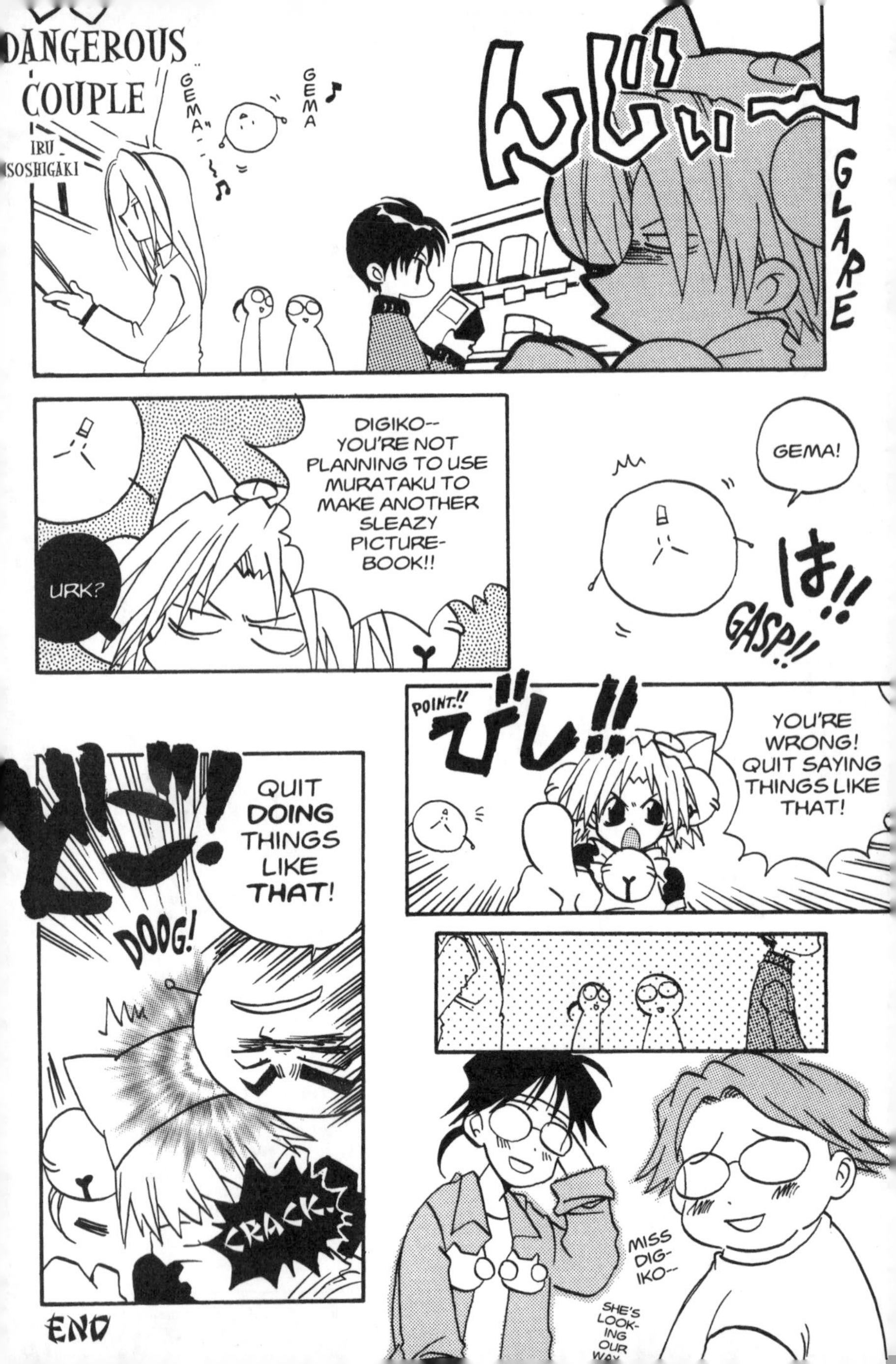
DANGEROUS COUPLE
IRU SOSHIGAKI
んじぃー
GLARE
GEMA GEMA ♪
GEMA~ ♪
GEMA!
は!!
GASP!!
DIGIKO-- YOU'RE NOT PLANNING TO USE MURATAKU TO MAKE ANOTHER SLEAZY PICTURE-BOOK!!
URK?
POINT!!
びし!!
YOU'RE WRONG! QUIT SAYING THINGS LIKE THAT!
MISS DIG-IKO--
SHE'S LOOK-ING OUR WAY
QUIT DOING THINGS LIKE THAT!
DOOG!
CRACK
END

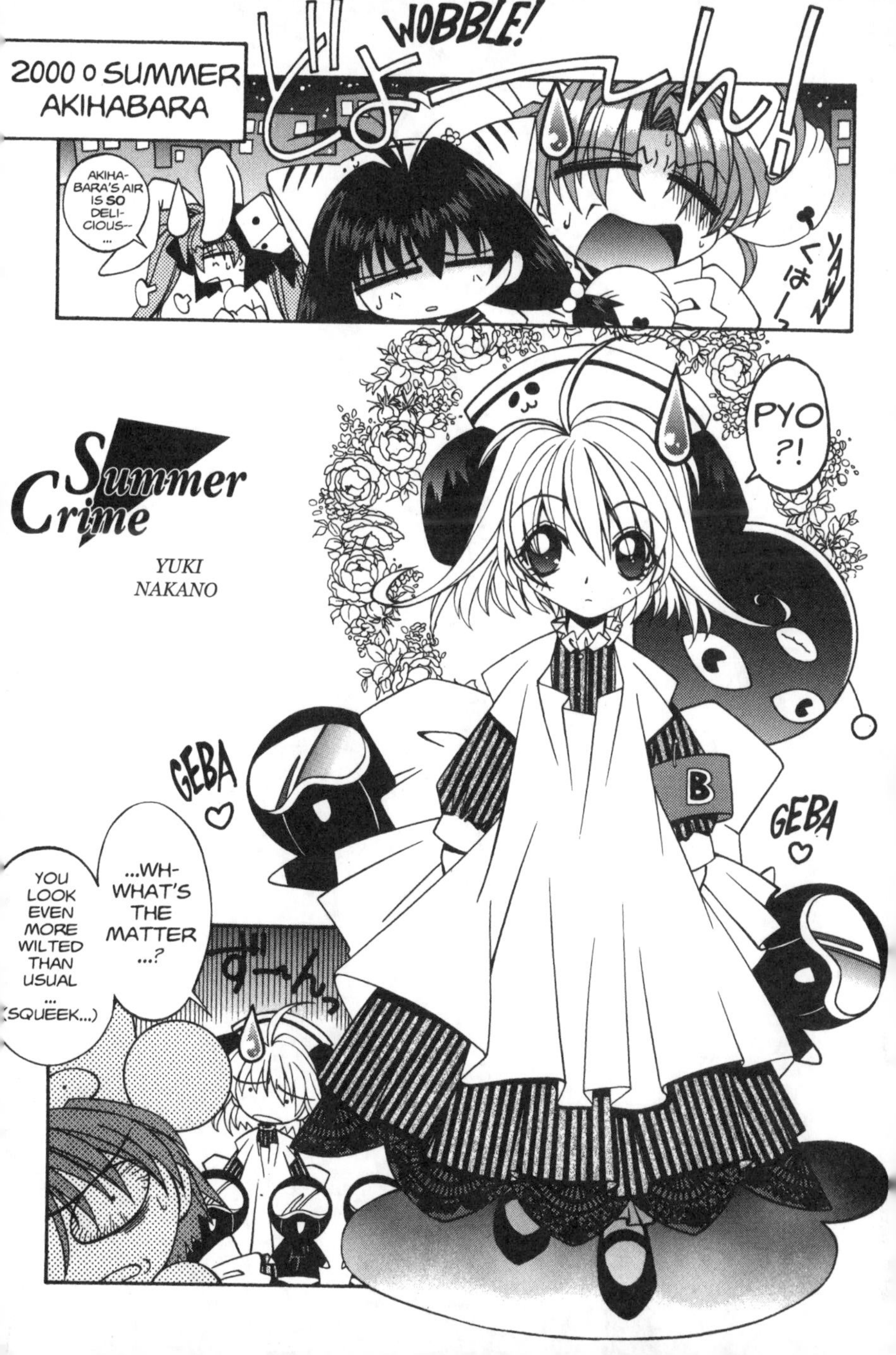

2000 ○ SUMMER AKIHABARA
WOBBLE!
YAWN
AKIHABARA'S AIR IS SO DELICIOUS-- ...
Summer Crime
YUKI NAKANO
PYO ?!
GEBA ♡
GEBA ♡
...WH-WHAT'S THE MATTER ...?
YOU LOOK EVEN MORE WILTED THAN USUAL ... (SQUEEK...)

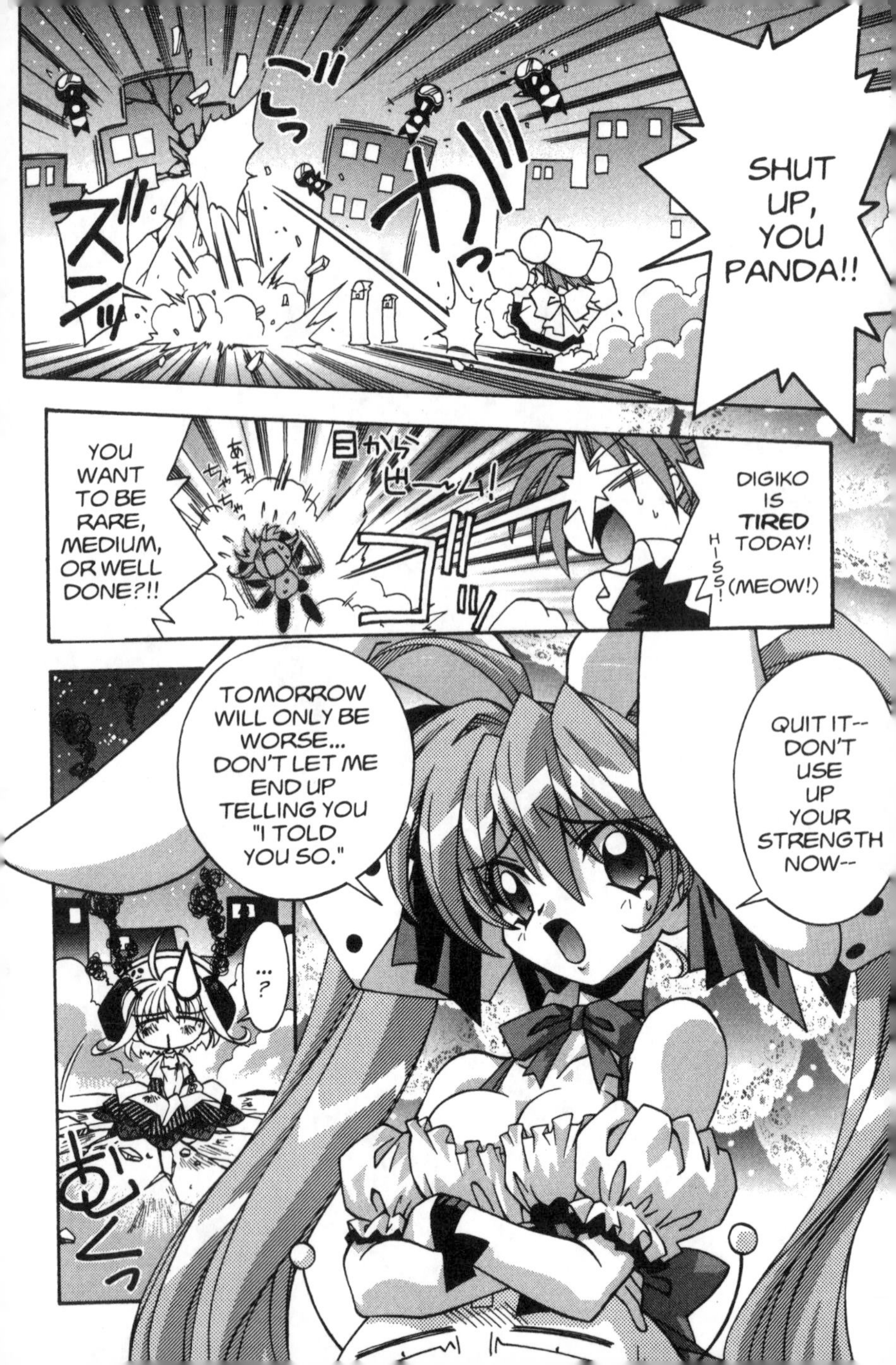
SHUT UP, YOU PANDA!!
DIGIKO IS TIRED TODAY!
HISS!
(MEOW!)
目からビーム!
YOU WANT TO BE RARE, MEDIUM, OR WELL DONE?!!
QUIT IT-- DON'T USE UP YOUR STRENGTH NOW--
TOMORROW WILL ONLY BE WORSE... DON'T LET ME END UP TELLING YOU "I TOLD YOU SO."
...?

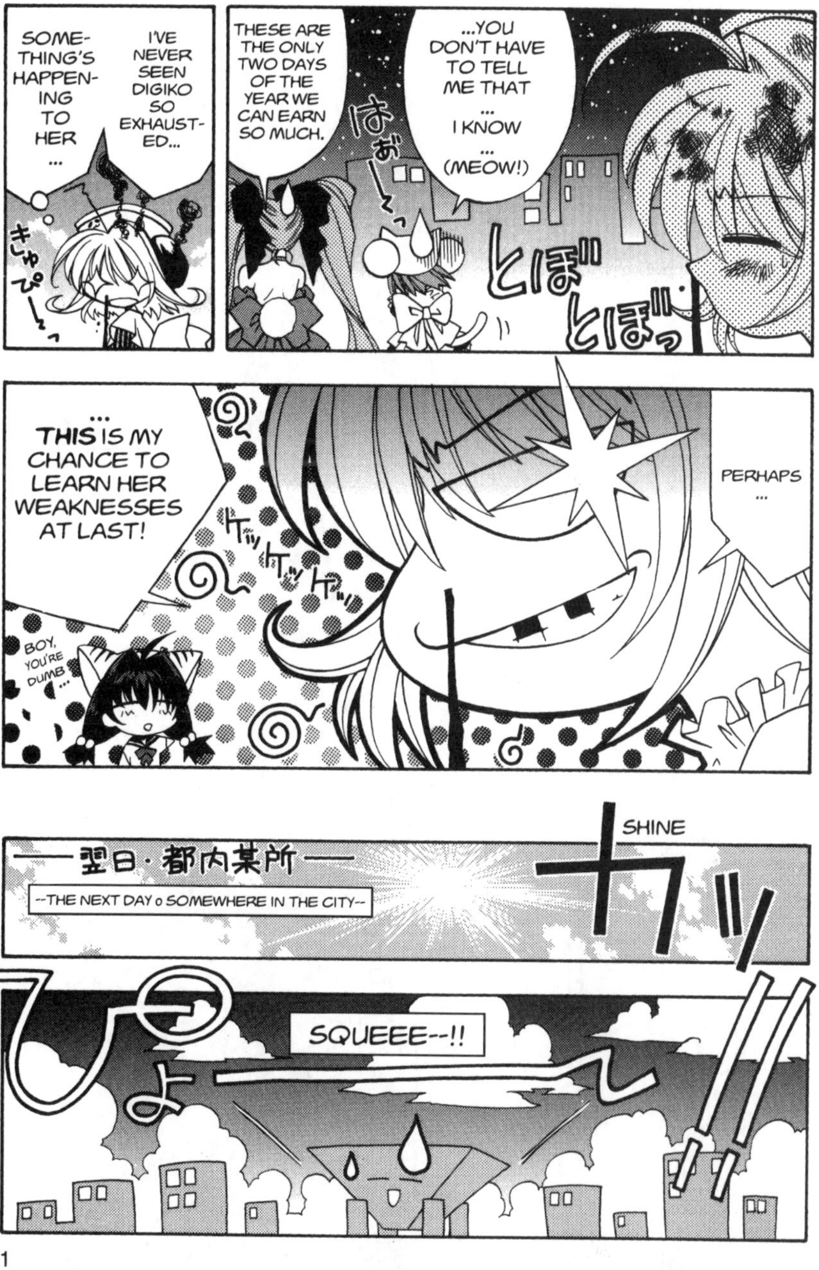

THESE ARE THE ONLY TWO DAYS OF THE YEAR WE CAN EARN SO MUCH.
...YOU DON'T HAVE TO TELL ME THAT ... I KNOW ... (MEOW!)
I'VE NEVER SEEN DIGIKO SO EXHAUST-ED...
SOME-THING'S HAPPEN-ING TO HER ...
PERHAPS ...
... THIS IS MY CHANCE TO LEARN HER WEAKNESSES AT LAST!
BOY, YOU'RE DUMB ...
SHINE
——翌日・都内某所——
--THE NEXT DAY o SOMEWHERE IN THE CITY--
SQUEEE--!!

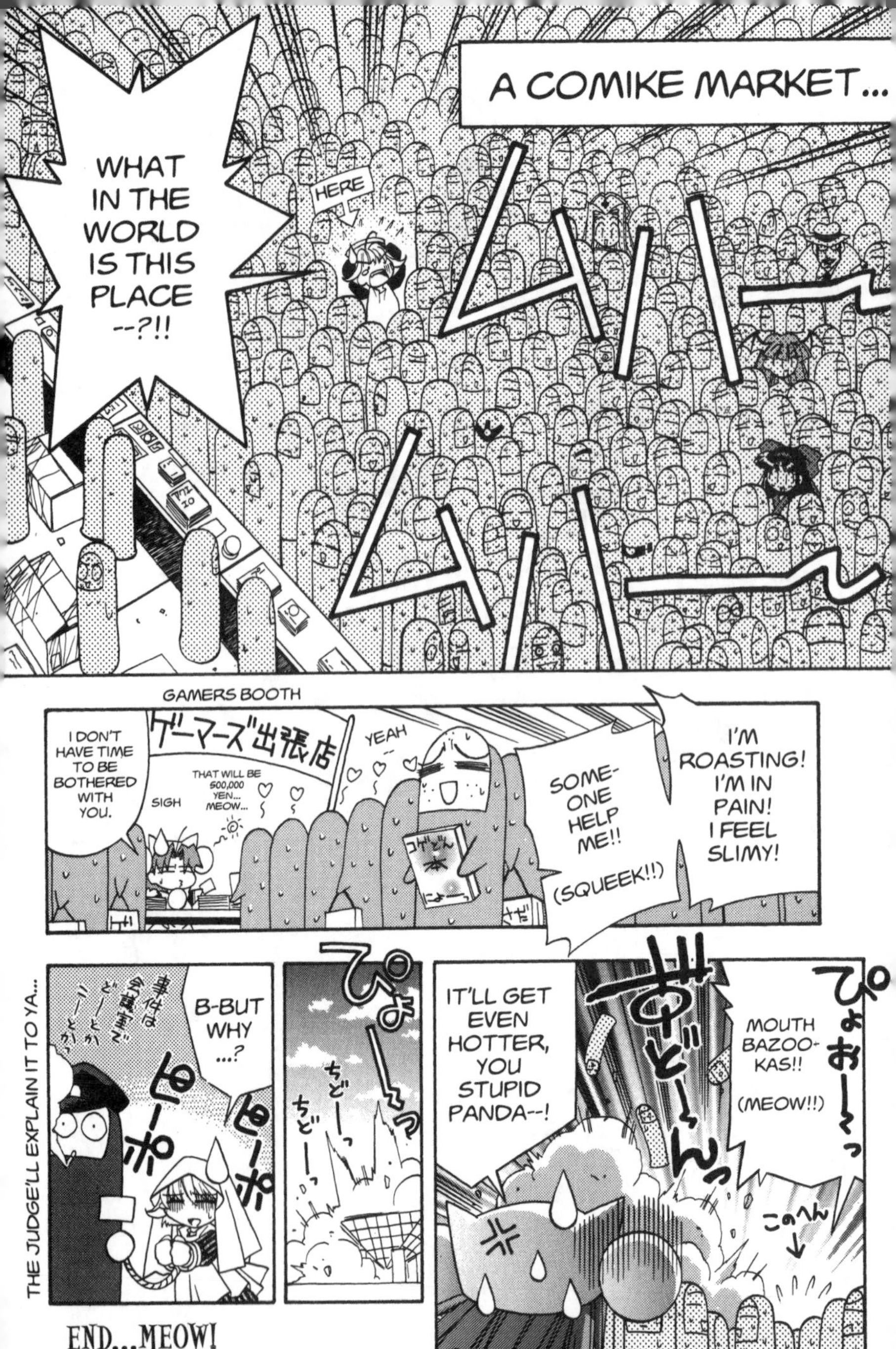
A COMIKE MARKET...
HERE
WHAT IN THE WORLD IS THIS PLACE --?!!
GAMERS BOOTH
I'M ROASTING! I'M IN PAIN! I FEEL SLIMY!
SOME-ONE HELP ME!! (SQUEEK!!)
YEAH --
ゲーマーズ出張店
THAT WILL BE 500,000 YEN... MEOW...
SIGH
I DON'T HAVE TIME TO BE BOTHERED WITH YOU.
ぴょおーっ
MOUTH BAZOO-KAS!! (MEOW!!)
ずどーんっ
このへん
IT'LL GET EVEN HOTTER, YOU STUPID PANDA--!
ぴょーっ
ちどーっ
ちどーっ
B-BUT WHY ...?
事件は会議室で どーとか こーとか
ピーポー
ピーポー
THE JUDGE'LL EXPLAIN IT TO YA...
END...MEOW!

WHAT WOULD YOU LIKE TO SEE HAPPEN AT GAMERS?

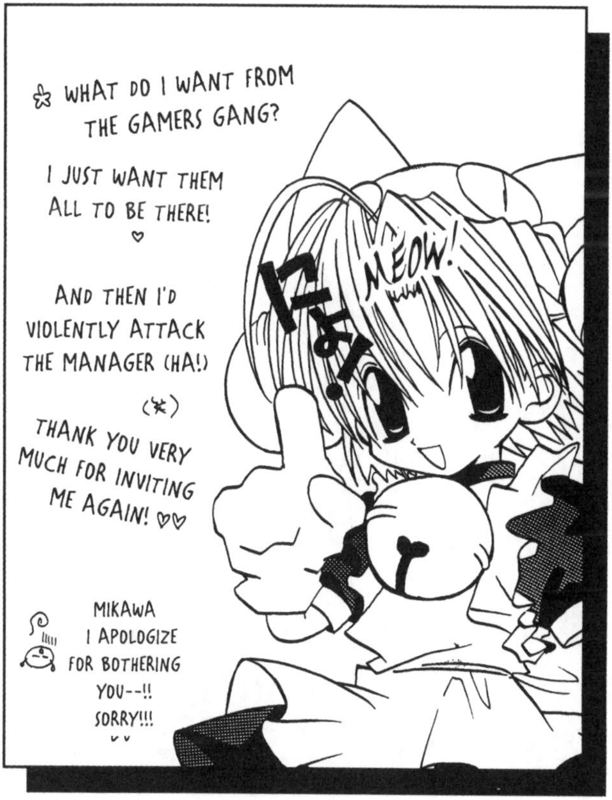
WHAT DO I WANT FROM THE GAMERS GANG?
I JUST WANT THEM ALL TO BE THERE! ♡
AND THEN I'D VIOLENTLY ATTACK THE MANAGER (HA!)
(*)
THANK YOU VERY MUCH FOR INVITING ME AGAIN! ♡♡
MEOW!
MIKAWA I APOLOGIZE FOR BOTHERING YOU--!! SORRY!!!

IRU ISOSHIGAKI

WHAT WOULD YOU LIKE TO SEE HAPPEN AT GAMERS?

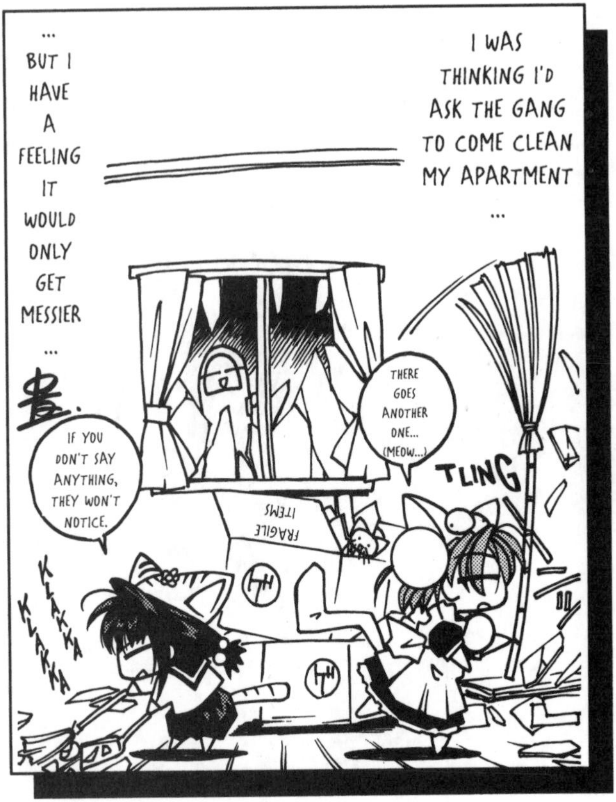
I WAS THINKING I'D ASK THE GANG TO COME CLEAN MY APARTMENT ...
... BUT I HAVE A FEELING IT WOULD ONLY GET MESSIER ...
THERE GOES ANOTHER ONE... (MEOW...)
TLING
FRAGILE ITEMS
IF YOU DON'T SAY ANYTHING, THEY WON'T NOTICE.
KLAKKA KLAKKA

YUKI NAKANO

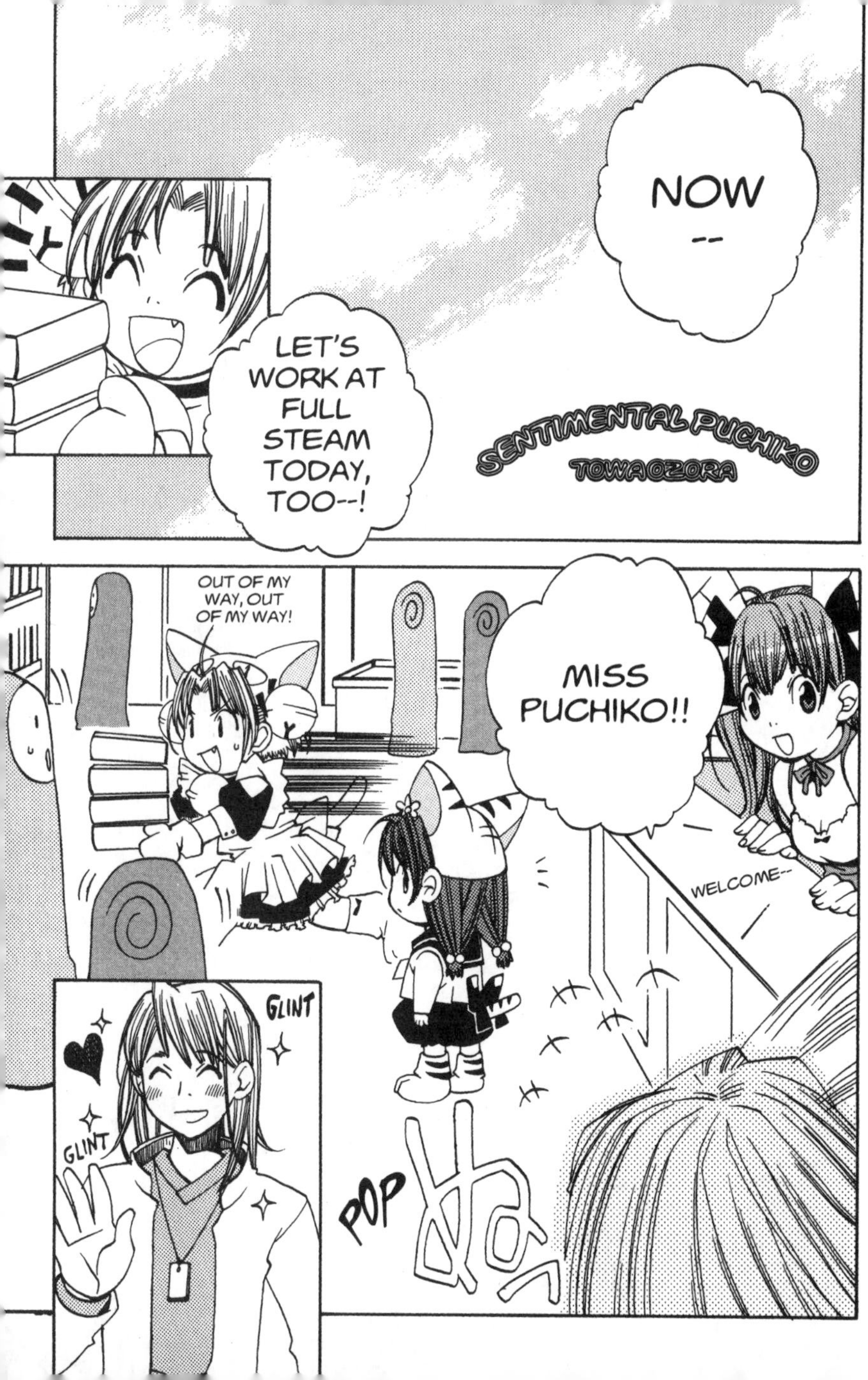
NOW --
SENTIMENTAL PUCHIKO
TOWA OZORA
LET'S WORK AT FULL STEAM TODAY, TOO--!
MISS PUCHIKO!!
WELCOME--
OUT OF MY WAY, OUT OF MY WAY!
POP
GLINT
GLINT

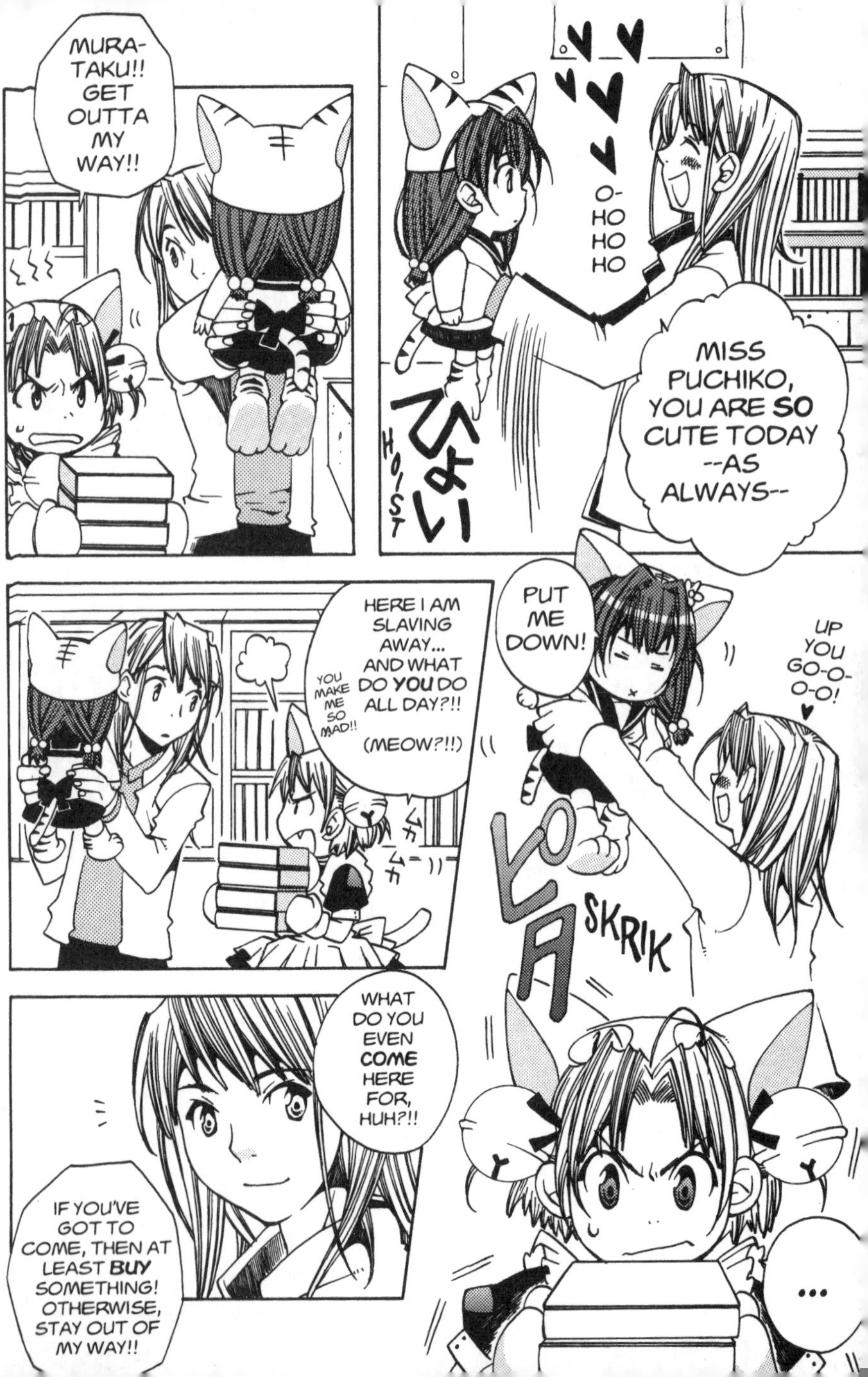
O-HO HO HO
MISS PUCHIKO, YOU ARE SO CUTE TODAY --AS ALWAYS--
ひょい
HOIST
MURA-TAKU!! GET OUTTA MY WAY!!
UP YOU GO-O-O-O-O!
PUT ME DOWN!
ぴょ
SKRIK
HERE I AM SLAVING AWAY... AND WHAT DO YOU DO ALL DAY?!!
(MEOW?!!)
YOU MAKE ME SO MAD!!
...
WHAT DO YOU EVEN COME HERE FOR, HUH?!!
IF YOU'VE GOT TO COME, THEN AT LEAST BUY SOMETHING! OTHERWISE, STAY OUT OF MY WAY!!

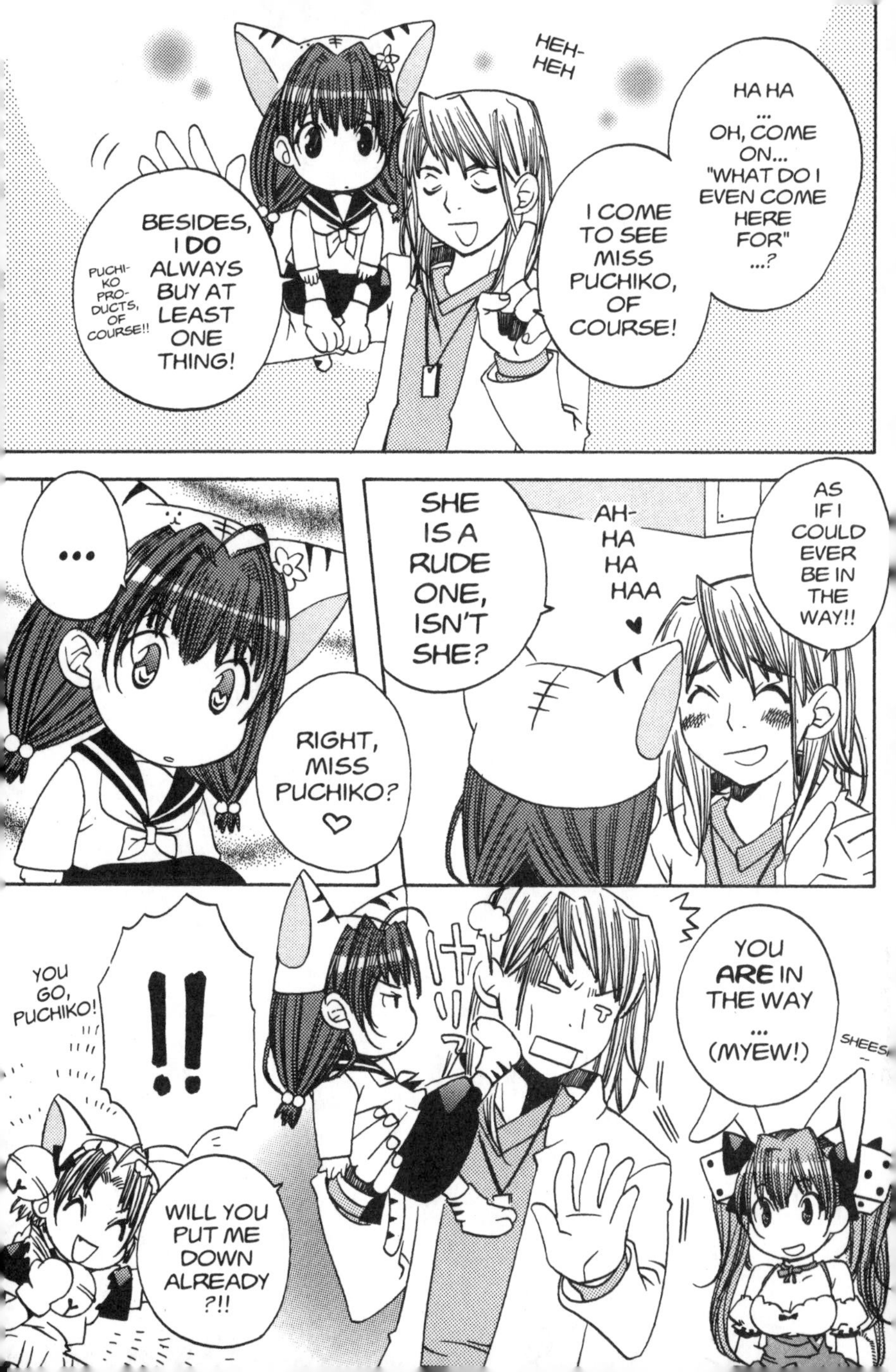

HEH-HEH
HA HA ... OH, COME ON... "WHAT DO I EVEN COME HERE FOR" ...?
I COME TO SEE MISS PUCHIKO, OF COURSE!
BESIDES, I **DO** ALWAYS BUY AT LEAST ONE THING!
PUCHIKO PRODUCTS, OF COURSE!!
AS IF I COULD EVER BE IN THE WAY!!
AH-HA HA HAA ♥
SHE IS A RUDE ONE, ISN'T SHE?
RIGHT, MISS PUCHIKO? ♡
...
YOU **ARE** IN THE WAY ... (MYEW!)
SHEES-
!!
YOU GO, PUCHIKO!
WILL YOU PUT ME DOWN ALREADY ?!!

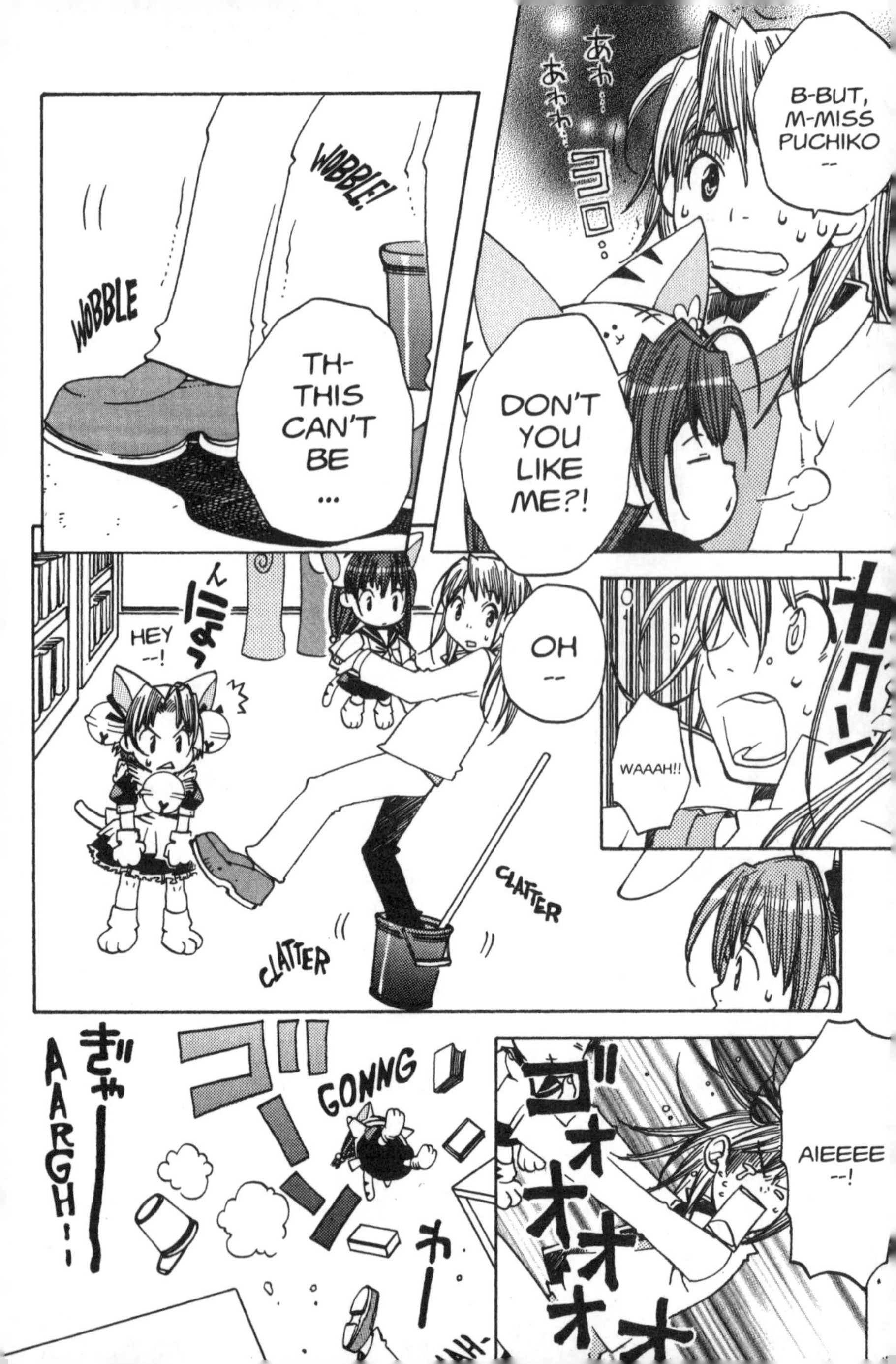
あわ…あわわ…
ヨロ
B-BUT, M-MISS PUCHIKO --
DON'T YOU LIKE ME?!
WOBBLE!
WOBBLE
TH-THIS CAN'T BE ...
WAAAH!!
OH --
HEY --!
CLATTER
CLATTER
AIEEEE --!
GONNG
AARGH!!

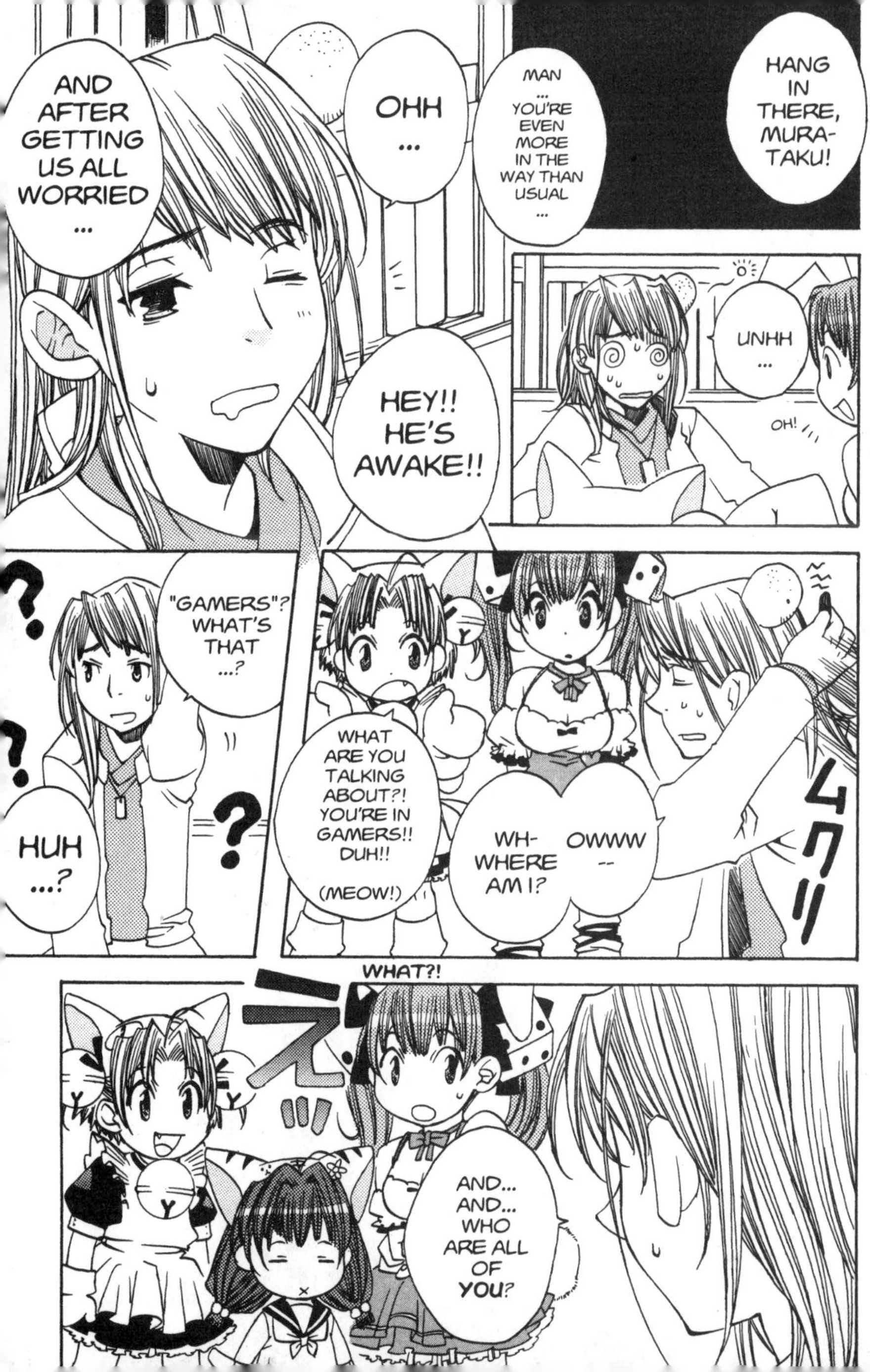
HANG IN THERE, MURA-TAKU!
MAN ... YOU'RE EVEN MORE IN THE WAY THAN USUAL ...
UNHH ...
OH!
OHH ...
AND AFTER GETTING US ALL WORRIED ...
HEY!! HE'S AWAKE!!
ムクリ
OWWW --
WH- WHERE AM I?
WHAT ARE YOU TALKING ABOUT?! YOU'RE IN GAMERS!! DUH!! (MEOW!)
"GAMERS"? WHAT'S THAT ...?
HUH ...?
WHAT?!
え
AND... AND... WHO ARE ALL OF YOU?

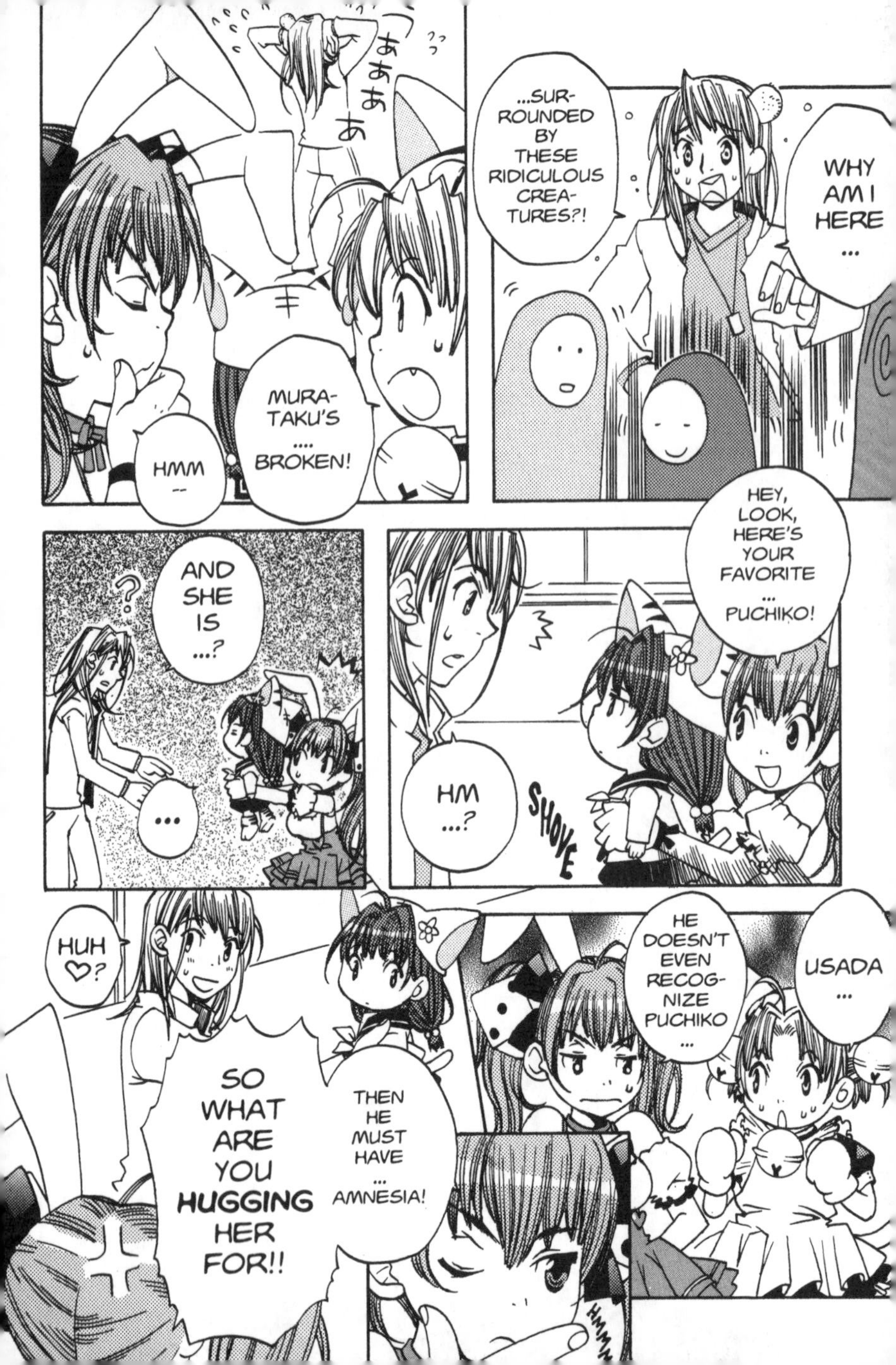
WHY AM I HERE ...
...SUR-ROUNDED BY THESE RIDICULOUS CREA-TURES?!
ああああ
MURA-TAKU'S .... BROKEN!
HMM --
HEY, LOOK, HERE'S YOUR FAVORITE ... PUCHIKO!
SHOVE
HM ...?
AND SHE IS ...?
...
USADA ...
HE DOESN'T EVEN RECOG-NIZE PUCHIKO ...
THEN HE MUST HAVE ... AMNESIA!
HMMM
HUH ♡?
SO WHAT ARE YOU **HUGGING** HER FOR!!

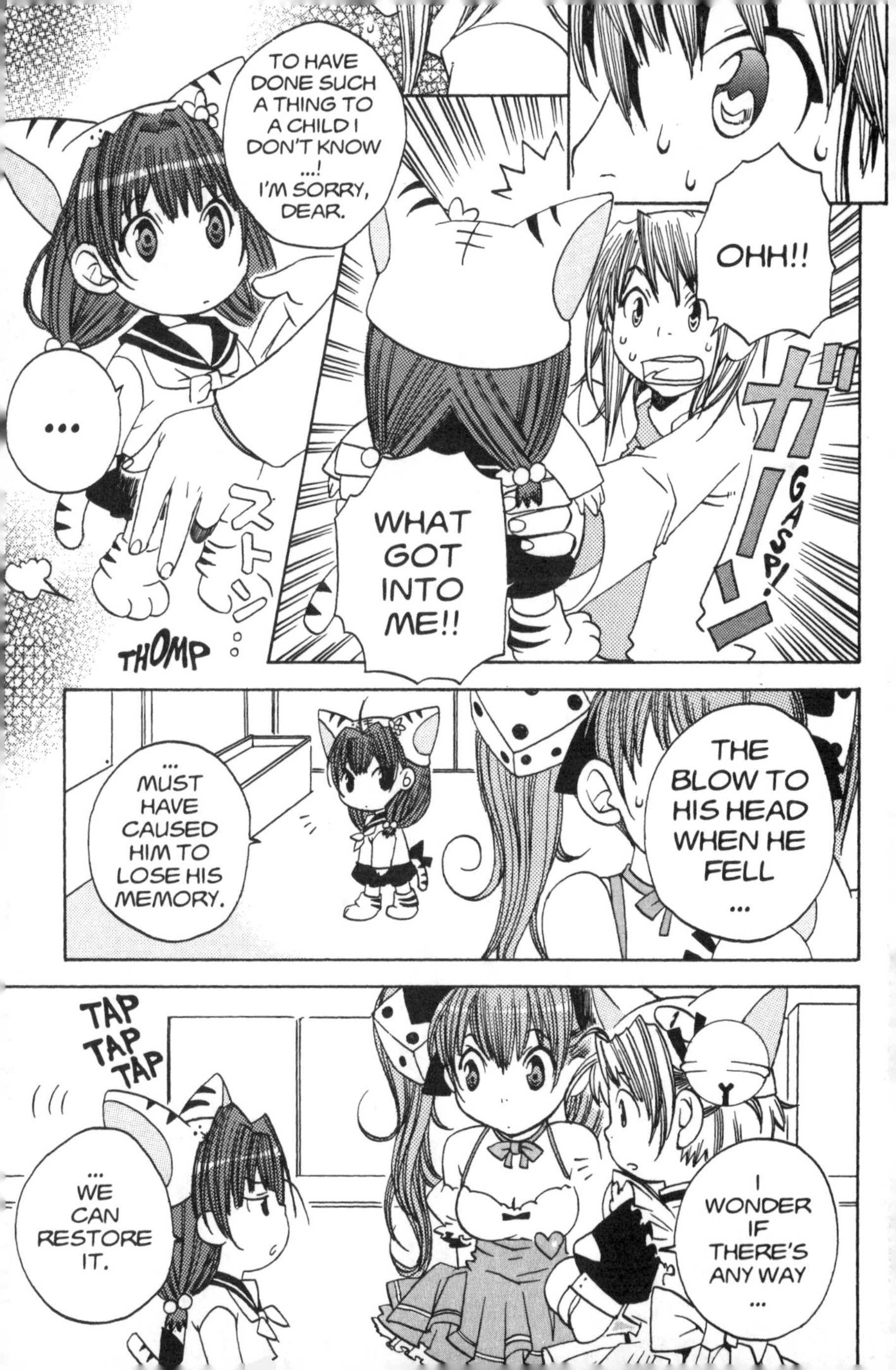
OHH!!
ガーン
GASP!
WHAT GOT INTO ME!!
TO HAVE DONE SUCH A THING TO A CHILD I DON'T KNOW ...! I'M SORRY, DEAR.
...
ストン
THOMP
THE BLOW TO HIS HEAD WHEN HE FELL ...
... MUST HAVE CAUSED HIM TO LOSE HIS MEMORY.
I WONDER IF THERE'S ANY WAY ...
TAP TAP TAP
... WE CAN RESTORE IT.

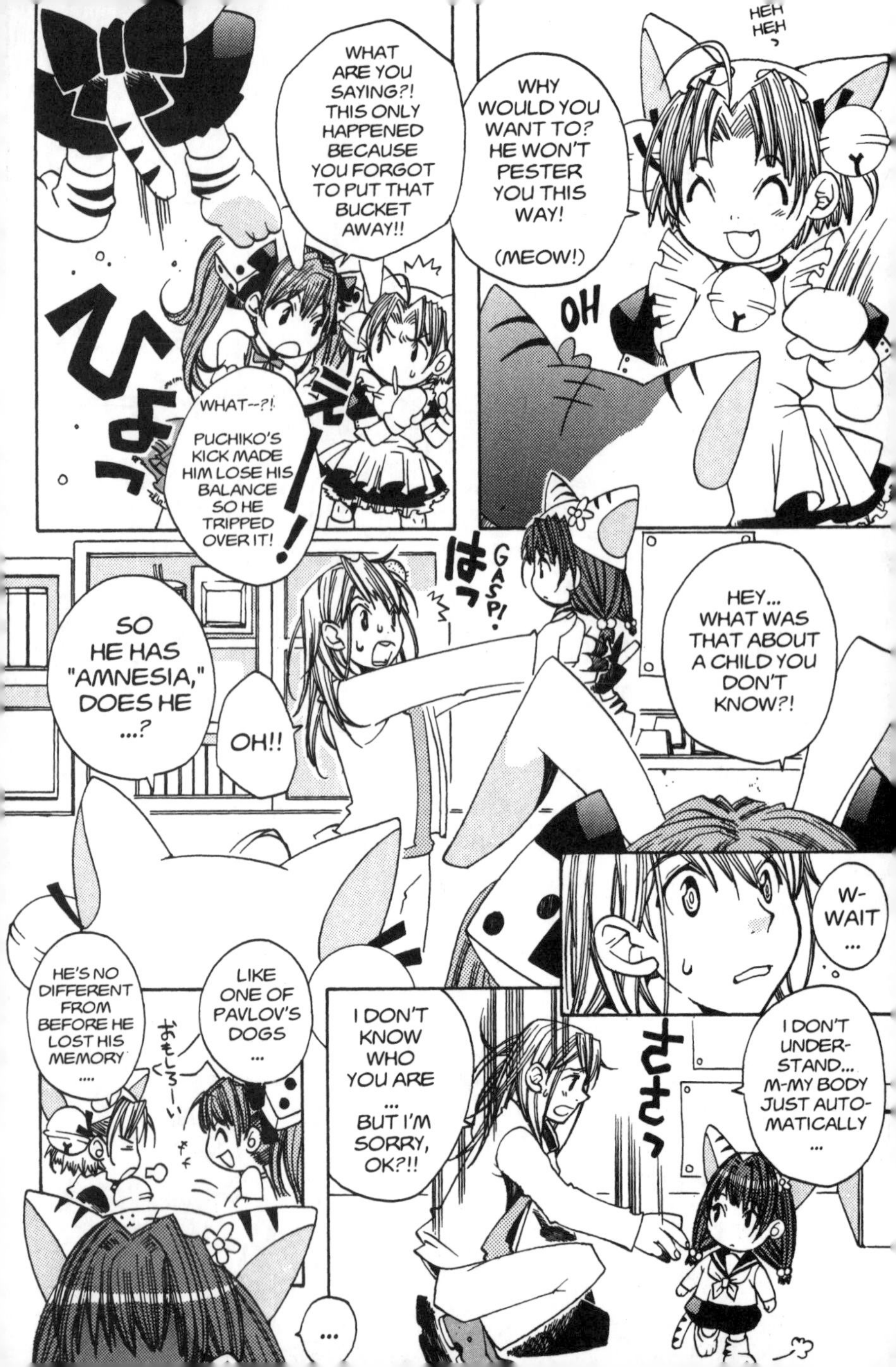
HEH HEH
WHY WOULD YOU WANT TO? HE WON'T PESTER YOU THIS WAY! (MEOW!)
OH
WHAT ARE YOU SAYING?! THIS ONLY HAPPENED BECAUSE YOU FORGOT TO PUT THAT BUCKET AWAY!!
ひょっ
えー!!
WHAT--?! PUCHIKO'S KICK MADE HIM LOSE HIS BALANCE SO HE TRIPPED OVER IT!
HEY... WHAT WAS THAT ABOUT A CHILD YOU DON'T KNOW?!
はっ
GASP!
SO HE HAS "AMNESIA," DOES HE ...?
OH!!
W-WAIT ...
I DON'T UNDER-STAND... M-MY BODY JUST AUTO-MATICALLY ...
さっ
I DON'T KNOW WHO YOU ARE ... BUT I'M SORRY, OK?!!
...
LIKE ONE OF PAVLOV'S DOGS ...
HE'S NO DIFFERENT FROM BEFORE HE LOST HIS MEMORY ....
おもしろーい

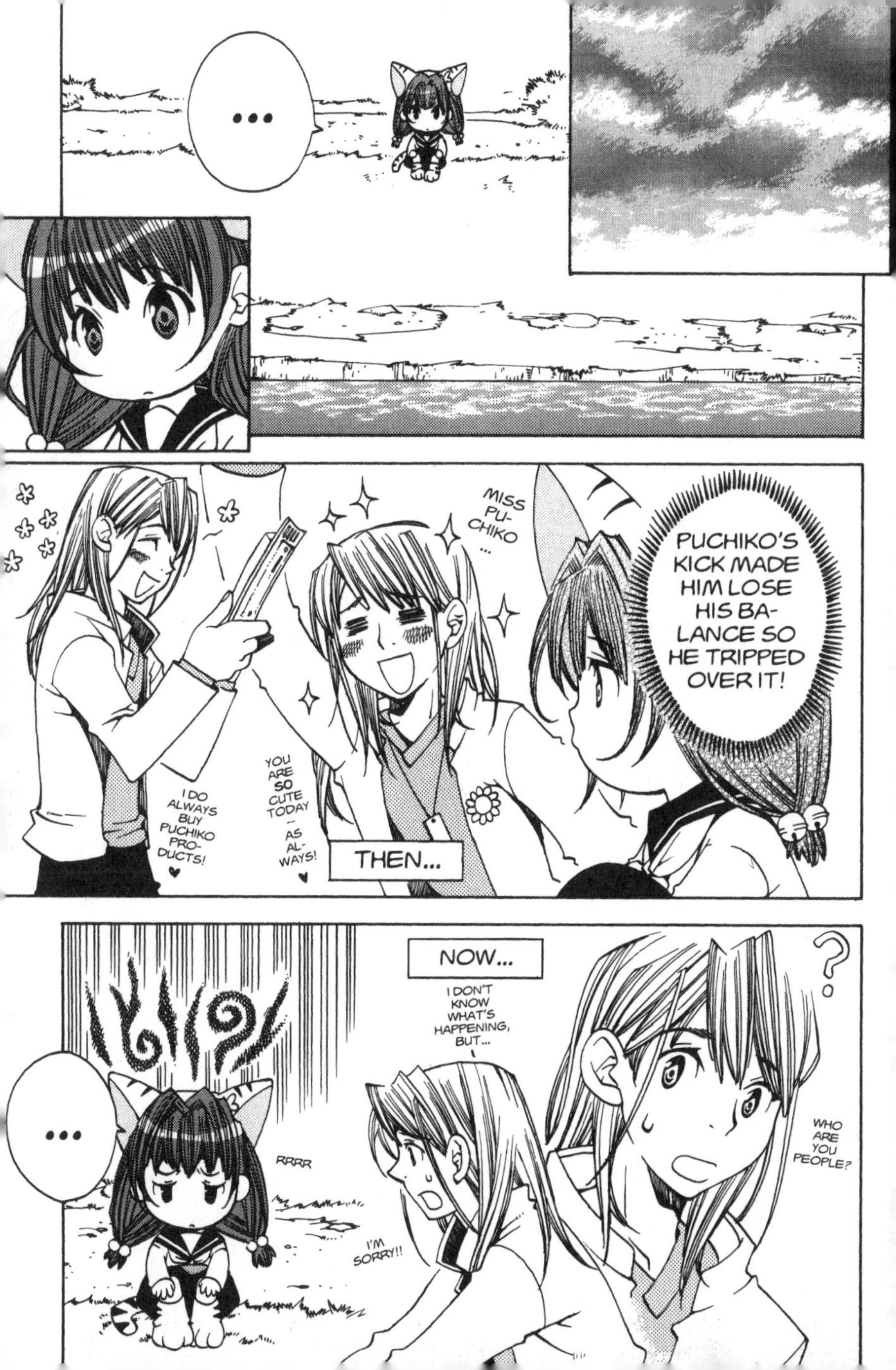
...
PUCHIKO'S KICK MADE HIM LOSE HIS BALANCE SO HE TRIPPED OVER IT!
MISS PUCHIKO...
YOU ARE SO CUTE TODAY -- AS ALWAYS!
THEN...
I DO ALWAYS BUY PUCHIKO PRODUCTS!
NOW...
?
WHO ARE YOU PEOPLE?
I DON'T KNOW WHAT'S HAPPENING, BUT...
I'M SORRY!!
RRRR
...

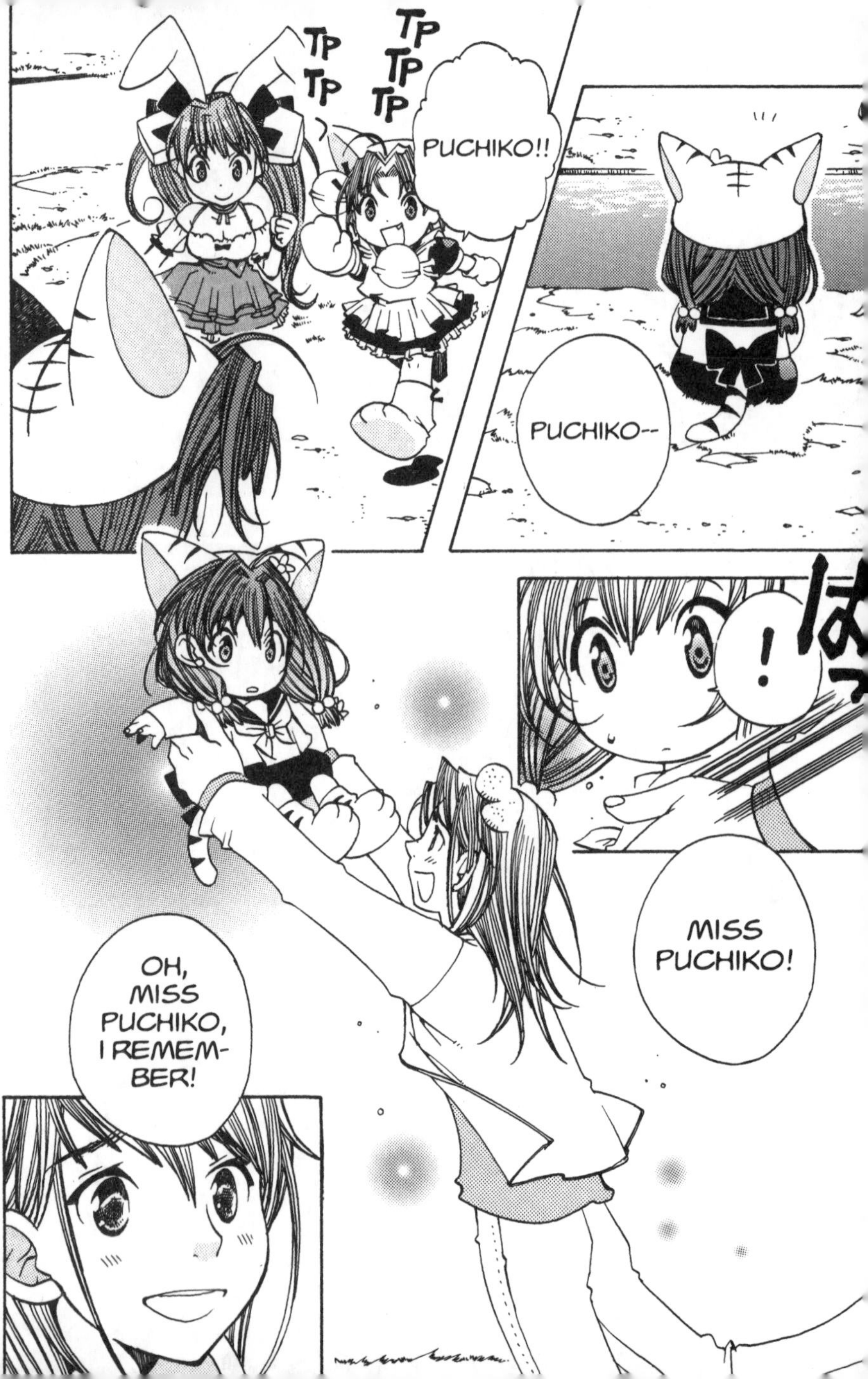
PUCHIKO--
TP TP TP
TP TP TP
PUCHIKO!!
!
MISS PUCHIKO!
OH, MISS PUCHIKO, I REMEMBER!

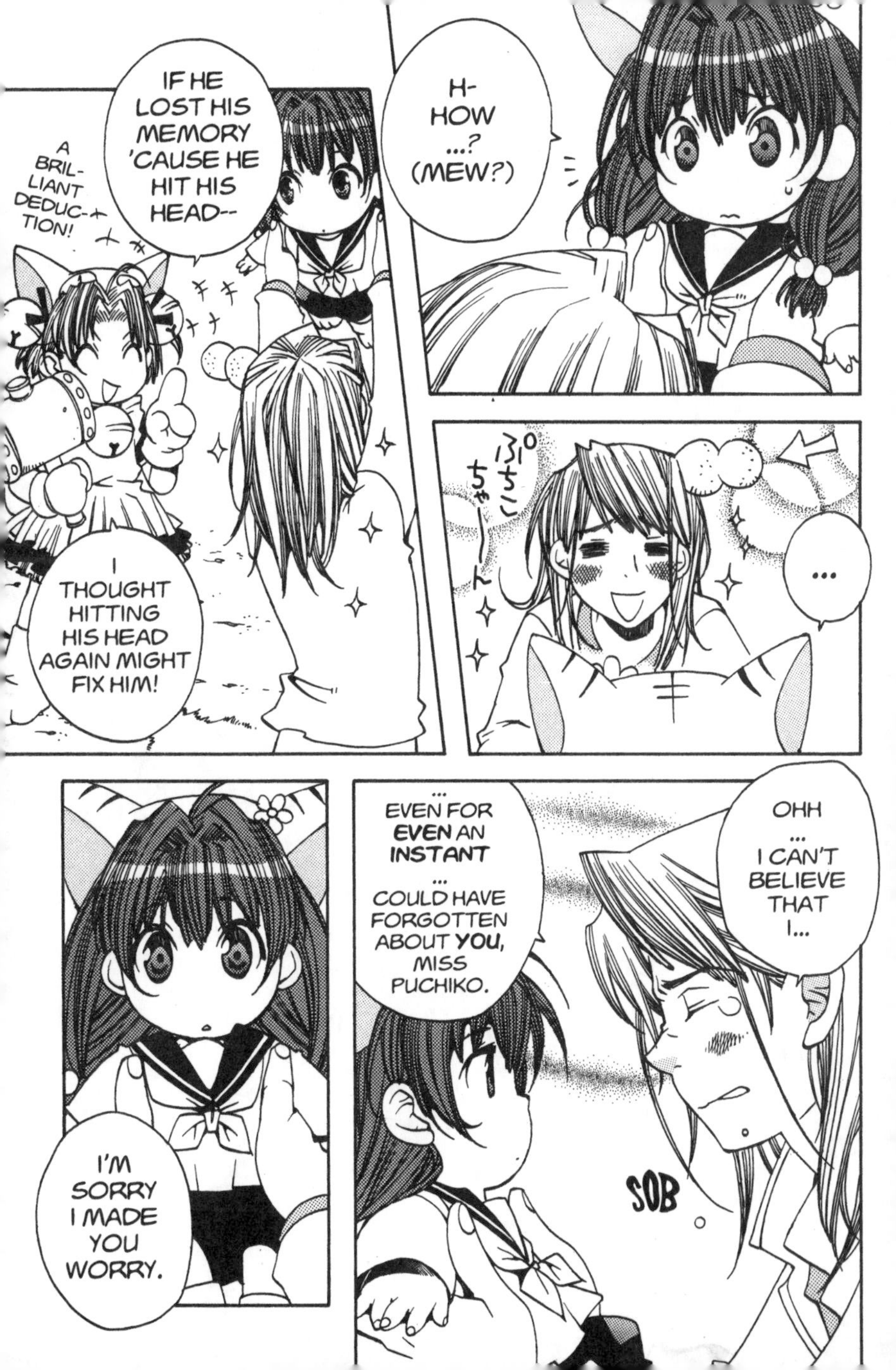

H-HOW ...? (MEW?)
ぷちこちゃーん
...
IF HE LOST HIS MEMORY 'CAUSE HE HIT HIS HEAD--
A BRIL-LIANT DEDUC-TION!
I THOUGHT HITTING HIS HEAD AGAIN MIGHT FIX HIM!
OHH ... I CAN'T BELIEVE THAT I...
... EVEN FOR **EVEN** AN **INSTANT** ... COULD HAVE FORGOTTEN ABOUT **YOU**, MISS PUCHIKO.
SOB
I'M SORRY I MADE YOU WORRY.

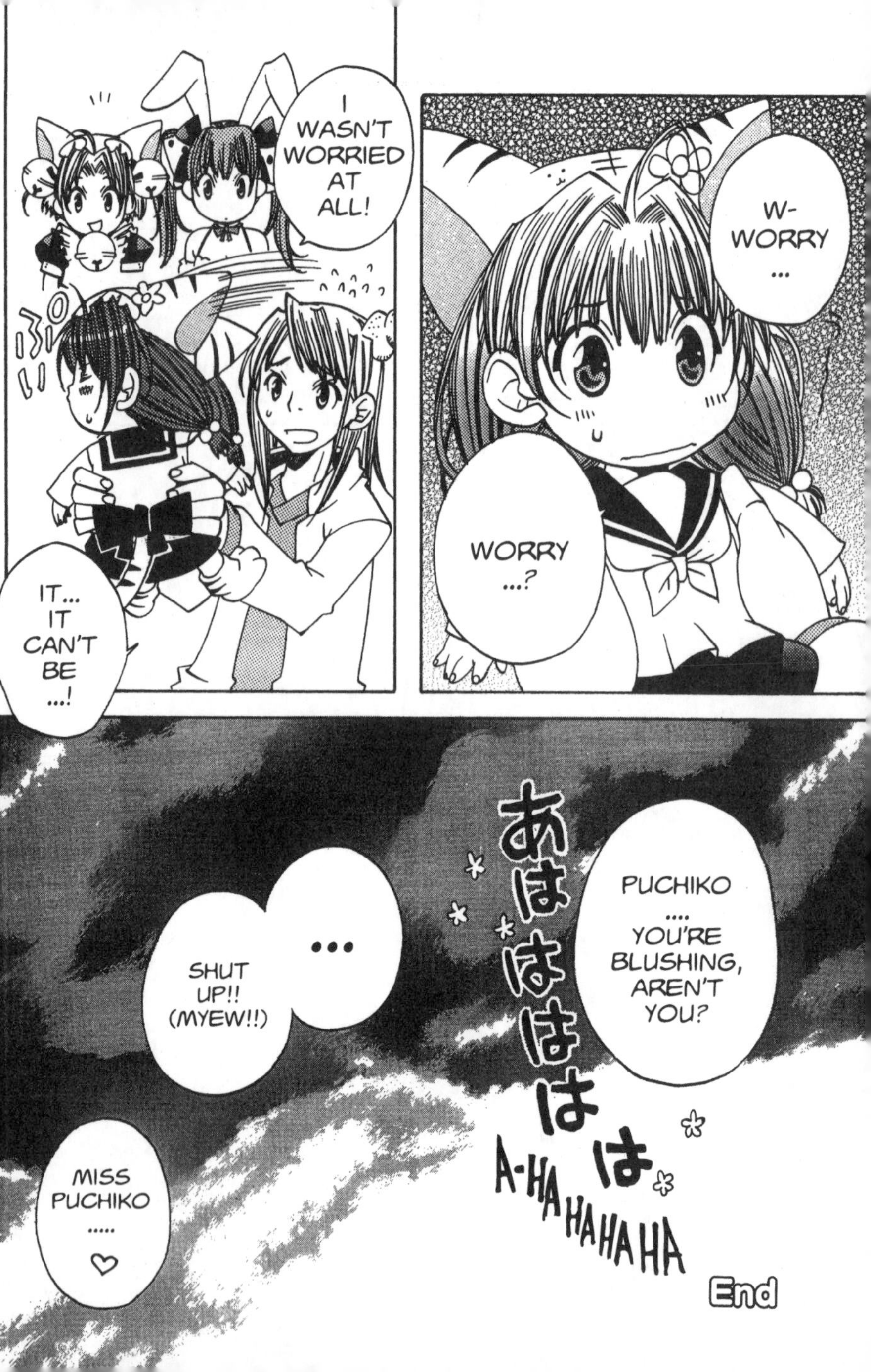
W-WORRY ...
WORRY ...?
I WASN'T WORRIED AT ALL!
IT... IT CAN'T BE ...!
PUCHIKO .... YOU'RE BLUSHING, AREN'T YOU?
あははは
A-HAHAHAHA
...
SHUT UP!! (MYEW!!)
MISS PUCHIKO ...... ♡
End

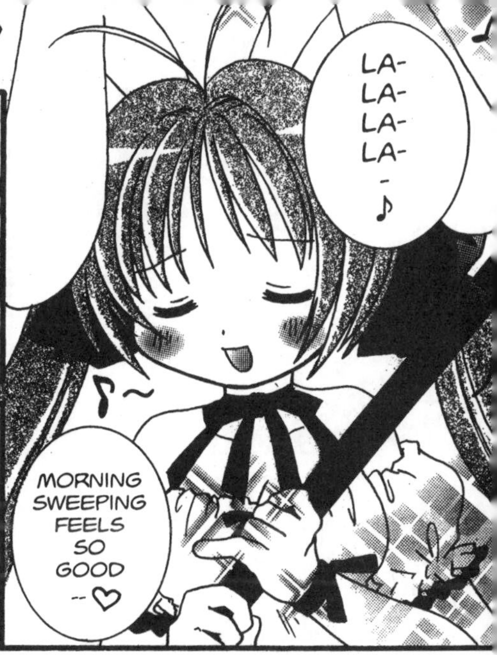
LA-LA-LA-LA-~♪
MORNING SWEEPING FEELS SO GOOD --♡

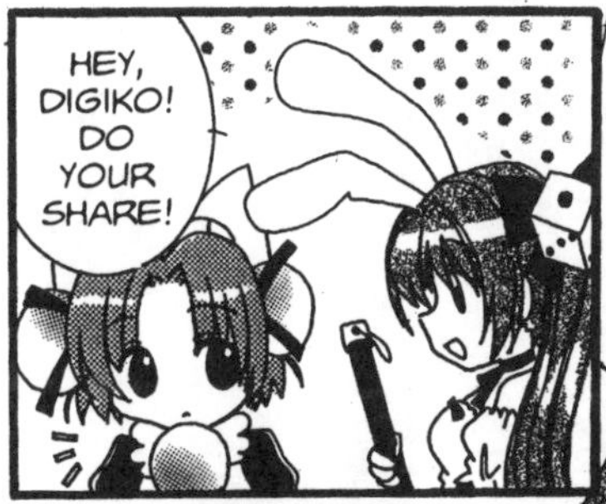
HEY, DIGIKO! DO YOUR SHARE!

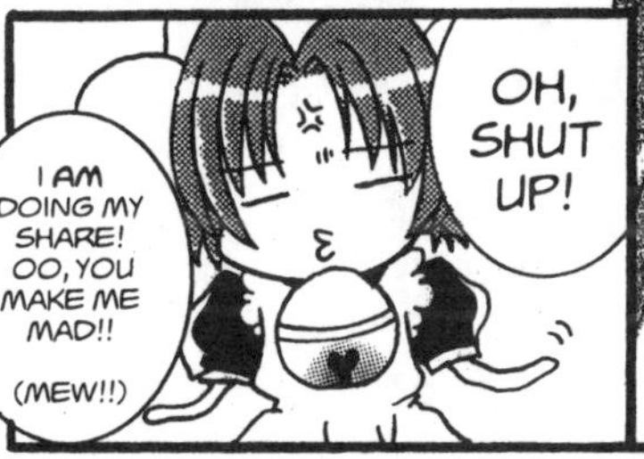
OH, SHUT UP!
I AM DOING MY SHARE! OO, YOU MAKE ME MAD!! (MEW!!)

MORNING☆FRESH

MAYUMI TAKAYANAGI

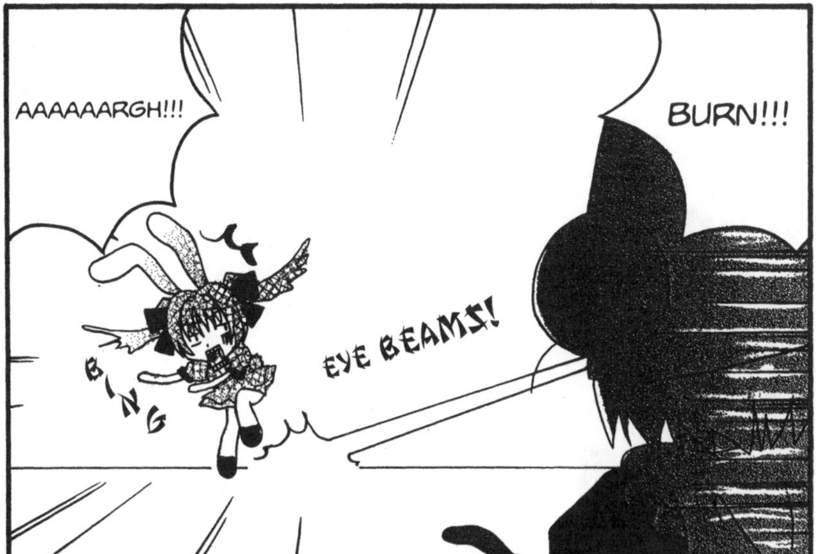
BURN!!!
AAAAAARGH!!!
EYE BEAMS!
BING

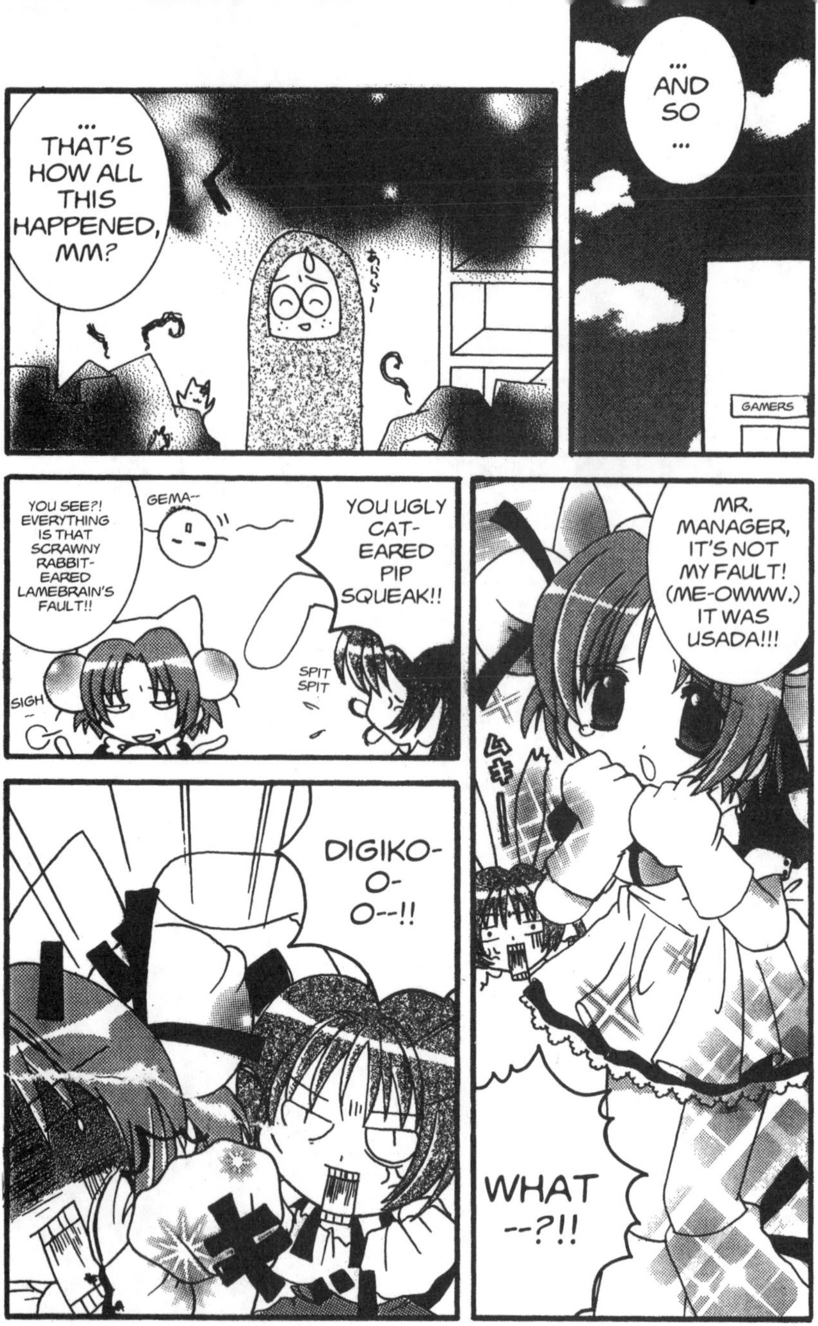

... AND SO ...
GAMERS
... THAT'S HOW ALL THIS HAPPENED, MM?
MR. MANAGER, IT'S NOT MY FAULT! (ME-OWWW.) IT WAS USADA!!!
WHAT --?!!
YOU UGLY CAT-EARED PIP SQUEAK!!
GEMA--
YOU SEE?! EVERYTHING IS THAT SCRAWNY RABBIT-EARED LAMEBRAIN'S FAULT!!
SPIT SPIT
SIGH --
DIGIKO-O-O--!!

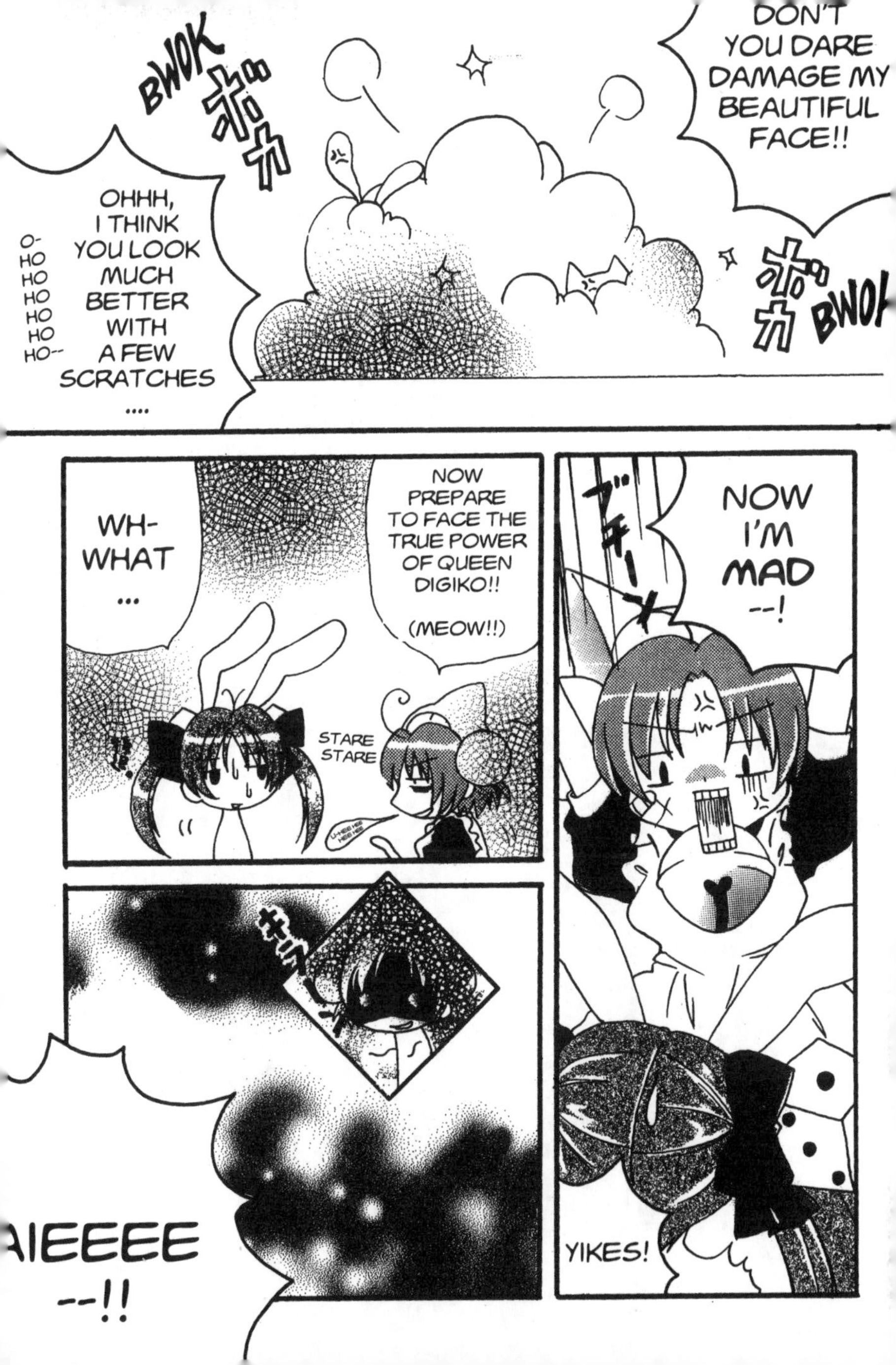
DON'T YOU DARE DAMAGE MY BEAUTIFUL FACE!!
BWOK
BWOK
OHHH, I THINK YOU LOOK MUCH BETTER WITH A FEW SCRATCHES ....
O-HO HO HO HO HO HO--
NOW I'M MAD --!
YIKES!
NOW PREPARE TO FACE THE TRUE POWER OF QUEEN DIGIKO!!
(MEOW!!)
STARE STARE
WH-WHAT ...
AIEEEE --!!

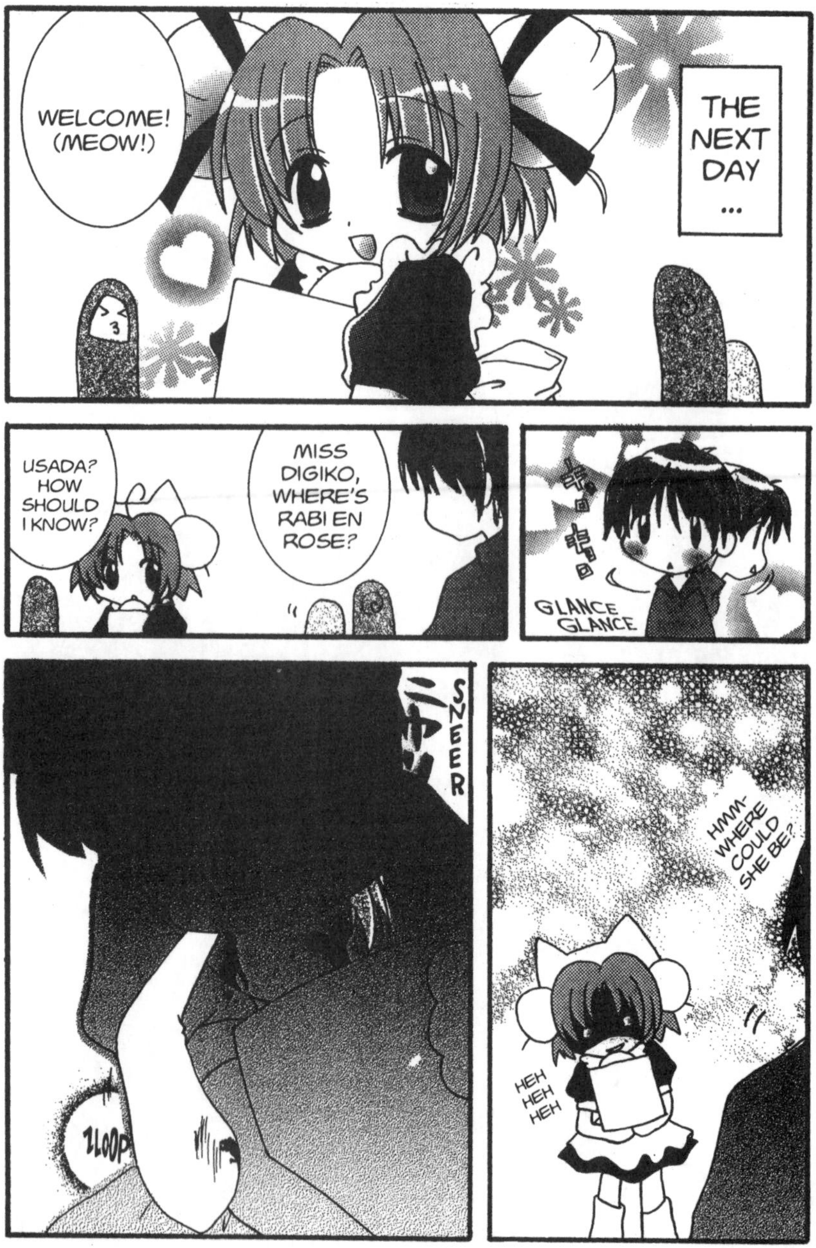
THE NEXT DAY ...
WELCOME! (MEOW!)
GLANCE GLANCE
MISS DIGIKO, WHERE'S RABI EN ROSE?
USADA? HOW SHOULD I KNOW?
HMM- WHERE COULD SHE BE?
HEH HEH HEH
SNEER
ZLOOP

End...

WHAT WOULD YOU LIKE TO SEE HAPPEN AT GAMERS?

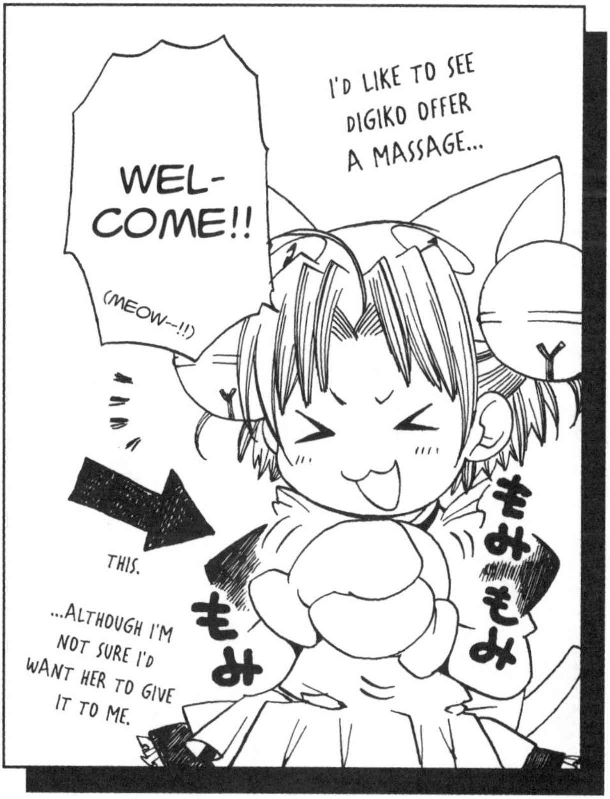
I'D LIKE TO SEE DIGIKO OFFER A MASSAGE...
WEL-COME!!
(MEOW--!!)
THIS.
...ALTHOUGH I'M NOT SURE I'D WANT HER TO GIVE IT TO ME.
もみもみ
もみ

TOWA OZORA

WHAT WOULD YOU LIKE TO SEE HAPPEN AT GAMERS?

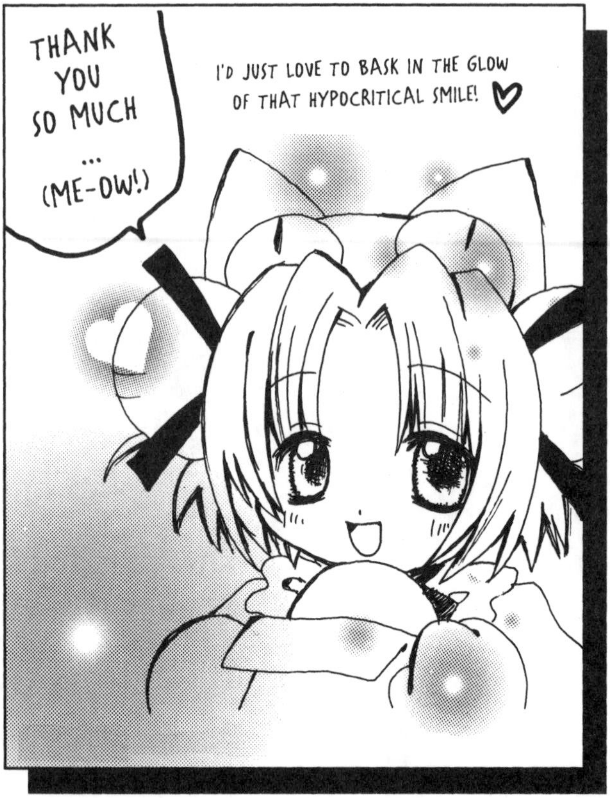
THANK YOU SO MUCH ... (ME-OW!)
I'D JUST LOVE TO BASK IN THE GLOW OF THAT HYPOCRITICAL SMILE!

MAYUMI TAKAYANAGI

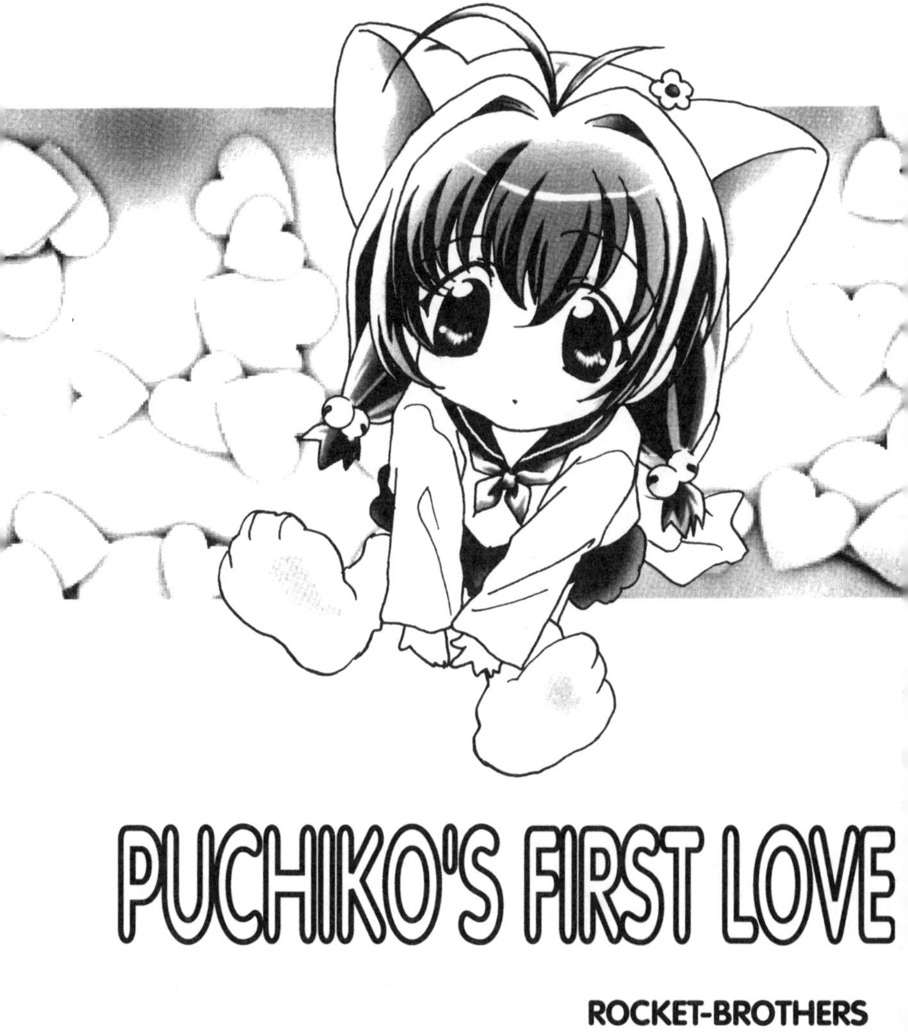

PUCHIKO'S FIRST LOVE

ROCKET-BROTHERS

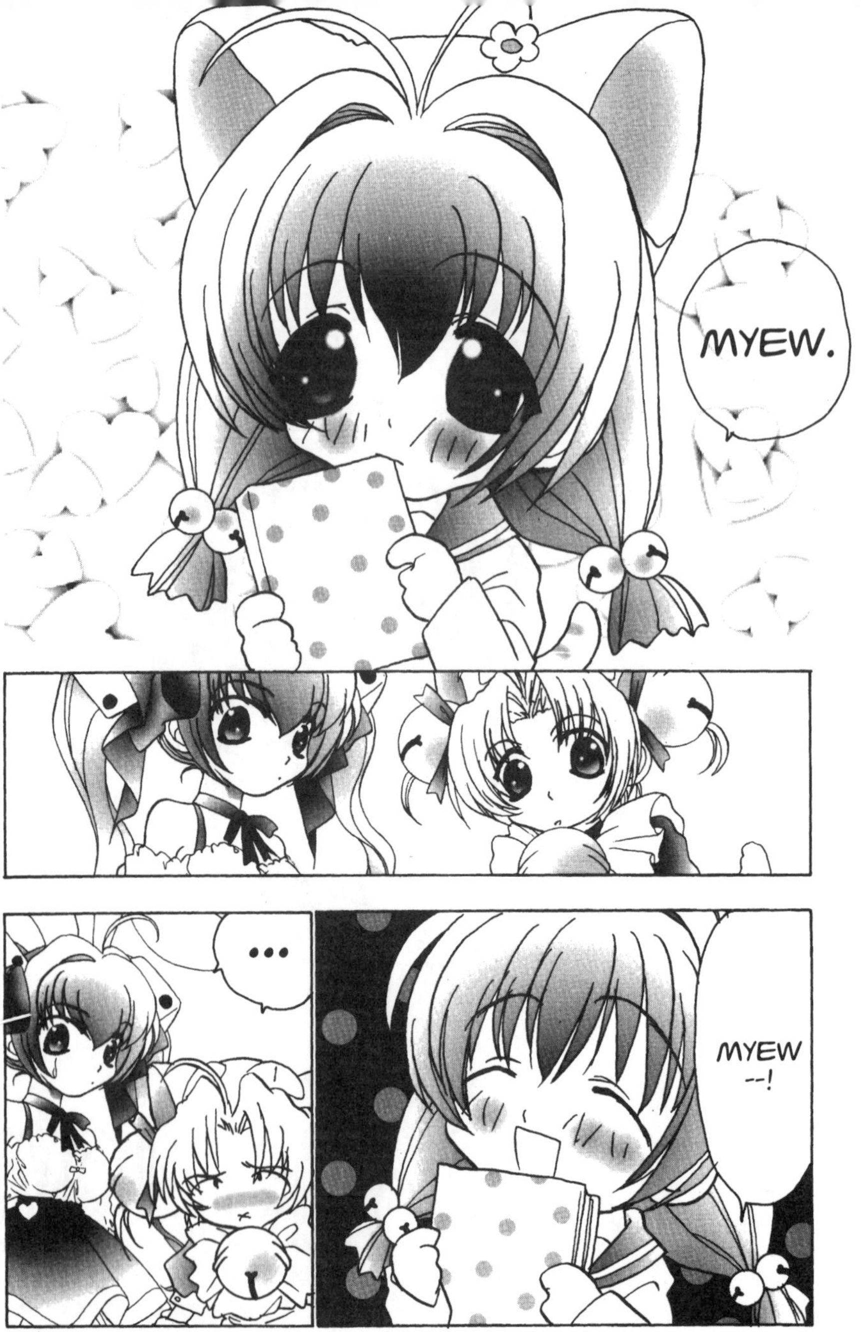
MYEW.
MYEW
--!
...

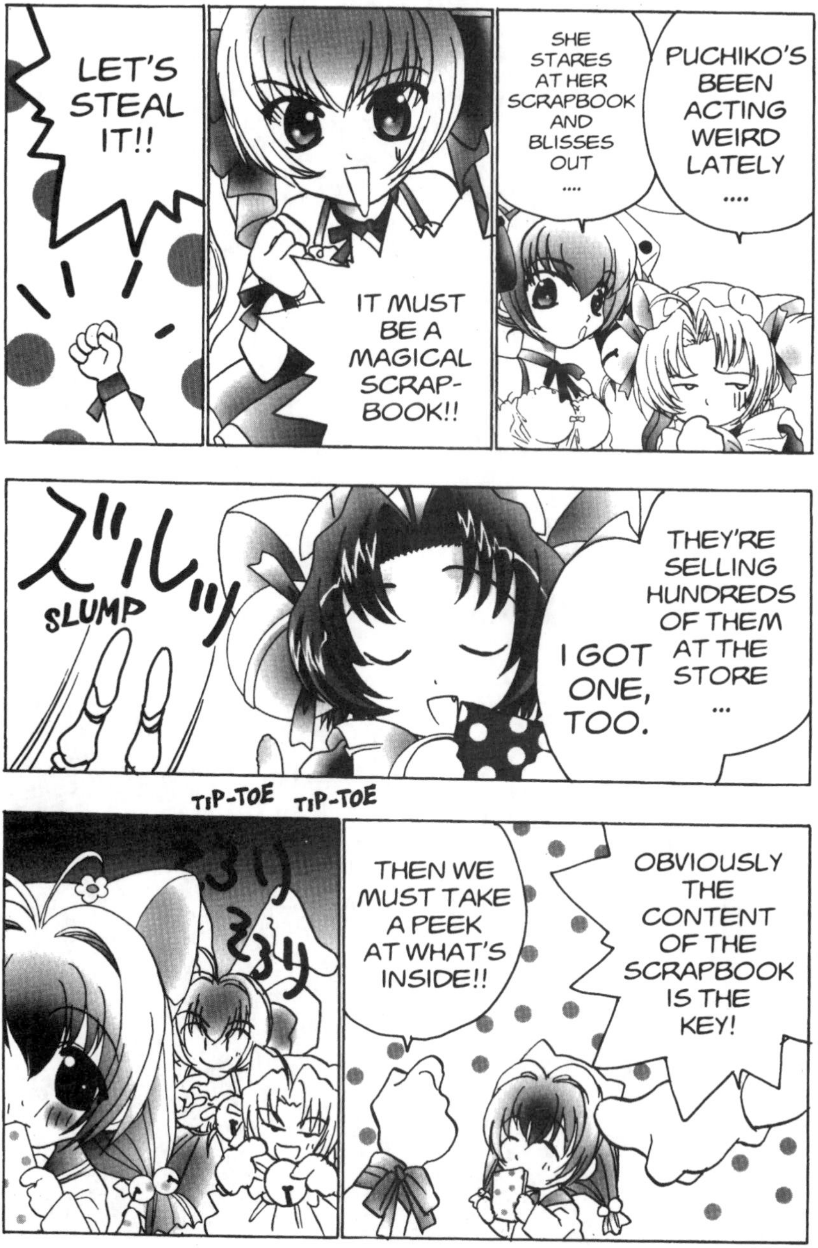
PUCHIKO'S BEEN ACTING WEIRD LATELY ....
SHE STARES AT HER SCRAPBOOK AND BLISSES OUT ....
IT MUST BE A MAGICAL SCRAP-BOOK!!
LET'S STEAL IT!!
THEY'RE SELLING HUNDREDS OF THEM AT THE STORE ...
I GOT ONE, TOO.
ズルッ
SLUMP
TIP-TOE TIP-TOE
OBVIOUSLY THE CONTENT OF THE SCRAPBOOK IS THE KEY!
THEN WE MUST TAKE A PEEK AT WHAT'S INSIDE!!

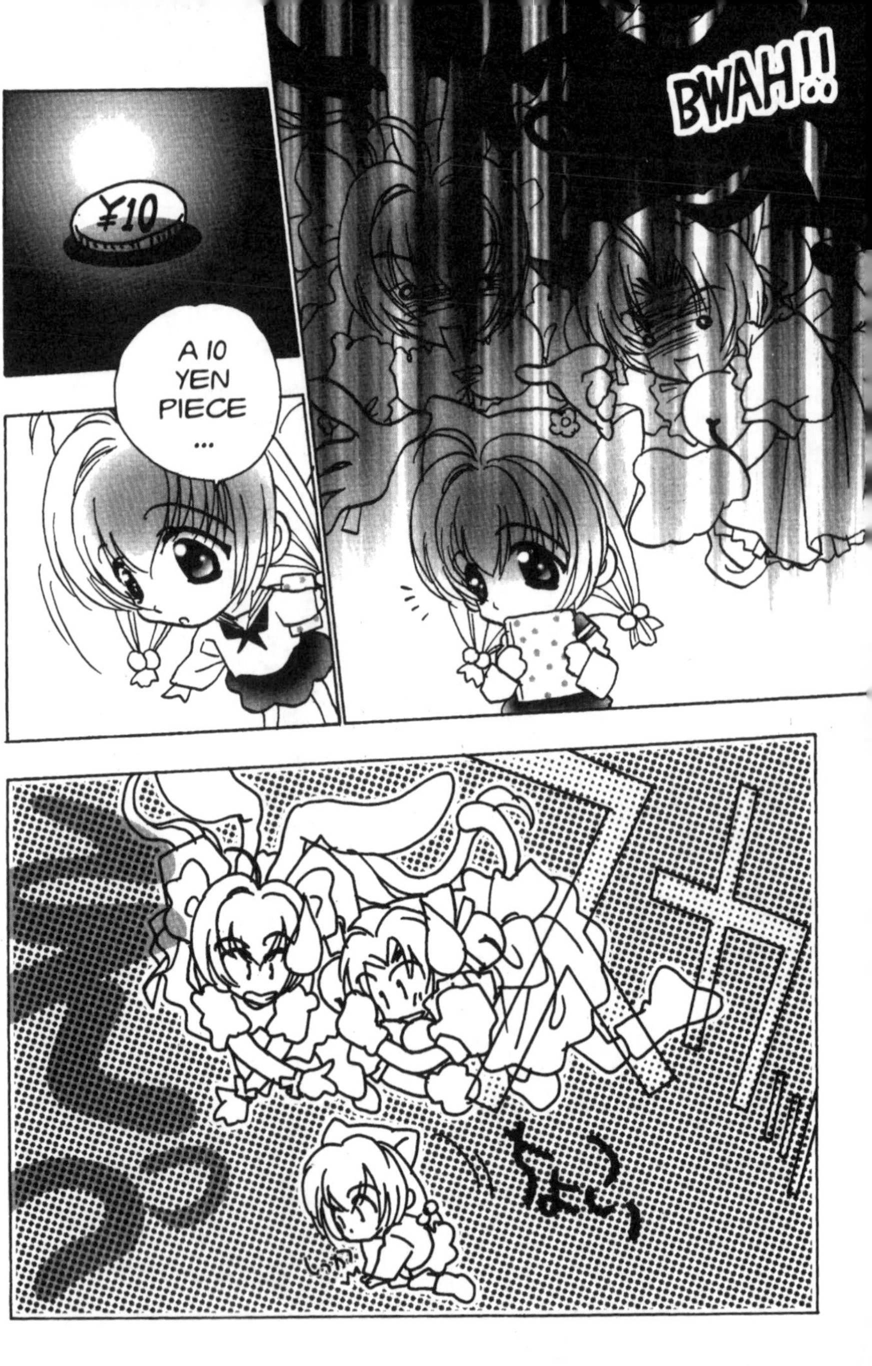
BWAH!!
A 10 YEN PIECE ...

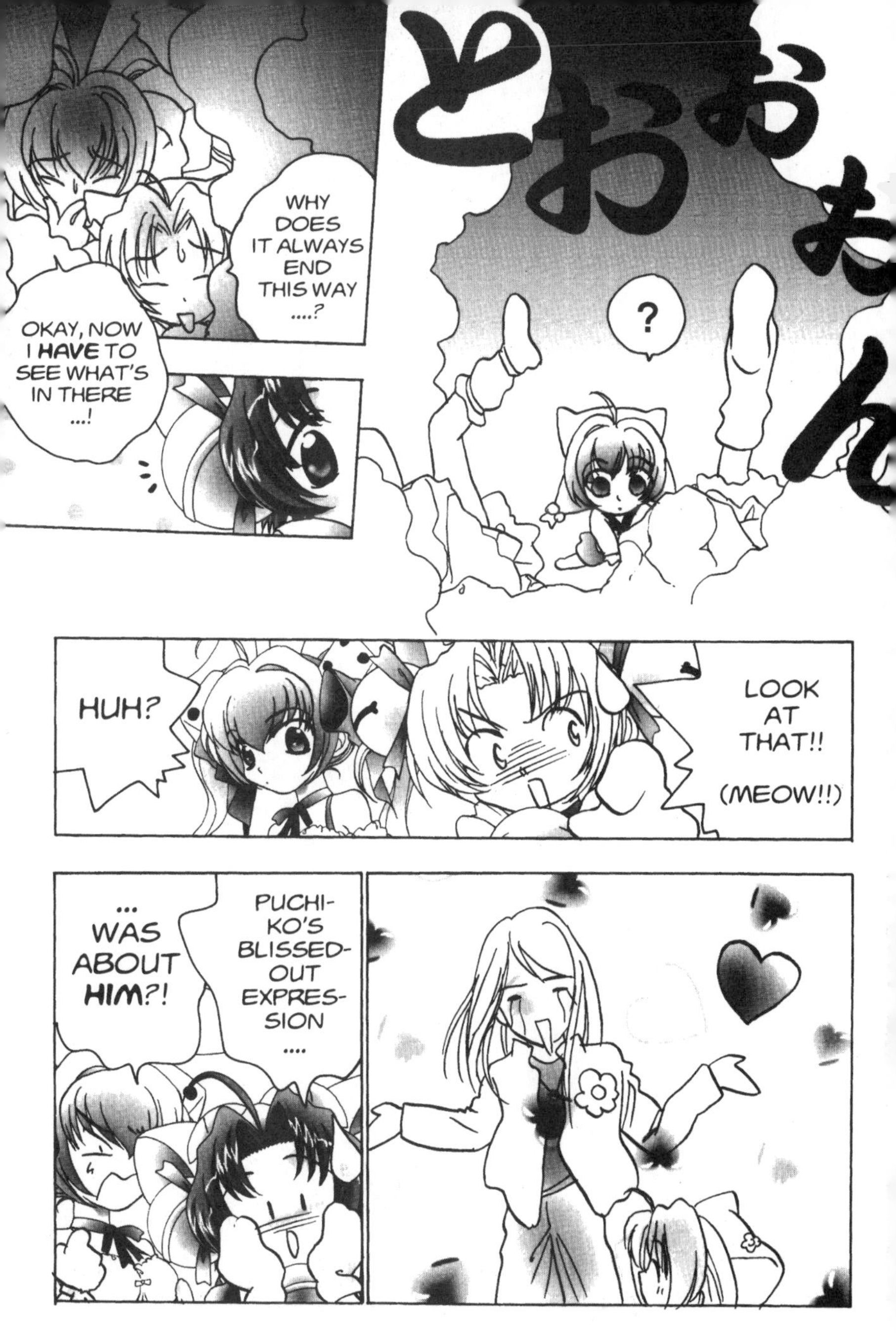

とぉおおん
?
WHY DOES IT ALWAYS END THIS WAY ....?
OKAY, NOW I **HAVE** TO SEE WHAT'S IN THERE ...!
LOOK AT THAT!!
(MEOW!!)
HUH?
PUCHIKO'S BLISSED-OUT EXPRESSION ....
... WAS ABOUT **HIM**?!

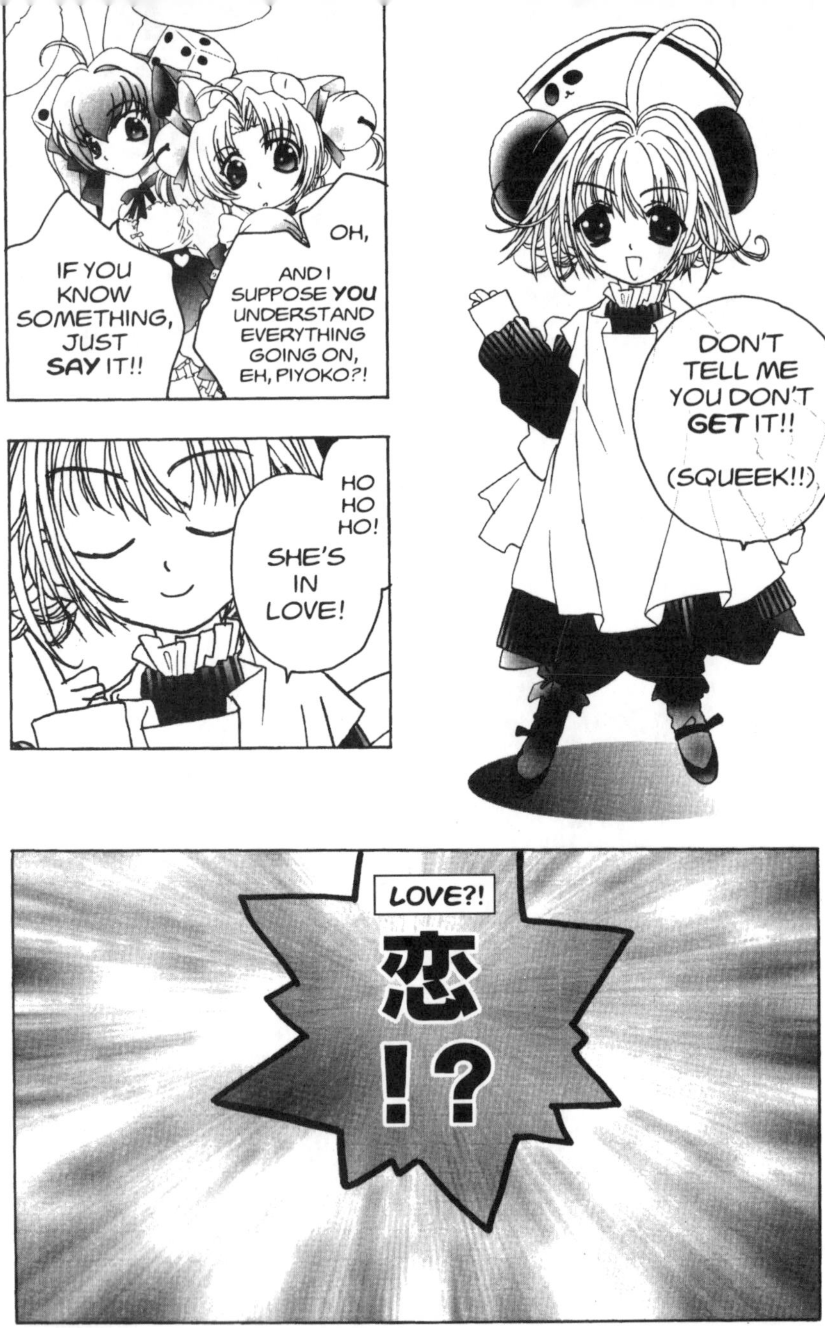
DON'T TELL ME YOU DON'T GET IT!!
(SQUEEK!!)
OH, AND I SUPPOSE YOU UNDERSTAND EVERYTHING GOING ON, EH, PIYOKO?!
IF YOU KNOW SOMETHING, JUST SAY IT!!
HO HO HO! SHE'S IN LOVE!
LOVE?!
恋!?

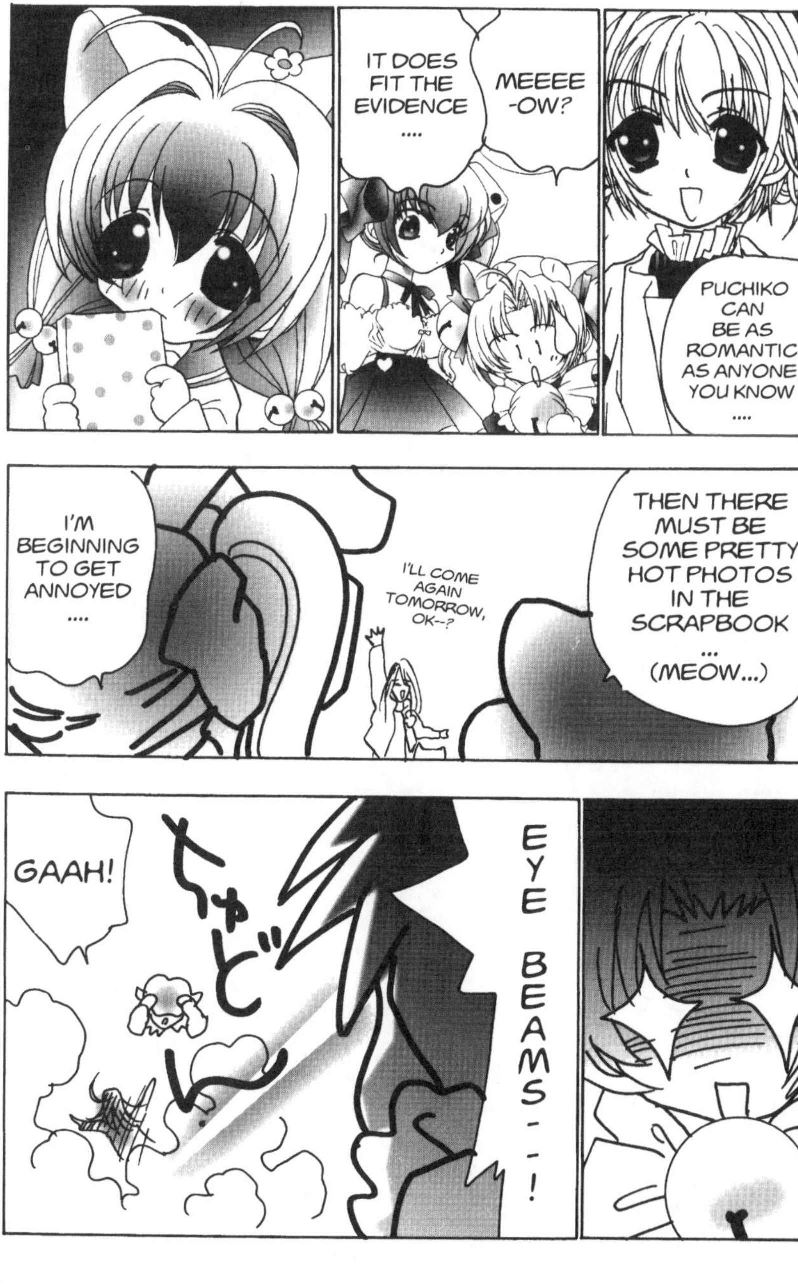
PUCHIKO CAN BE AS ROMANTIC AS ANYONE, YOU KNOW ....
MEEEE -OW?
IT DOES FIT THE EVIDENCE ....
THEN THERE MUST BE SOME PRETTY HOT PHOTOS IN THE SCRAPBOOK ... (MEOW...)
I'LL COME AGAIN TOMORROW, OK--?
I'M BEGINNING TO GET ANNOYED ....
EYE BEAMS---!
GAAH!

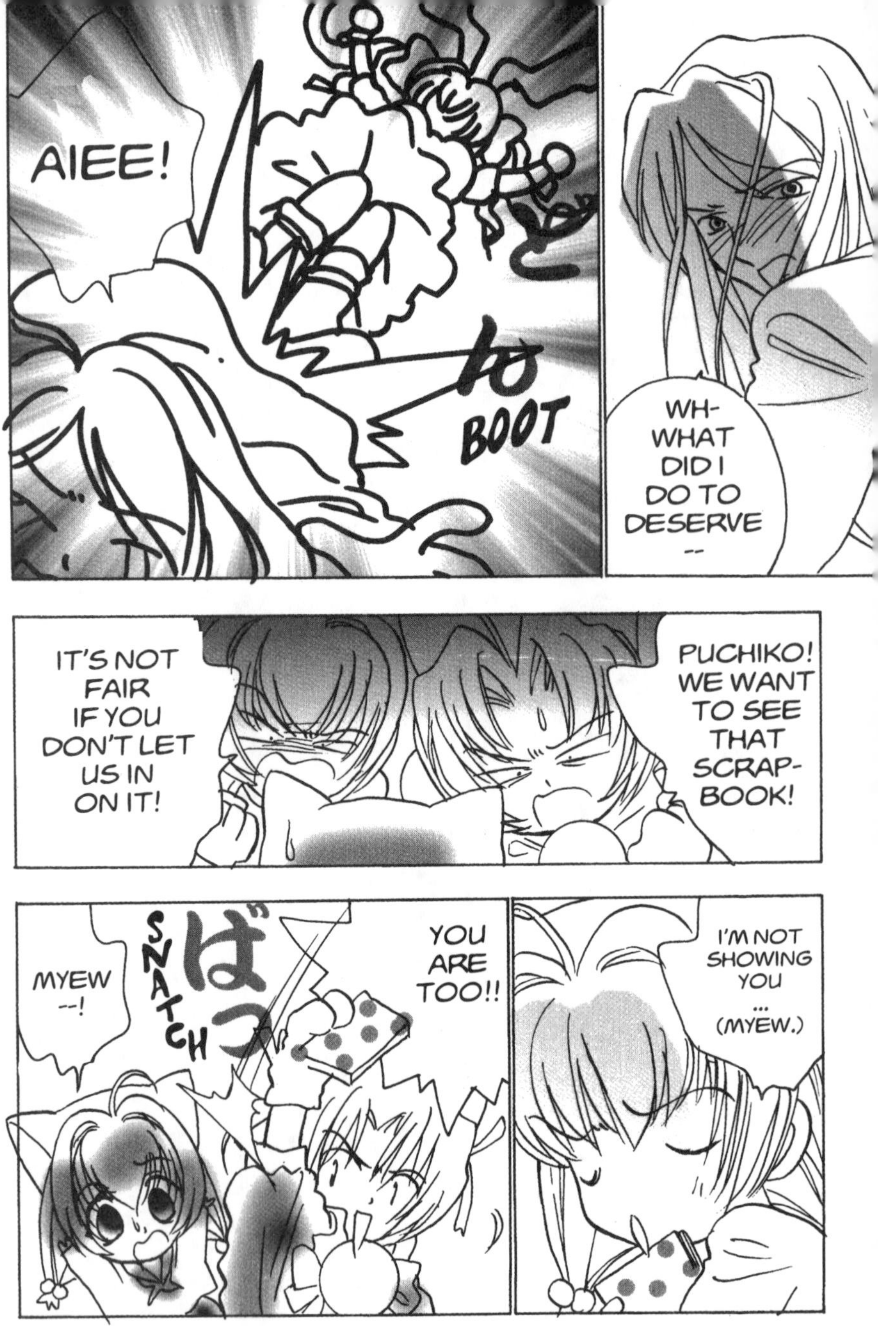
WH-WHAT DID I DO TO DESERVE --
AIEE!
BOOT
PUCHIKO! WE WANT TO SEE THAT SCRAP-BOOK!
IT'S NOT FAIR IF YOU DON'T LET US IN ON IT!
I'M NOT SHOWING YOU ... (MYEW.)
YOU ARE TOO!!
ばっ
SNATCH
MYEW --!

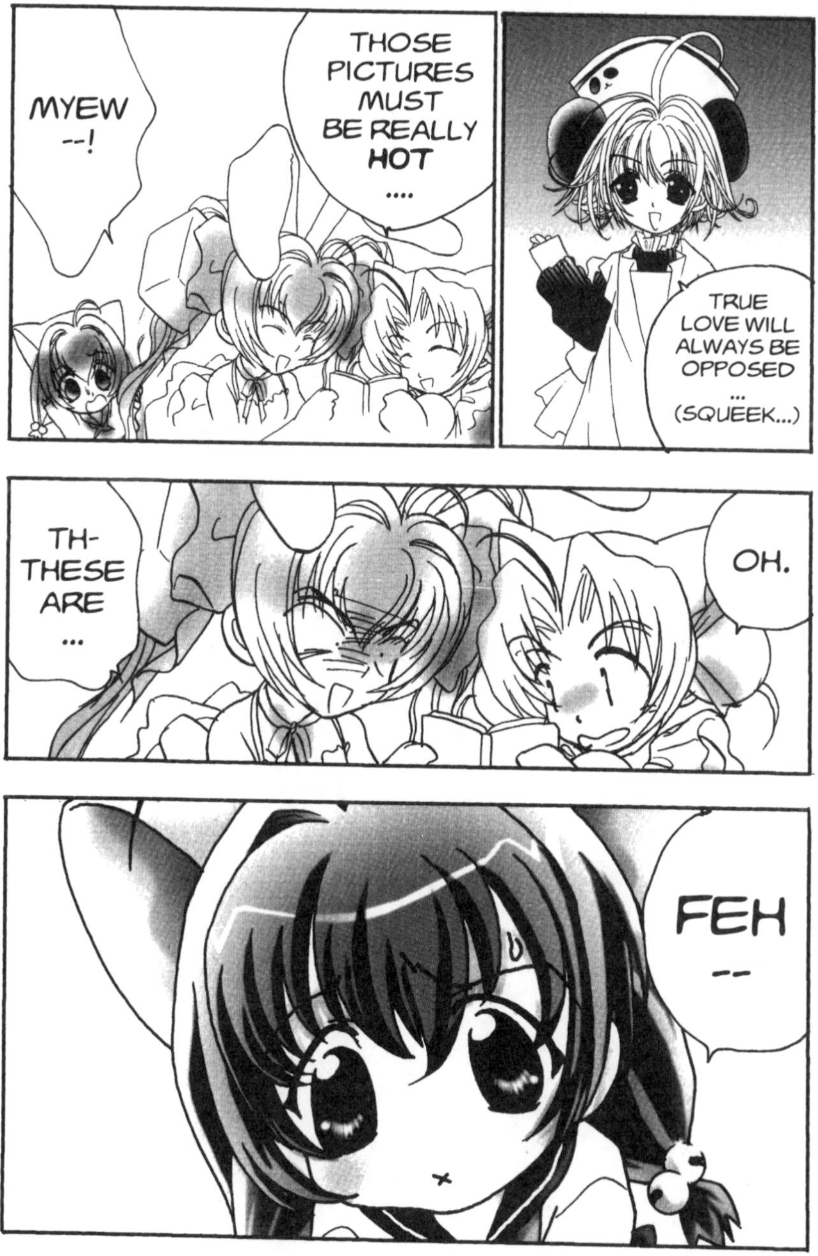
TRUE LOVE WILL ALWAYS BE OPPOSED ... (SQUEEK...)
THOSE PICTURES MUST BE REALLY **HOT** ....
MYEW --!
OH.
TH-THESE ARE ...
FEH --

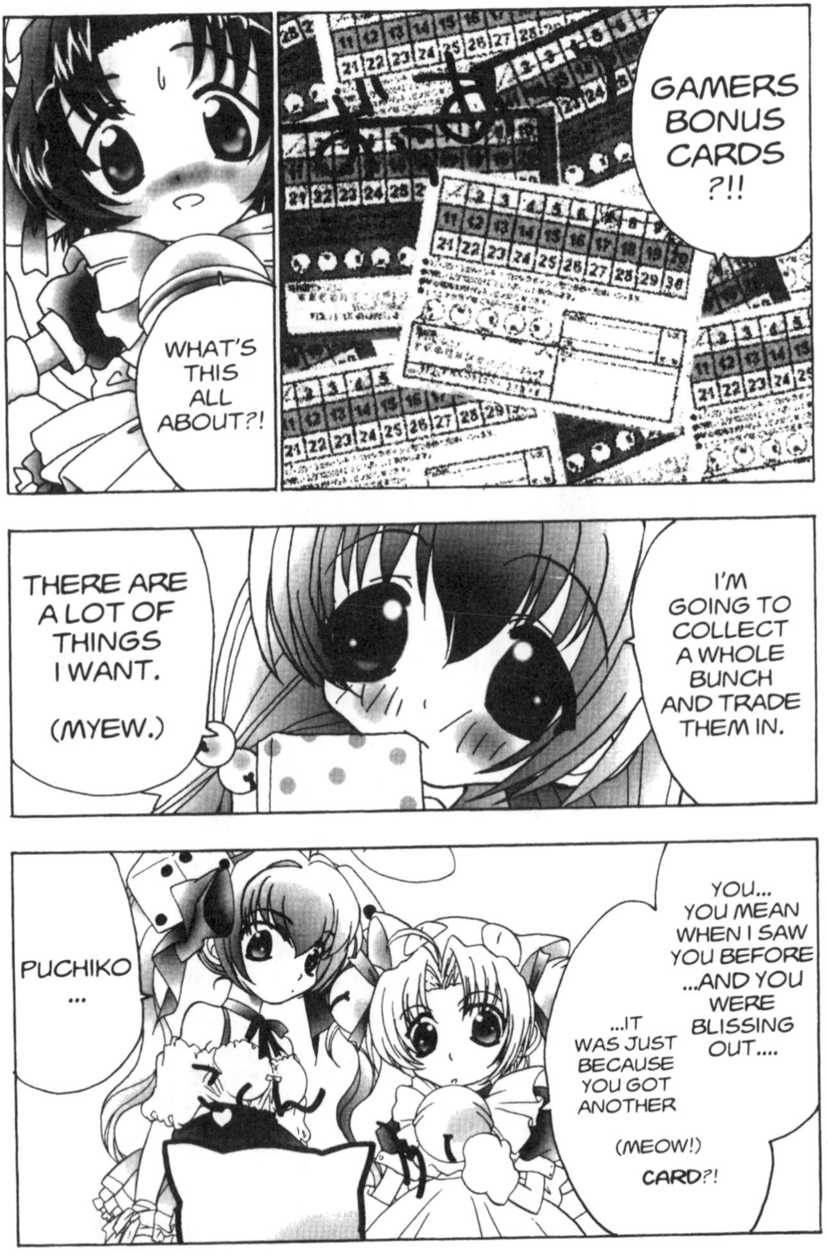
GAMERS BONUS CARDS ?!!
WHAT'S THIS ALL ABOUT?!
I'M GOING TO COLLECT A WHOLE BUNCH AND TRADE THEM IN.
THERE ARE A LOT OF THINGS I WANT.
(MYEW.)
YOU... YOU MEAN WHEN I SAW YOU BEFORE ...AND YOU WERE BLISSING OUT....
...IT WAS JUST BECAUSE YOU GOT ANOTHER
(MEOW!)
CARD?!
PUCHIKO ...

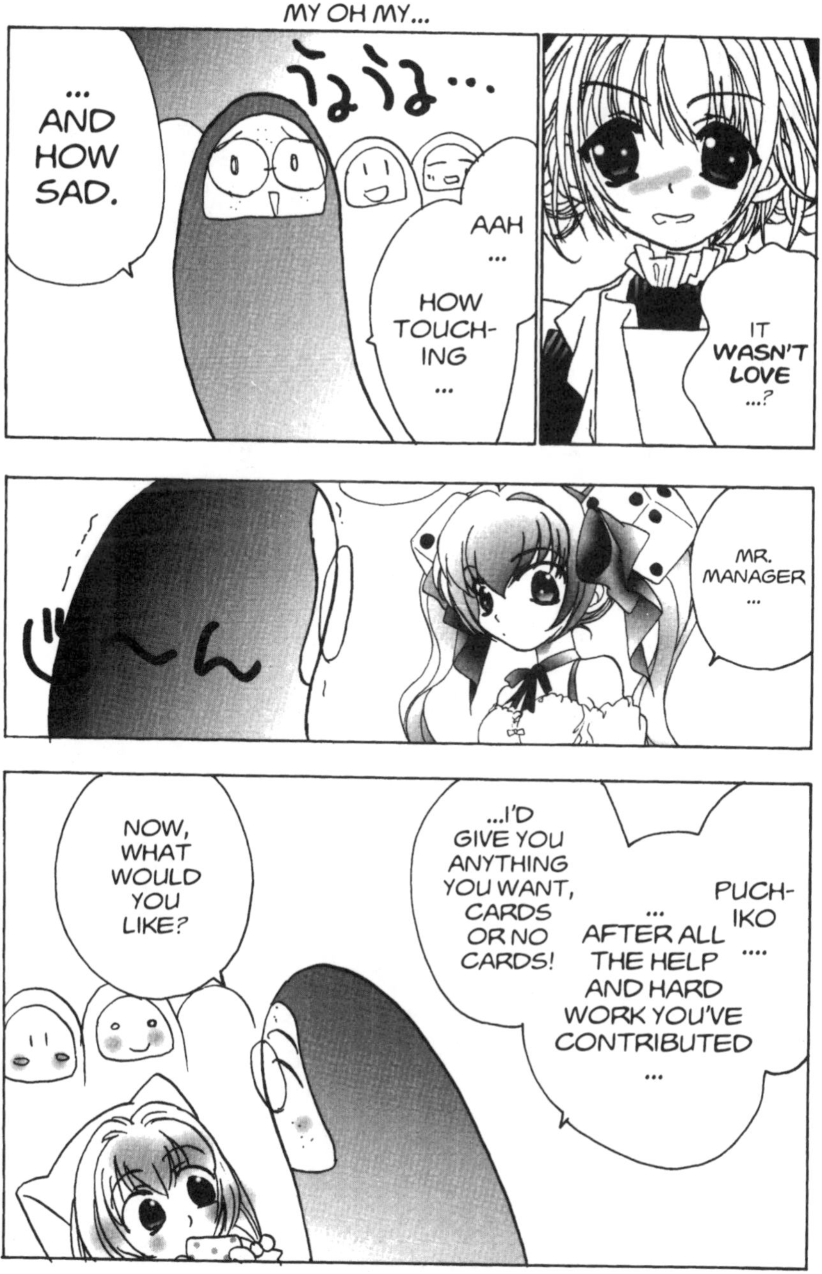
IT WASN'T LOVE ...?
MY OH MY...
AAH ... HOW TOUCHING ...
... AND HOW SAD.
MR. MANAGER ...
じ〜ん
PUCHIKO ....
... AFTER ALL THE HELP AND HARD WORK YOU'VE CONTRIBUTED ...
...I'D GIVE YOU ANYTHING YOU WANT, CARDS OR NO CARDS!
NOW, WHAT WOULD YOU LIKE?

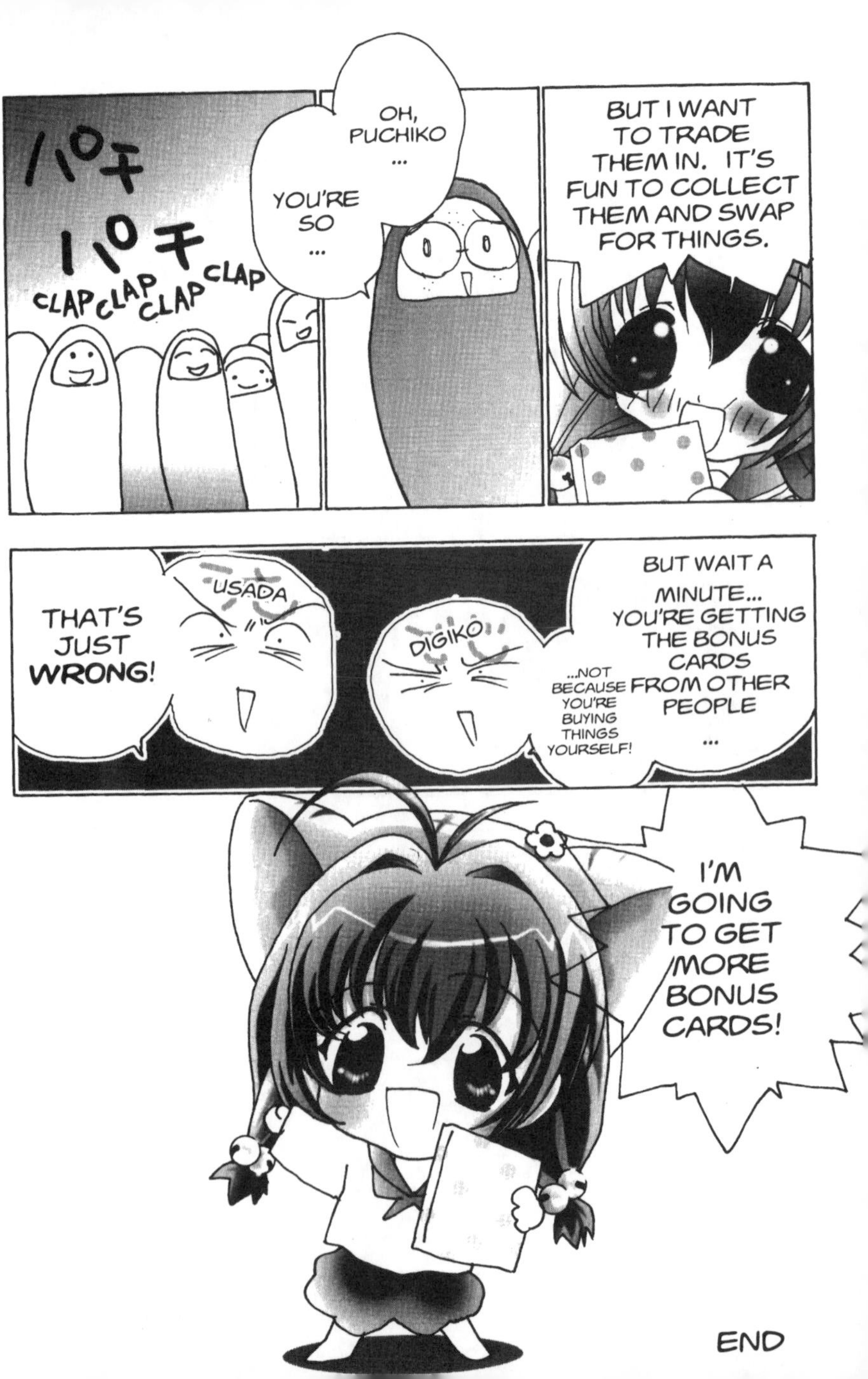
BUT I WANT TO TRADE THEM IN. IT'S FUN TO COLLECT THEM AND SWAP FOR THINGS.
OH, PUCHIKO ...
YOU'RE SO ...
パチ
パチ
CLAP CLAP CLAP CLAP
BUT WAIT A MINUTE... YOU'RE GETTING THE BONUS CARDS FROM OTHER PEOPLE ...
...NOT BECAUSE YOU'RE BUYING THINGS YOURSELF!
DIGIKO
USADA
THAT'S JUST WRONG!
I'M GOING TO GET MORE BONUS CARDS!

END

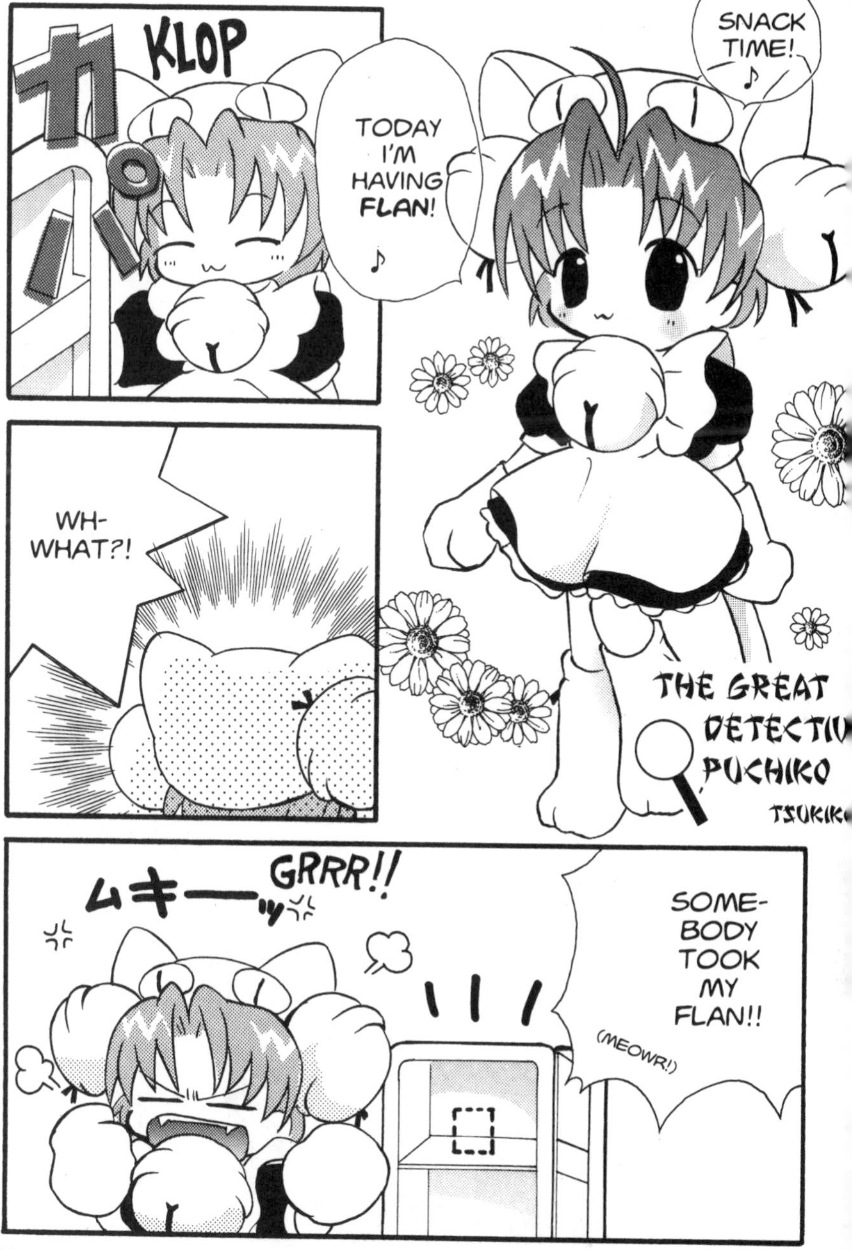
SNACK TIME! ♪
TODAY I'M HAVING FLAN! ♪
THE GREAT DETECTIV
PUCHIKO
TSUKIK
カパッ
KLOP
WH-WHAT?!
ムキーーッ
GRRR!!
SOME-BODY TOOK MY FLAN!!
(MEOWR!)

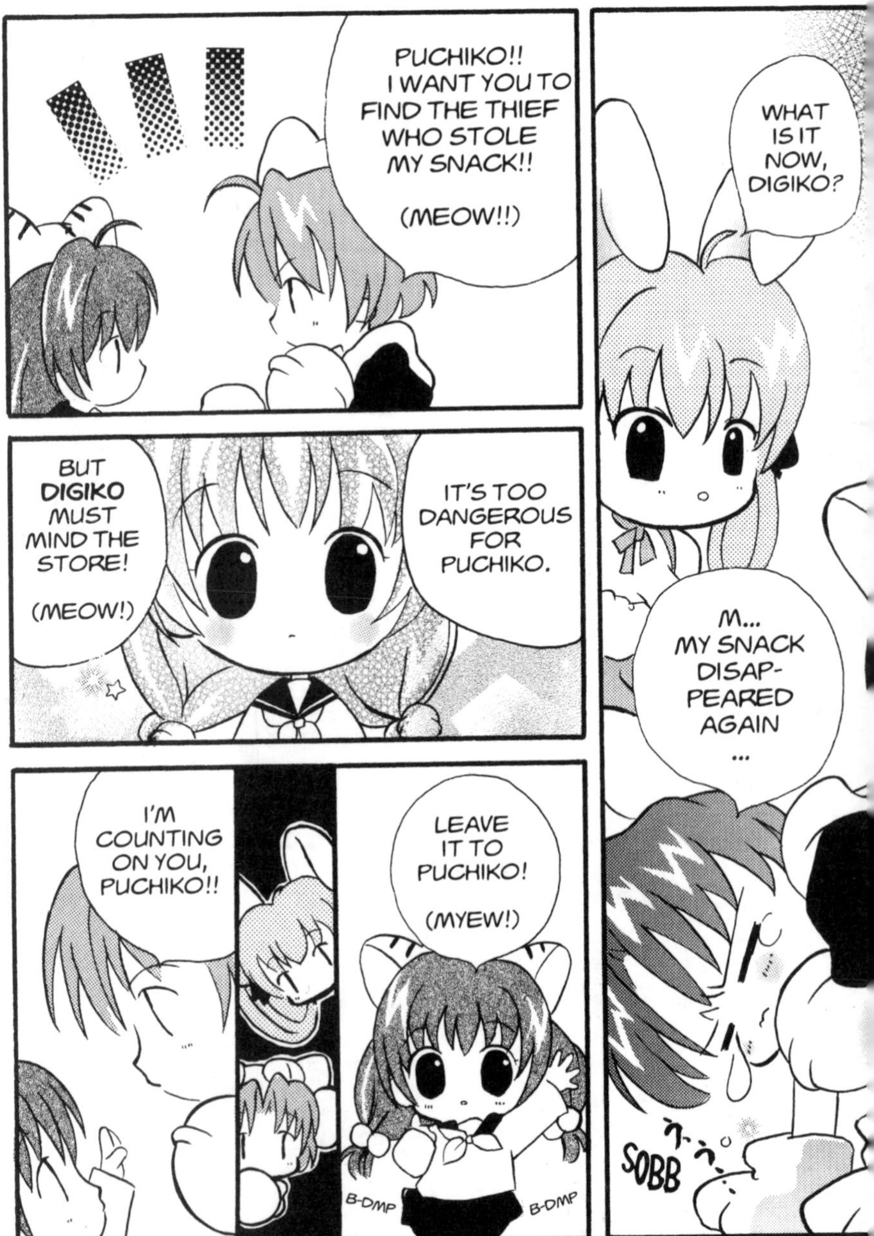
WHAT IS IT NOW, DIGIKO?
M... MY SNACK DISAP-PEARED AGAIN ...
SOBB
PUCHIKO!! I WANT YOU TO FIND THE THIEF WHO STOLE MY SNACK!! (MEOW!!)
IT'S TOO DANGEROUS FOR PUCHIKO.
BUT **DIGIKO** MUST MIND THE STORE! (MEOW!)
LEAVE IT TO PUCHIKO! (MYEW!)
B-DMP
B-DMP
I'M COUNTING ON YOU, PUCHIKO!!

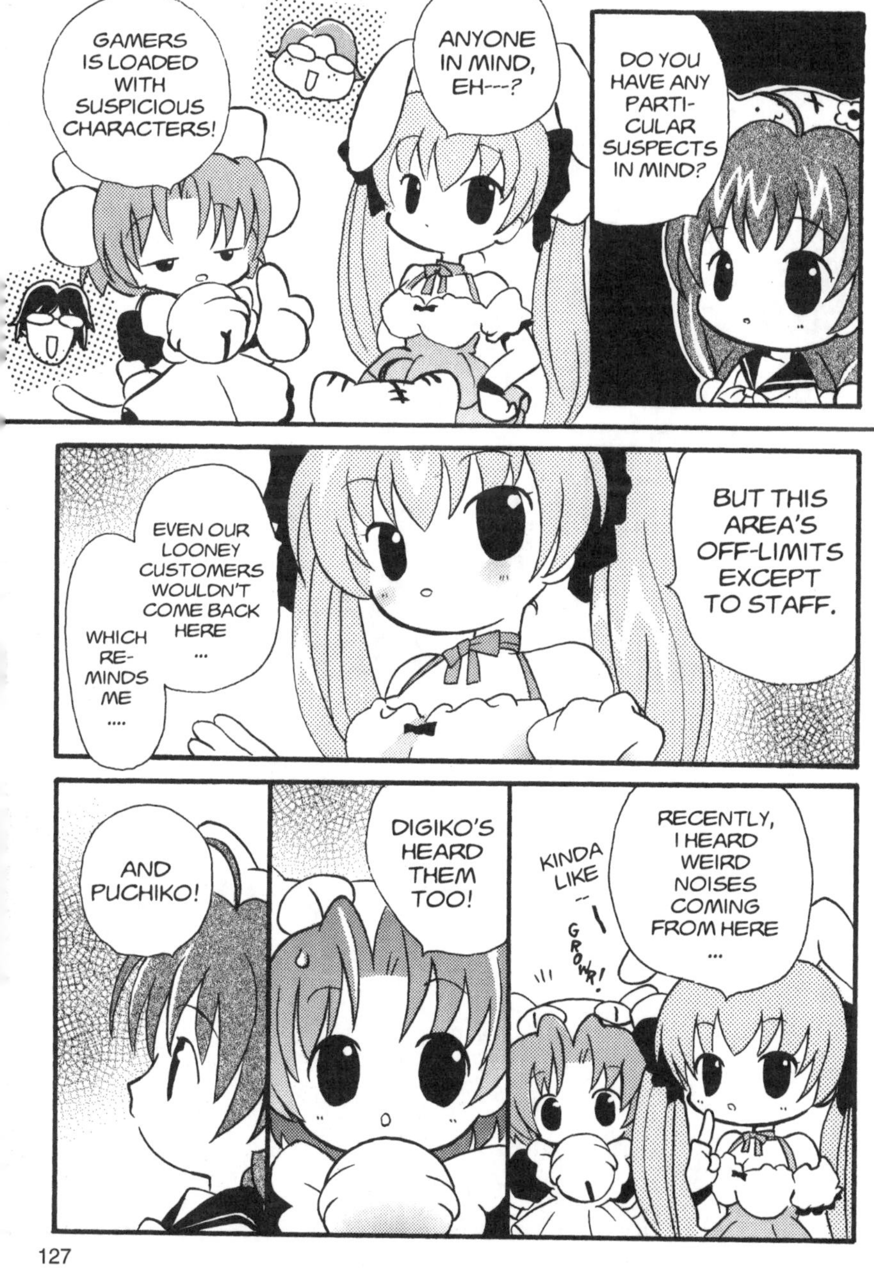
DO YOU HAVE ANY PARTI-CULAR SUSPECTS IN MIND?
ANYONE IN MIND, EH---?
GAMERS IS LOADED WITH SUSPICIOUS CHARACTERS!
BUT THIS AREA'S OFF-LIMITS EXCEPT TO STAFF.
EVEN OUR LOONEY CUSTOMERS WOULDN'T COME BACK HERE ...
WHICH RE-MINDS ME ....
RECENTLY, I HEARD WEIRD NOISES COMING FROM HERE ...
KINDA LIKE -- !
GROWR!
DIGIKO'S HEARD THEM TOO!
AND PUCHIKO!

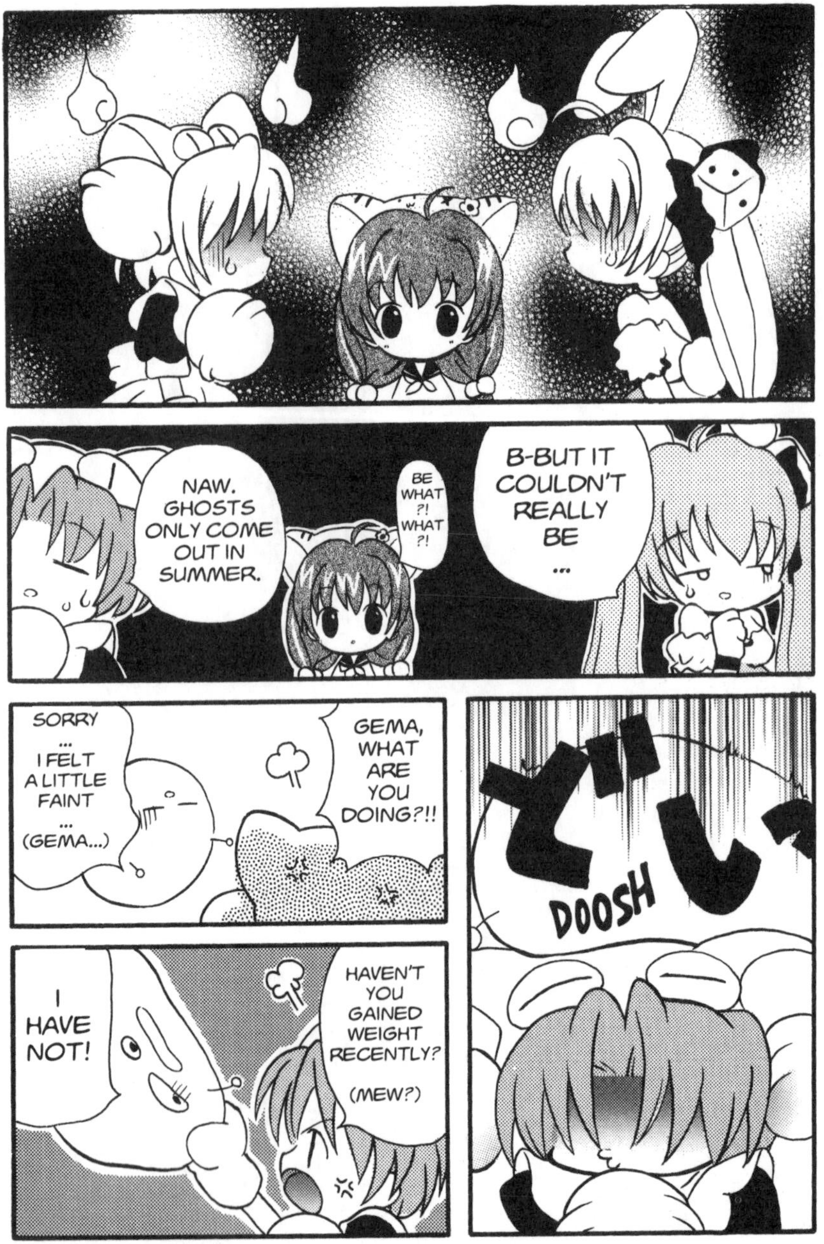
B-BUT IT COULDN'T REALLY BE ...
BE WHAT ?! WHAT ?!
NAW. GHOSTS ONLY COME OUT IN SUMMER.
DOOSH
GEMA, WHAT ARE YOU DOING?!!
SORRY ... I FELT A LITTLE FAINT ... (GEMA...)
HAVEN'T YOU GAINED WEIGHT RECENTLY?
(MEW?)
I HAVE NOT!

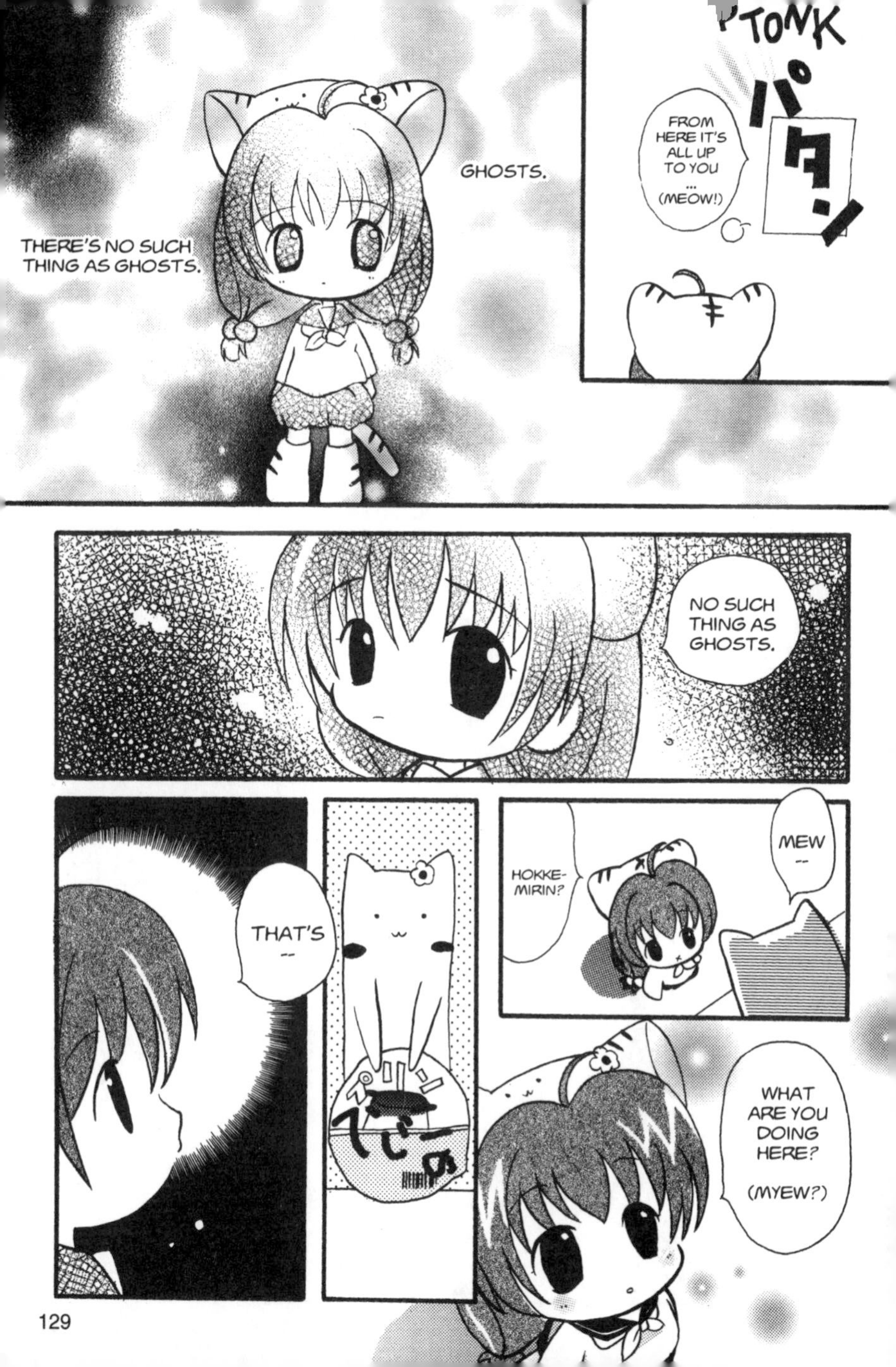

TONK
パタン!
FROM HERE IT'S ALL UP TO YOU ... (MEOW!)
GHOSTS.
THERE'S NO SUCH THING AS GHOSTS.
NO SUCH THING AS GHOSTS.
MEW --
HOKKE-MIRIN?
WHAT ARE YOU DOING HERE? (MYEW?)
THAT'S --

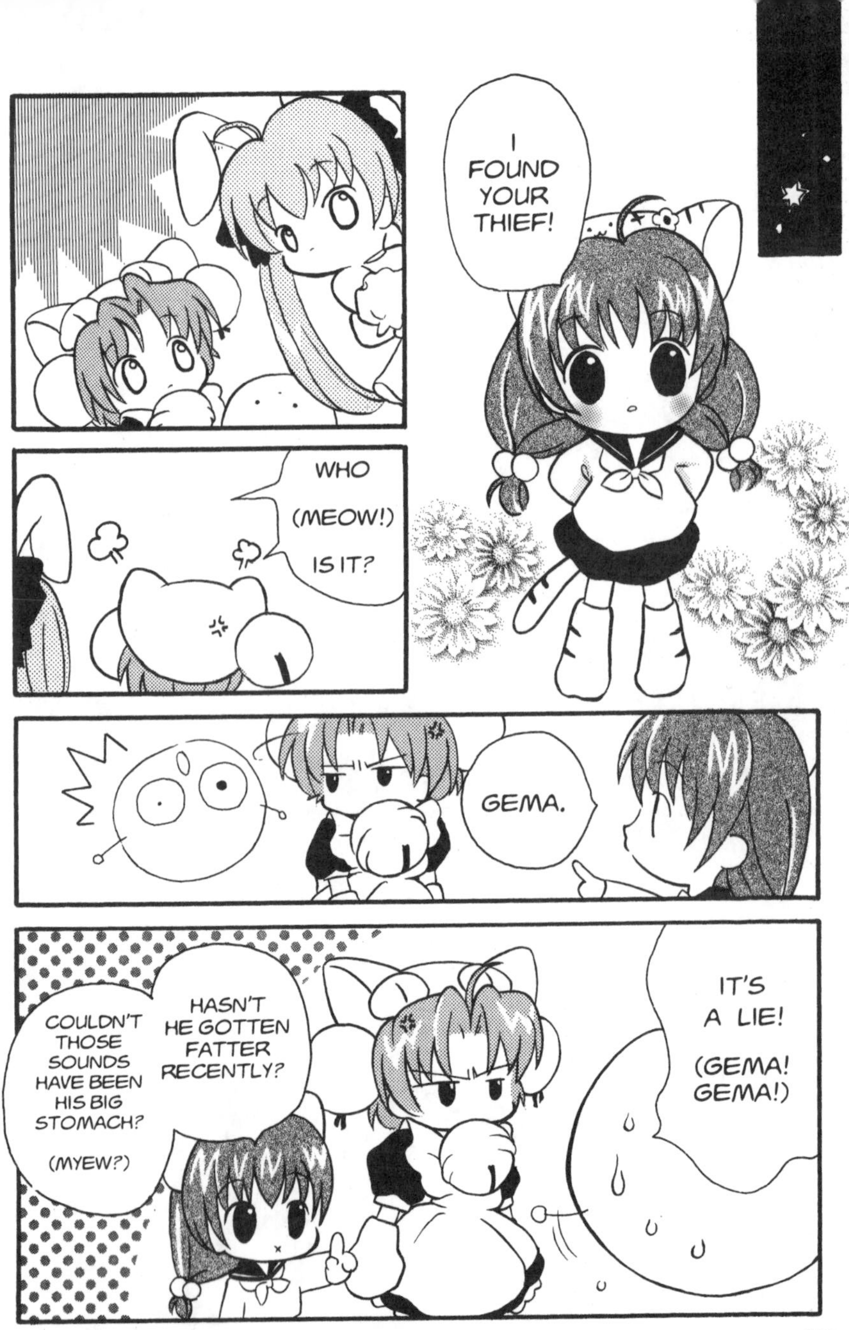
I FOUND YOUR THIEF!
WHO (MEOW!) IS IT?
GEMA.
IT'S A LIE!
(GEMA! GEMA!)
HASN'T HE GOTTEN FATTER RECENTLY?
COULDN'T THOSE SOUNDS HAVE BEEN HIS BIG STOMACH?
(MYEW?)

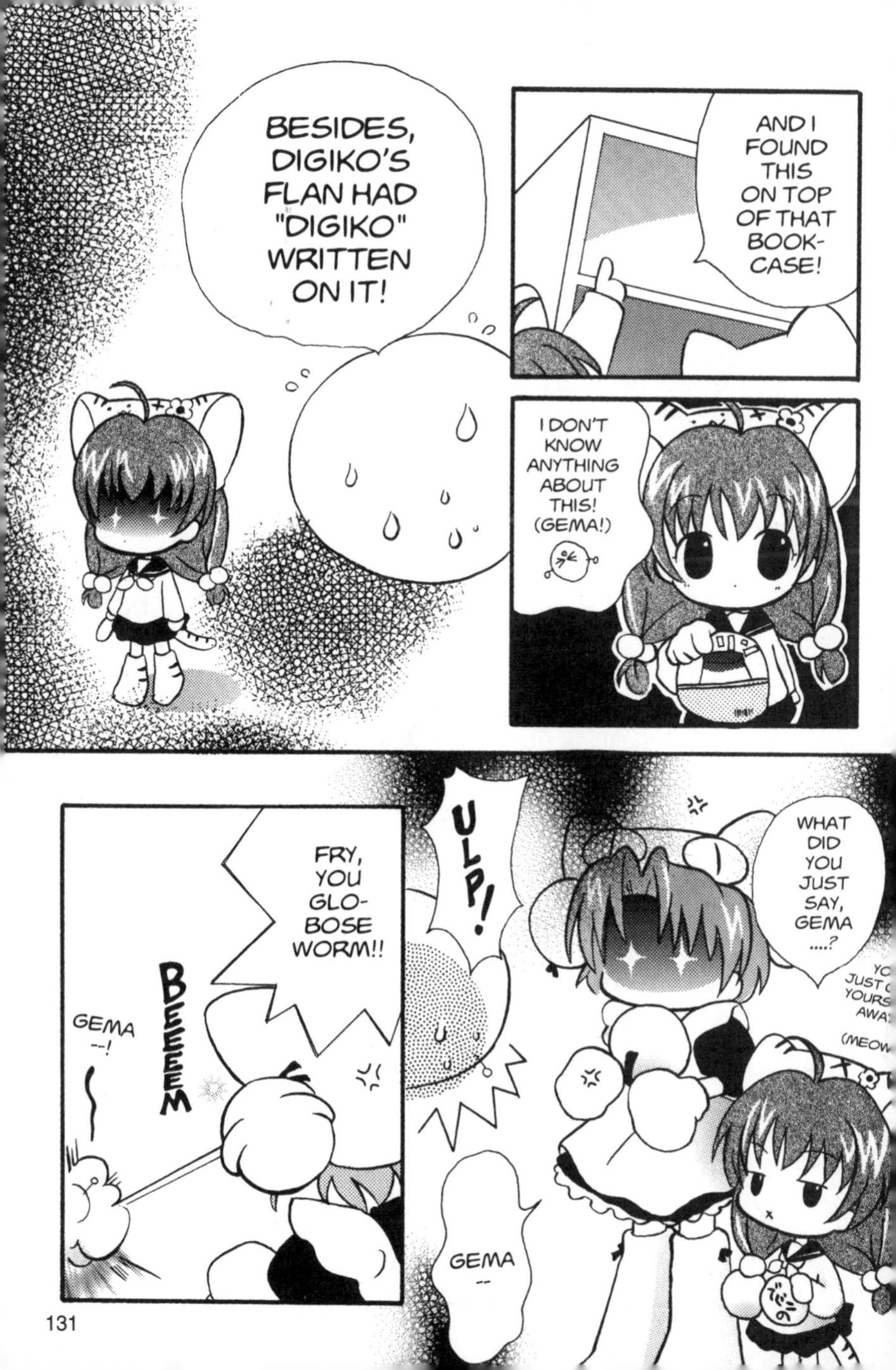
AND I FOUND THIS ON TOP OF THAT BOOK-CASE!
I DON'T KNOW ANYTHING ABOUT THIS! (GEMA!)
BESIDES, DIGIKO'S FLAN HAD "DIGIKO" WRITTEN ON IT!
WHAT DID YOU JUST SAY, GEMA ....?
ULP!
GEMA --
FRY, YOU GLO-BOSE WORM!!
BEEEEM
GEMA --!

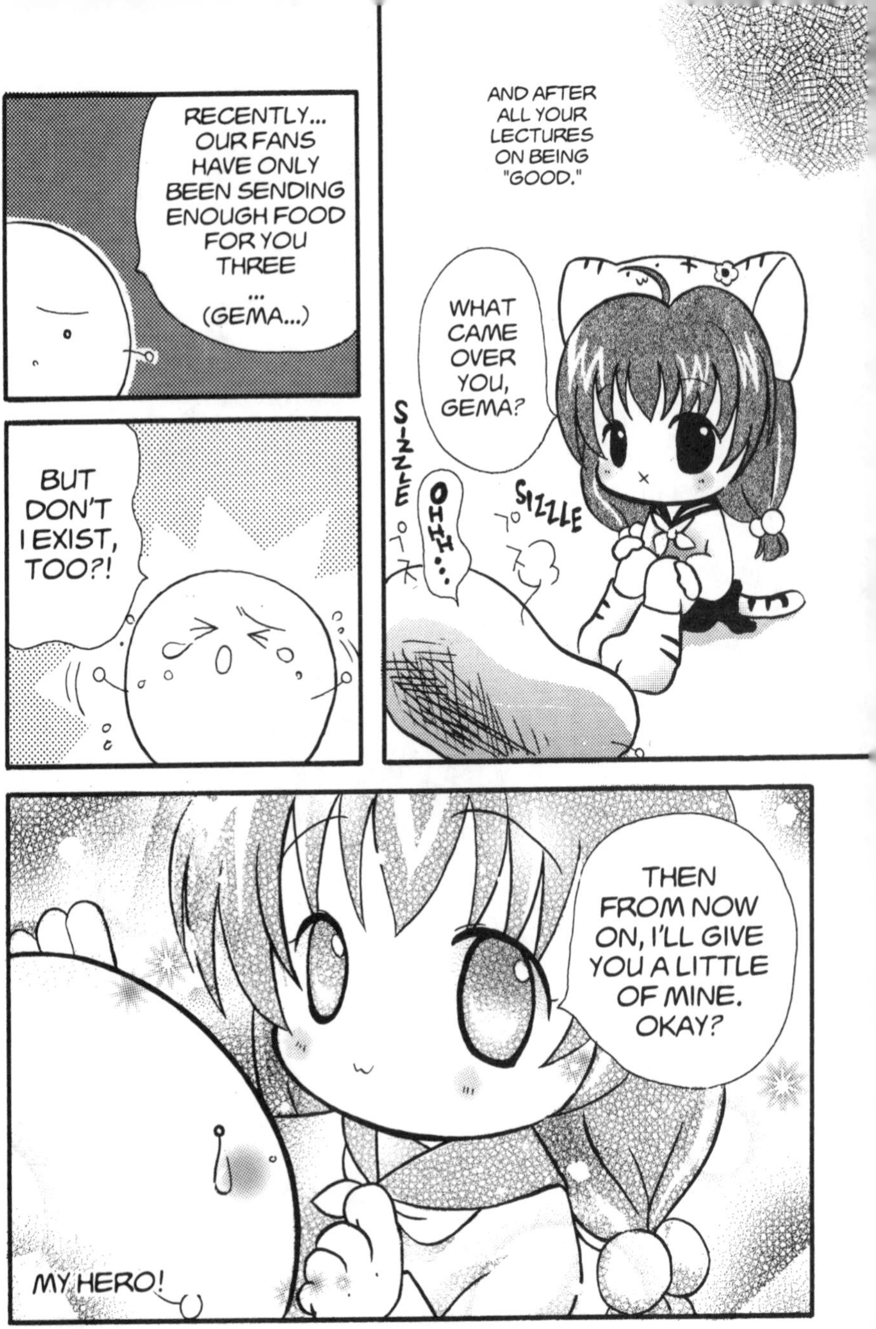
AND AFTER ALL YOUR LECTURES ON BEING "GOOD."
WHAT CAME OVER YOU, GEMA?
SIZZLE
OHHH...
SIZZLE
RECENTLY... OUR FANS HAVE ONLY BEEN SENDING ENOUGH FOOD FOR YOU THREE ... (GEMA...)
BUT DON'T I EXIST, TOO?!
THEN FROM NOW ON, I'LL GIVE YOU A LITTLE OF MINE. OKAY?
MY HERO!

END

WHAT WOULD YOU LIKE TO SEE HAPPEN AT GAMERS?

WE'D LIKE TO PLAY THE "DAIFUGO" CARD GAME WITH EVERYONE! (HA HA!)

ROCKET-BROTHERS

WHAT WOULD YOU LIKE TO SEE HAPPEN AT GAMERS?

I'D LIKE TO HAVE A SOUVENIR PHOTO

SHOOT WITH PETIToCHARAT

EVEN ONE OF THOSE PHOTO BOOTHS WOULD BE FINE.

TSUKIKO

TSUKIKO

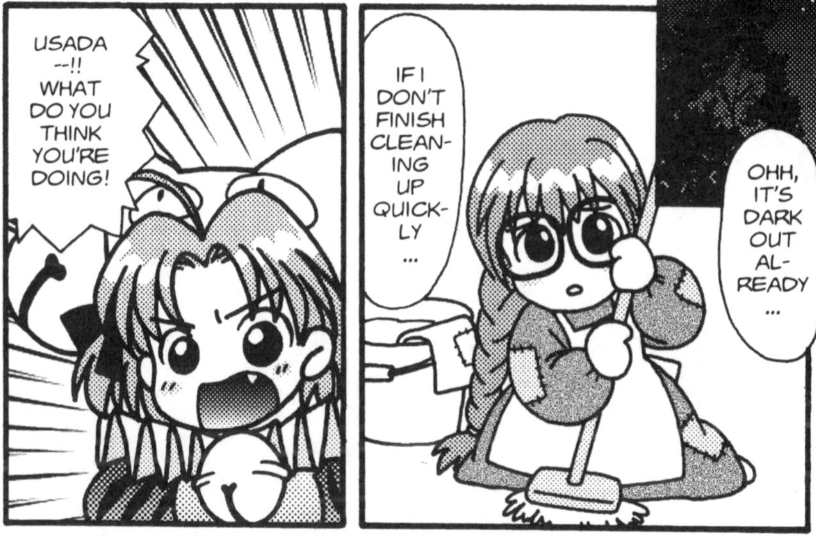
OHH, IT'S DARK OUT AL-READY ...
IF I DON'T FINISH CLEAN-ING UP QUICK-LY ...
USADA --!! WHAT DO YOU THINK YOU'RE DOING!

CINDERELLA SYNDROME

MARUMI YAMAMOTO

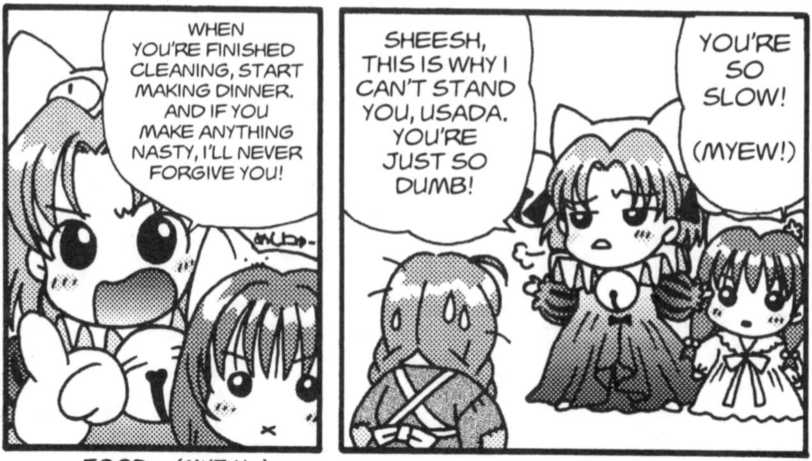
YOU'RE SO SLOW!
(MYEW!)
SHEESH, THIS IS WHY I CAN'T STAND YOU, USADA. YOU'RE JUST SO DUMB!
WHEN YOU'RE FINISHED CLEANING, START MAKING DINNER. AND IF YOU MAKE ANYTHING NASTY, I'LL NEVER FORGIVE YOU!

FOOD.... (MYEW...)

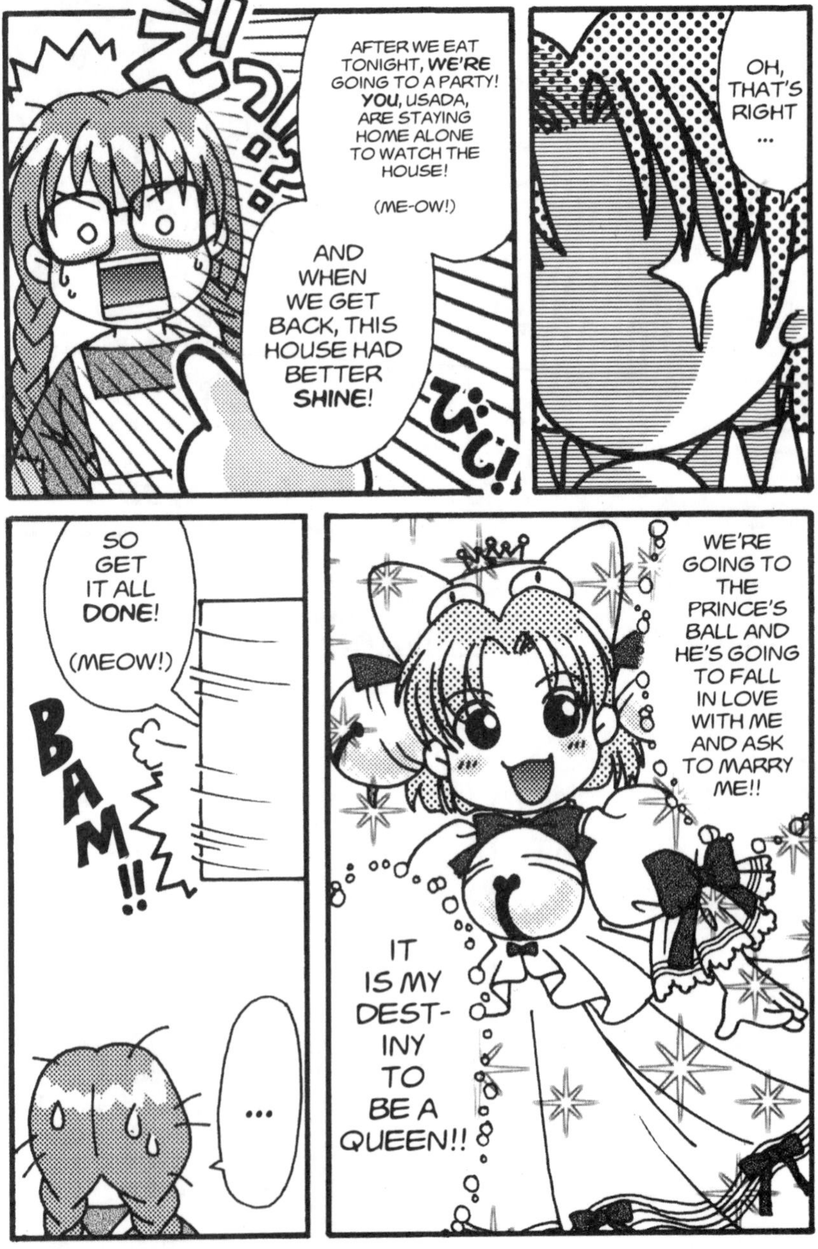
OH, THAT'S RIGHT ...
AFTER WE EAT TONIGHT, WE'RE GOING TO A PARTY! YOU, USADA, ARE STAYING HOME ALONE TO WATCH THE HOUSE!
(ME-OW!)
AND WHEN WE GET BACK, THIS HOUSE HAD BETTER SHINE!
WE'RE GOING TO THE PRINCE'S BALL AND HE'S GOING TO FALL IN LOVE WITH ME AND ASK TO MARRY ME!!
IT IS MY DEST-INY TO BE A QUEEN!!
SO GET IT ALL DONE!
(MEOW!)
BAM!!
...

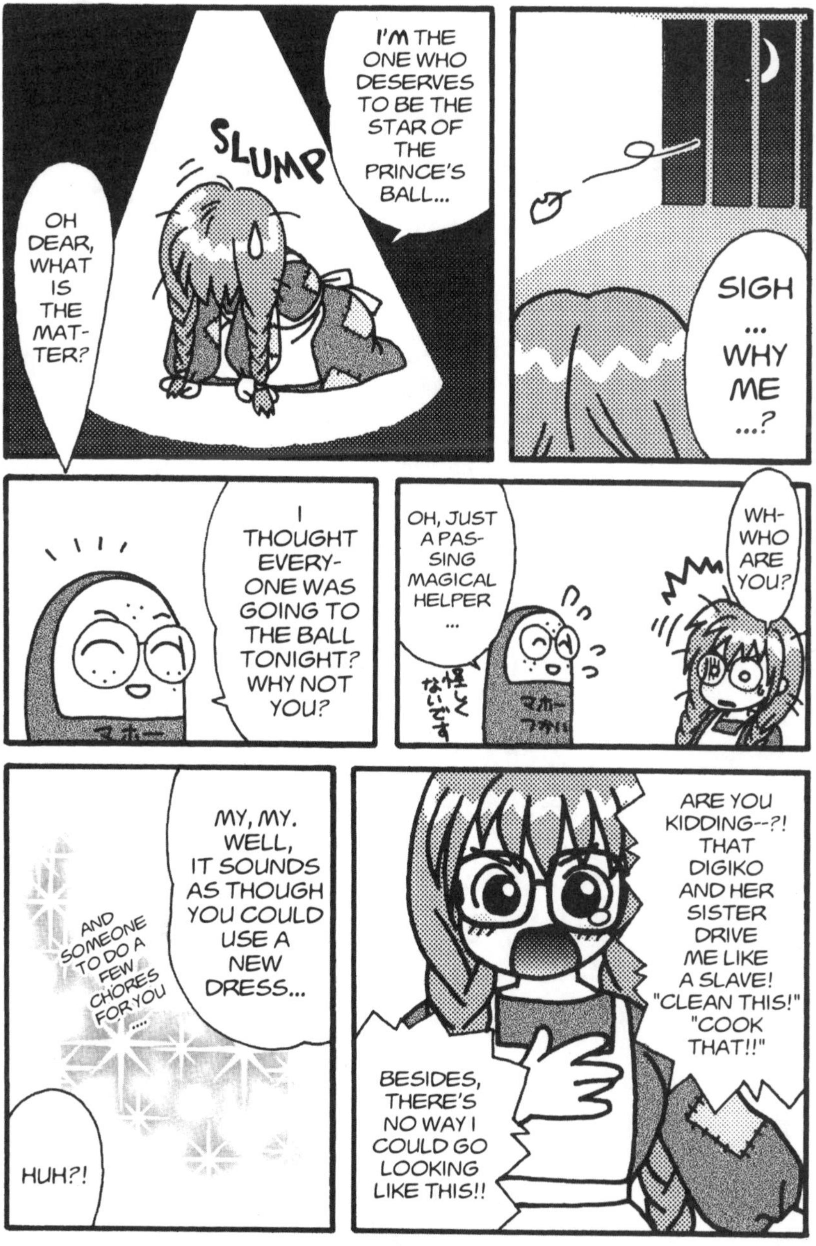

SIGH ... WHY ME ...?
I'M THE ONE WHO DESERVES TO BE THE STAR OF THE PRINCE'S BALL...
SLUMP
OH DEAR, WHAT IS THE MATTER?
WH-WHO ARE YOU?
OH, JUST A PASSING MAGICAL HELPER ...
怪しくないです
I THOUGHT EVERYONE WAS GOING TO THE BALL TONIGHT? WHY NOT YOU?
ARE YOU KIDDING--?! THAT DIGIKO AND HER SISTER DRIVE ME LIKE A SLAVE! "CLEAN THIS!" "COOK THAT!!"
BESIDES, THERE'S NO WAY I COULD GO LOOKING LIKE THIS!!
MY, MY. WELL, IT SOUNDS AS THOUGH YOU COULD USE A NEW DRESS...
AND SOMEONE TO DO A FEW CHORES FOR YOU ....
HUH?!

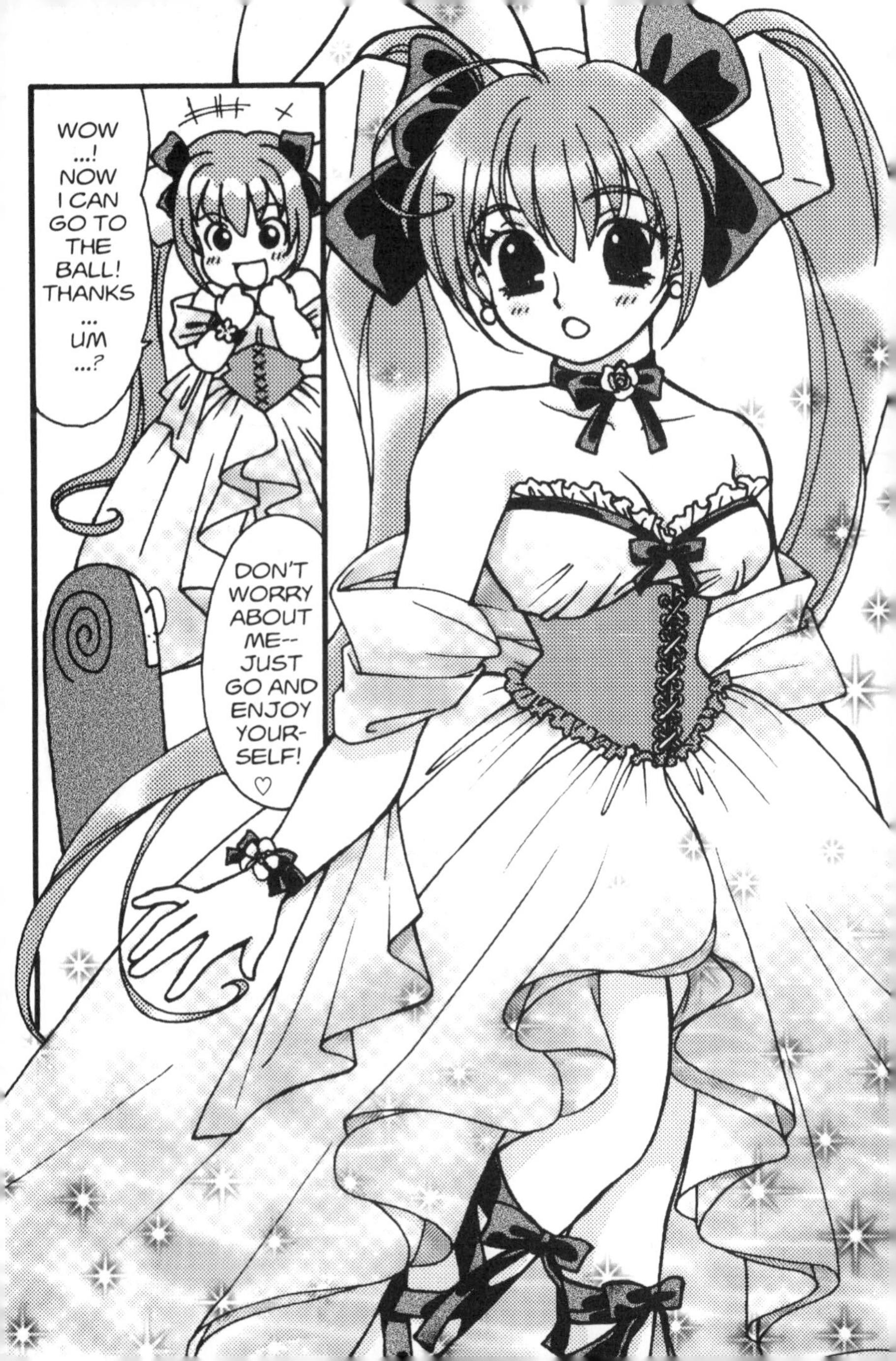
WOW ...! NOW I CAN GO TO THE BALL! THANKS ... UM ...?
DON'T WORRY ABOUT ME-- JUST GO AND ENJOY YOURSELF! ♡

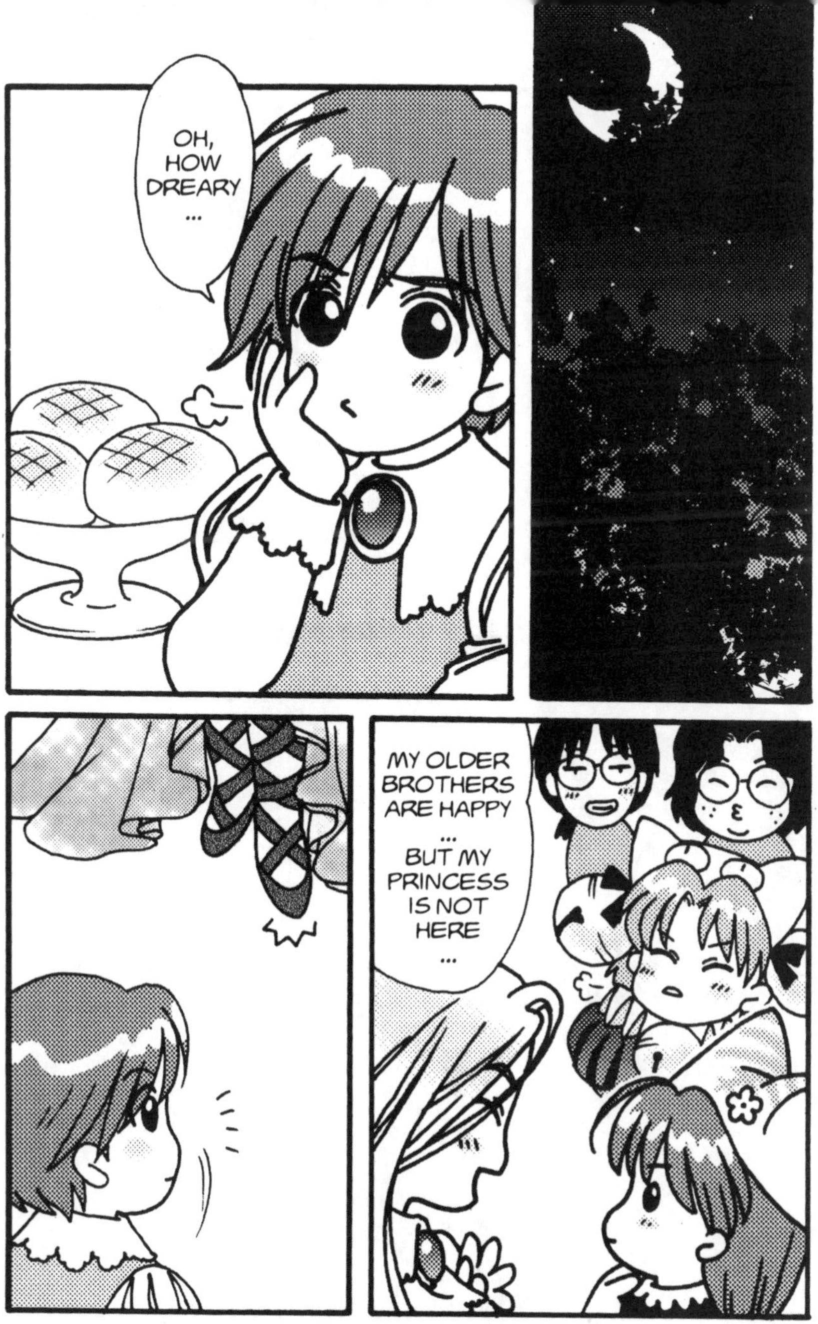
OH, HOW DREARY ...
MY OLDER BROTHERS ARE HAPPY ... BUT MY PRINCESS IS NOT HERE ...

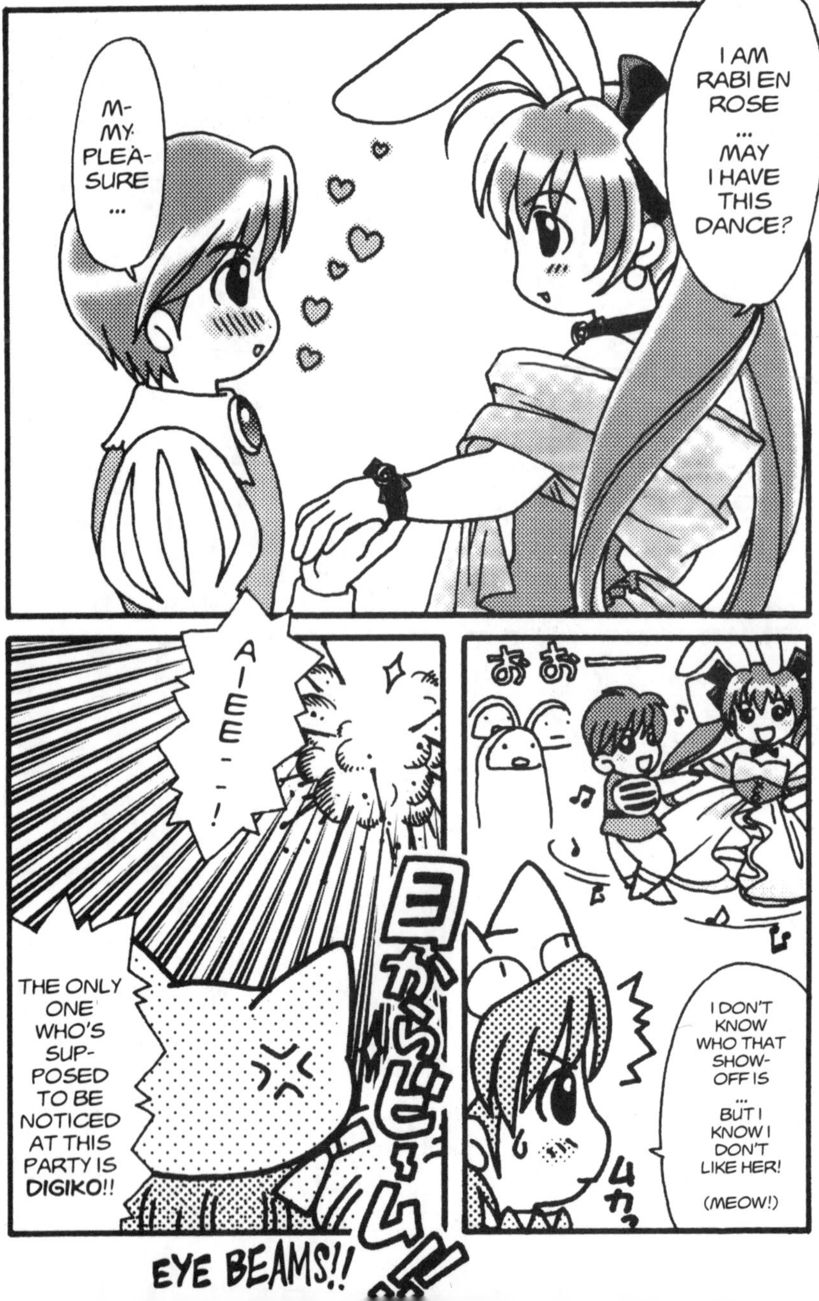
I AM RABI EN ROSE ... MAY I HAVE THIS DANCE?
M-MY PLEASURE ...
おおー
I DON'T KNOW WHO THAT SHOW-OFF IS ... BUT I KNOW I DON'T LIKE HER! (MEOW!)
ムカッ
AIEE--!
THE ONLY ONE WHO'S SUPPOSED TO BE NOTICED AT THIS PARTY IS **DIGIKO**!!
目からビーム!!
EYE BEAMS!!

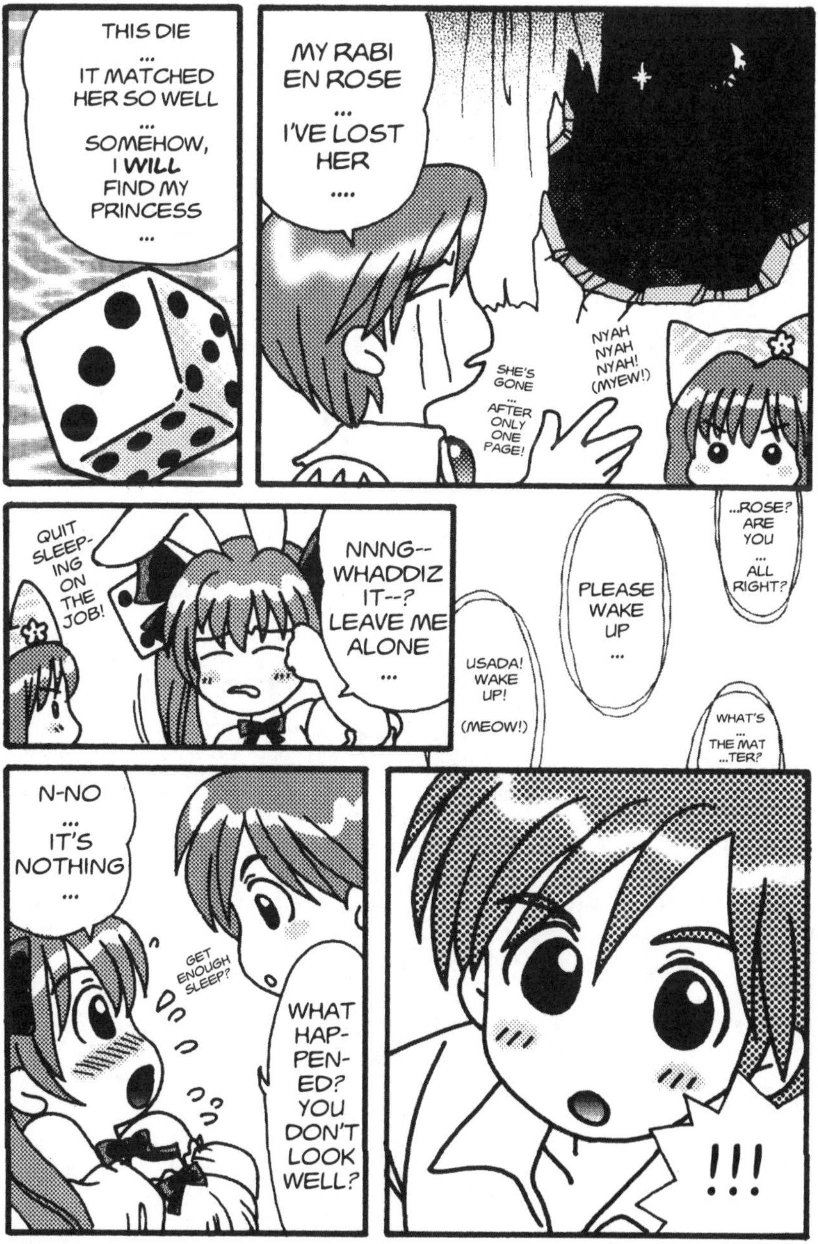
MY RABI EN ROSE ... I'VE LOST HER ....
NYAH NYAH NYAH! (MYEW!)
SHE'S GONE ... AFTER ONLY ONE PAGE!
THIS DIE ... IT MATCHED HER SO WELL ... SOMEHOW, I **WILL** FIND MY PRINCESS ...
...ROSE? ARE YOU ... ALL RIGHT?
PLEASE WAKE UP ...
USADA! WAKE UP! (MEOW!)
WHAT'S ... THE MAT ...TER?
NNNG-- WHADDIZ IT--? LEAVE ME ALONE ...
QUIT SLEEPING ON THE JOB!
!!!
WHAT HAP-PEN-ED? YOU DON'T LOOK WELL?
N-NO ... IT'S NOTHING ...
GET ENOUGH SLEEP?

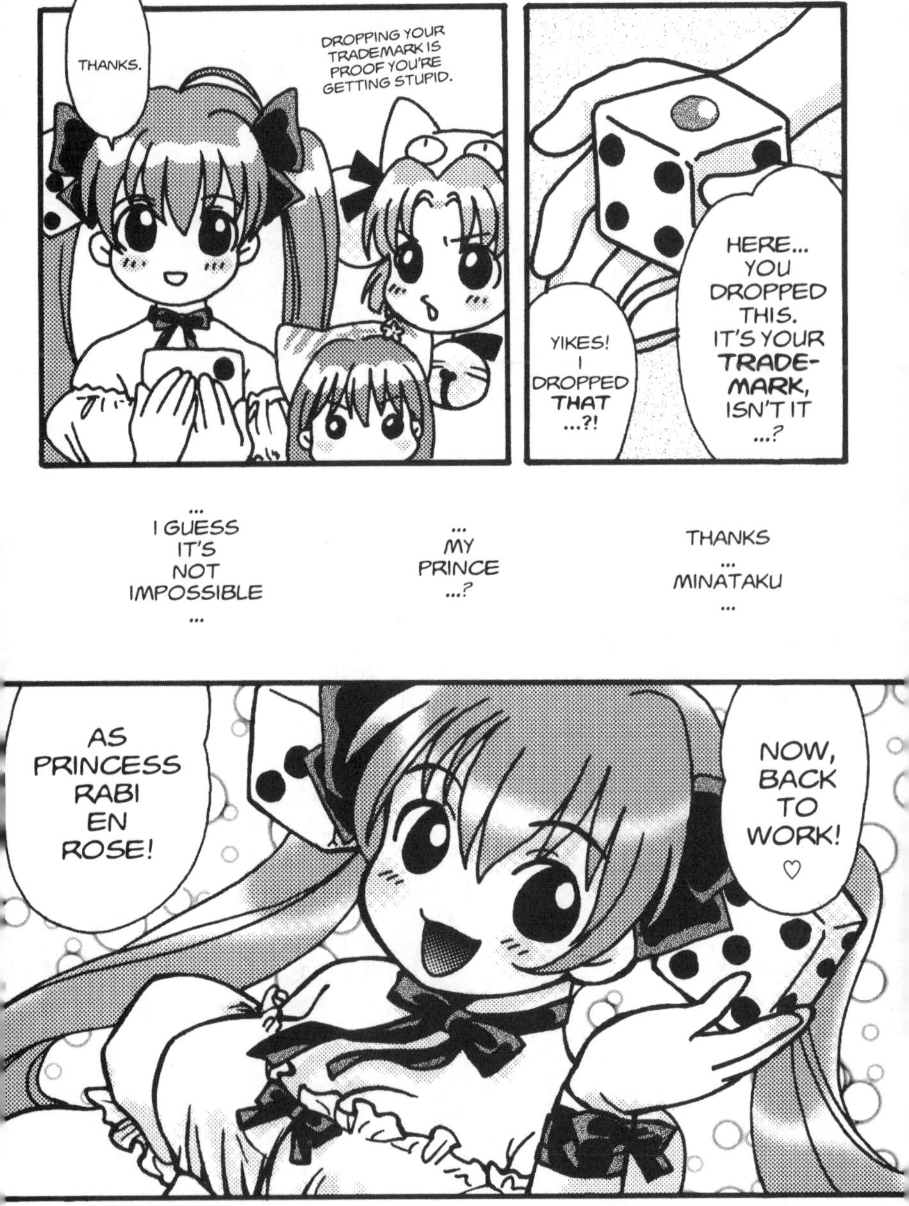
HERE... YOU DROPPED THIS. IT'S YOUR TRADEMARK, ISN'T IT ...?
YIKES! I DROPPED THAT ...?!
DROPPING YOUR TRADEMARK IS PROOF YOU'RE GETTING STUPID.
THANKS.
THANKS ... MINATAKU ...
... MY PRINCE ...?
... I GUESS IT'S NOT IMPOSSIBLE ...
NOW, BACK TO WORK! ♡
AS PRINCESS RABI EN ROSE!

End

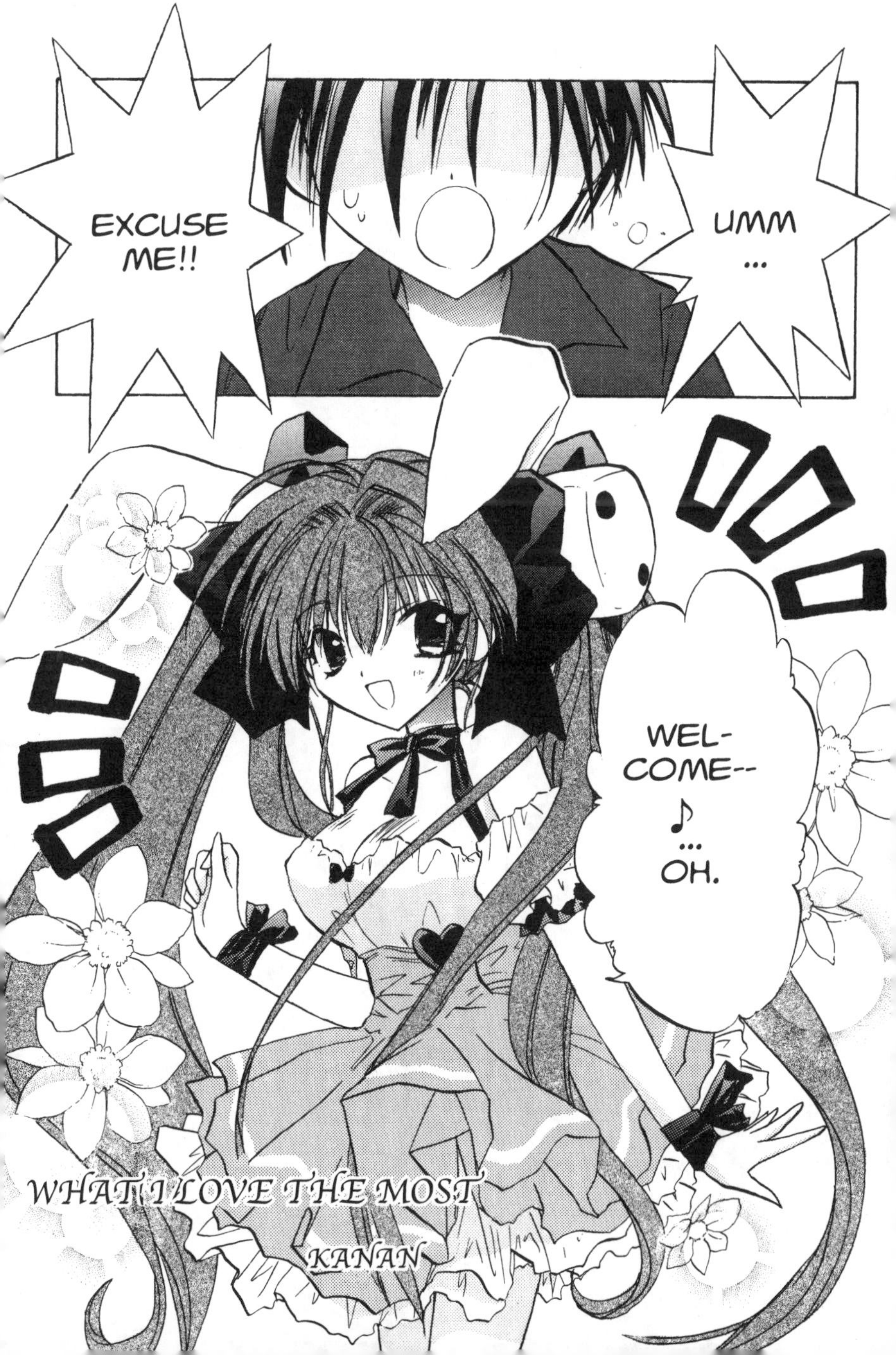

UMM ...
EXCUSE ME!!
WEL-COME-- ♪ ... OH.
WHAT I LOVE THE MOST
KANAN

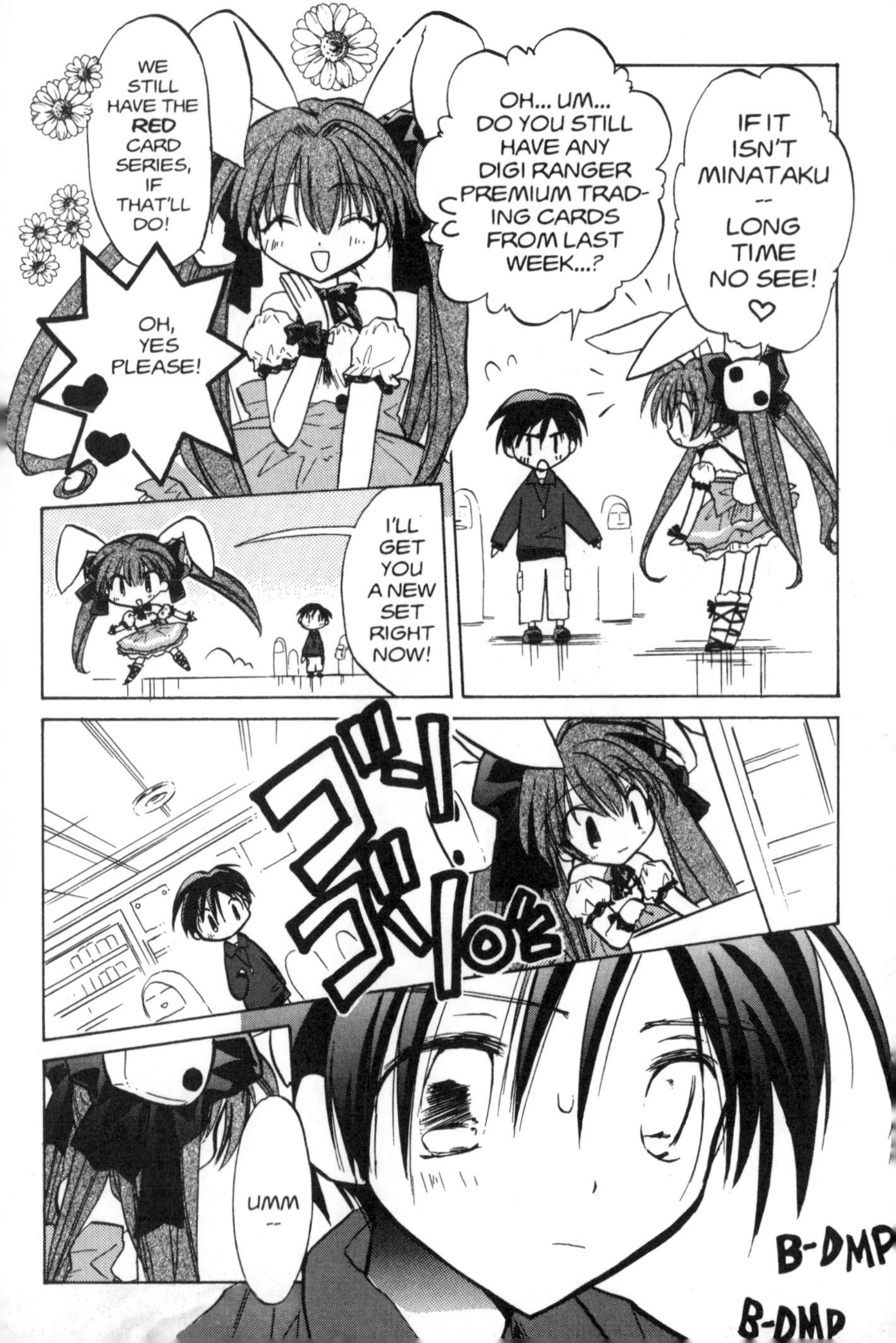
IF IT ISN'T MINATAKU -- LONG TIME NO SEE! ♡
OH... UM... DO YOU STILL HAVE ANY DIGI RANGER PREMIUM TRAD-ING CARDS FROM LAST WEEK...?
WE STILL HAVE THE **RED** CARD SERIES, IF THAT'LL DO!
OH, YES PLEASE!
I'LL GET YOU A NEW SET RIGHT NOW!
UMM --
B-DMP
B-DMP

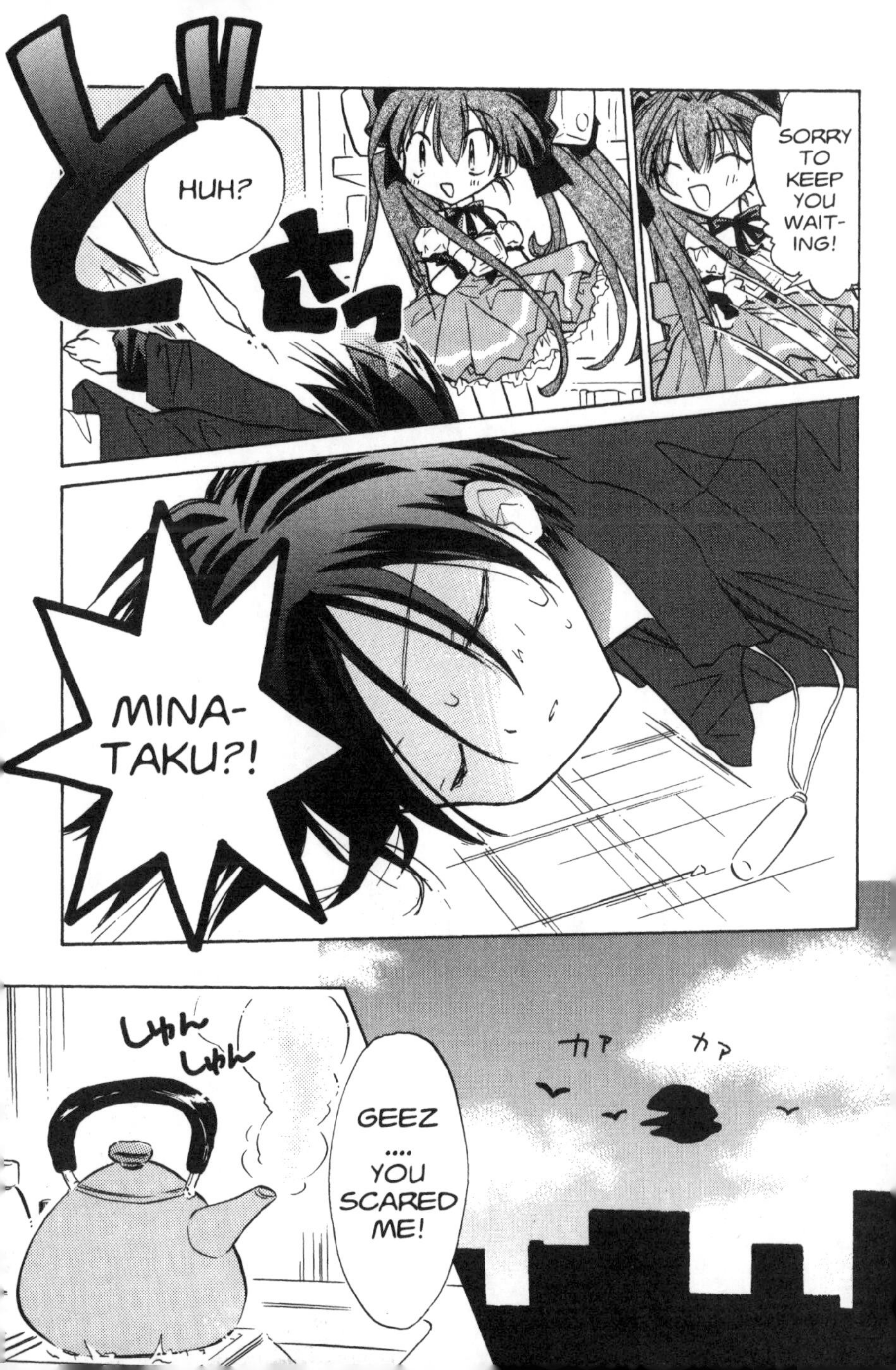

SORRY TO KEEP YOU WAIT-ING!
HUH?
どさっ
MINA-TAKU?!
カア カア
GEEZ .... YOU SCARED ME!
しゅん しゅん

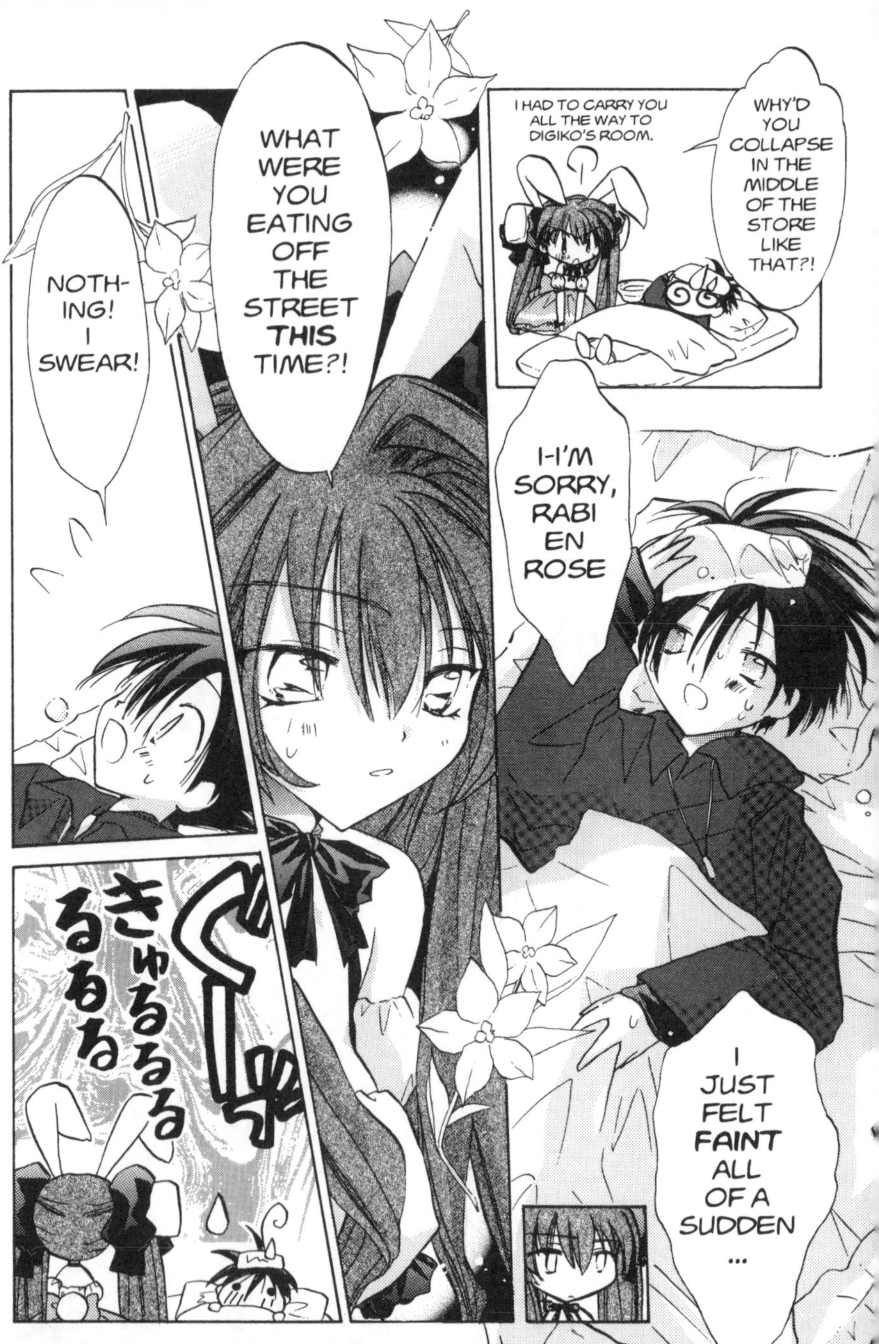
WHY'D YOU COLLAPSE IN THE MIDDLE OF THE STORE LIKE THAT?!
I HAD TO CARRY YOU ALL THE WAY TO DIGIKO'S ROOM.
I-I'M SORRY, RABI EN ROSE
I JUST FELT FAINT ALL OF A SUDDEN ...
WHAT WERE YOU EATING OFF THE STREET THIS TIME?!
NOTH-ING! I SWEAR!
ぐ〜
きゅるるるる
るるるる

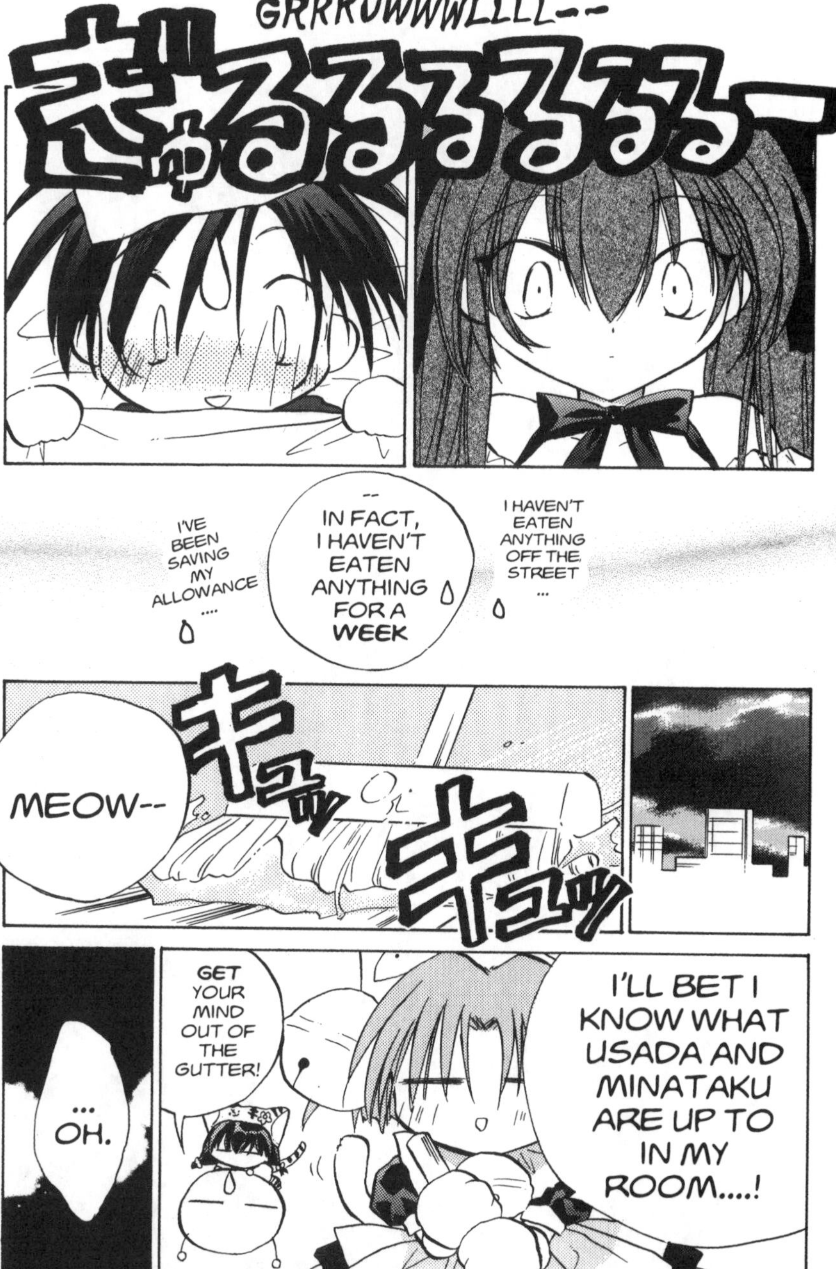
GRRROWWWLLLL--
ぎゅるるるるるるー
I HAVEN'T EATEN ANYTHING OFF THE STREET ...
-- IN FACT, I HAVEN'T EATEN ANYTHING FOR A WEEK
I'VE BEEN SAVING MY ALLOWANCE ....
キュッ
キュッ
MEOW--
I'LL BET I KNOW WHAT USADA AND MINATAKU ARE UP TO IN MY ROOM....!
GET YOUR MIND OUT OF THE GUTTER!
... OH.

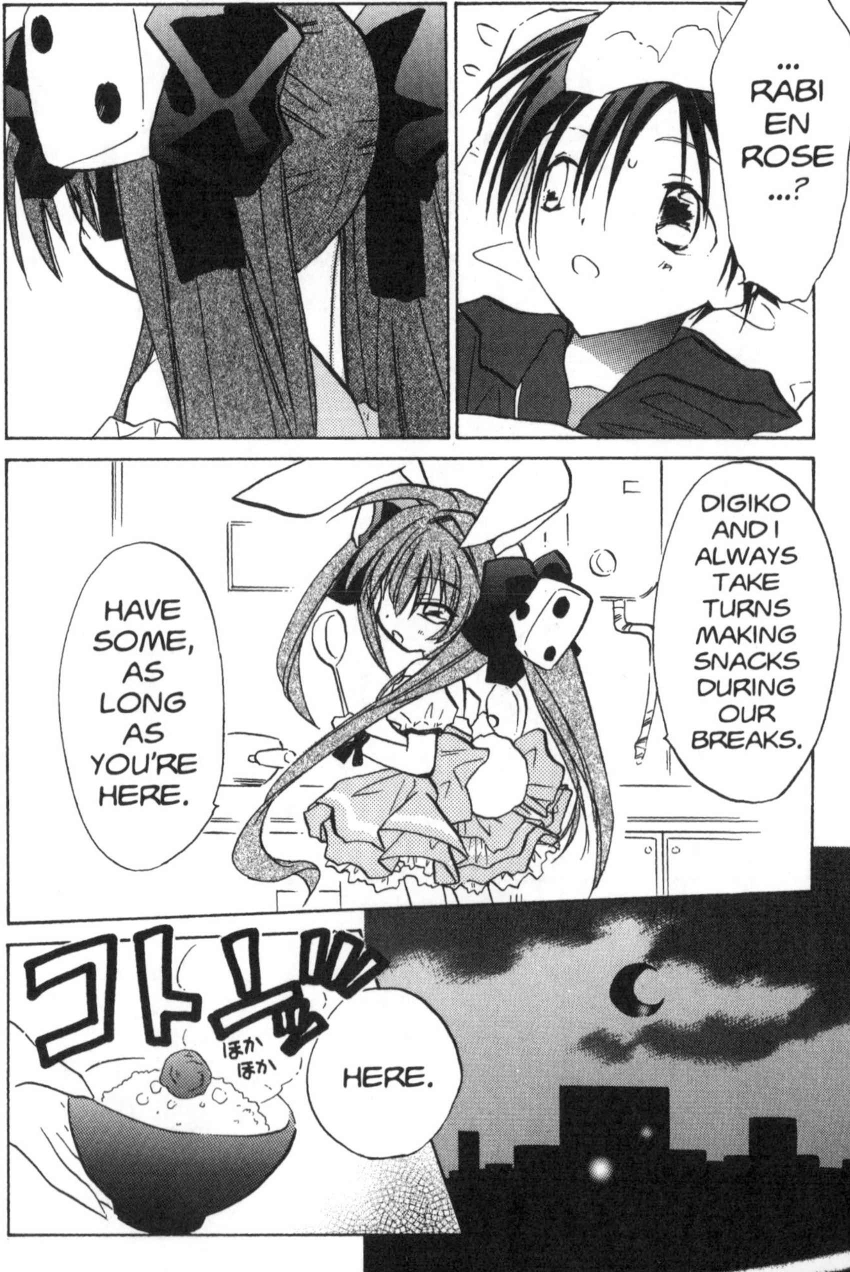
... RABI EN ROSE ...?
DIGIKO AND I ALWAYS TAKE TURNS MAKING SNACKS DURING OUR BREAKS.
HAVE SOME, AS LONG AS YOU'RE HERE.
コトッ
ほかほか
HERE.

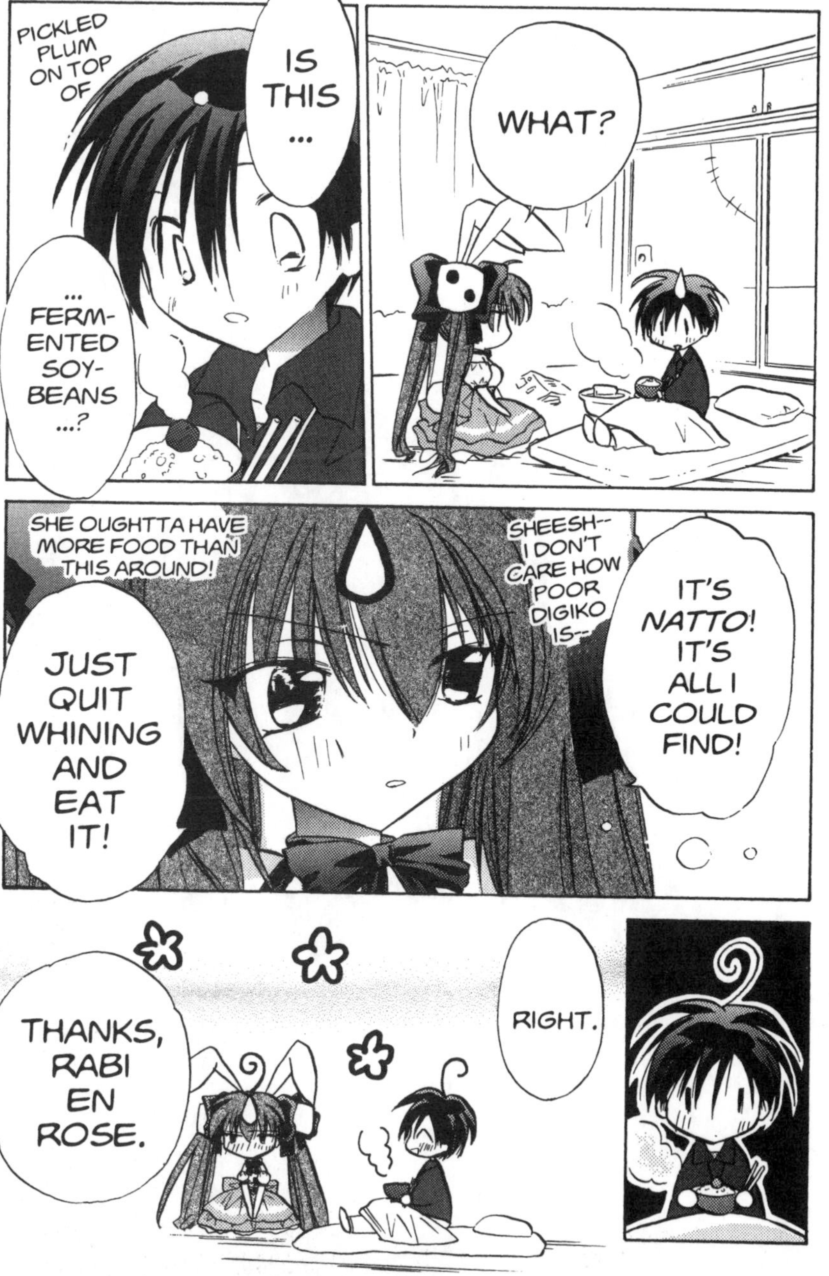
WHAT?
IS THIS ...
PICKLED PLUM ON TOP OF
... FERMENTED SOYBEANS ...?
IT'S NATTO! IT'S ALL I COULD FIND!
SHEESH-- I DON'T CARE HOW POOR DIGIKO IS--
SHE OUGHTTA HAVE MORE FOOD THAN THIS AROUND!
JUST QUIT WHINING AND EAT IT!
RIGHT.
THANKS, RABI EN ROSE.

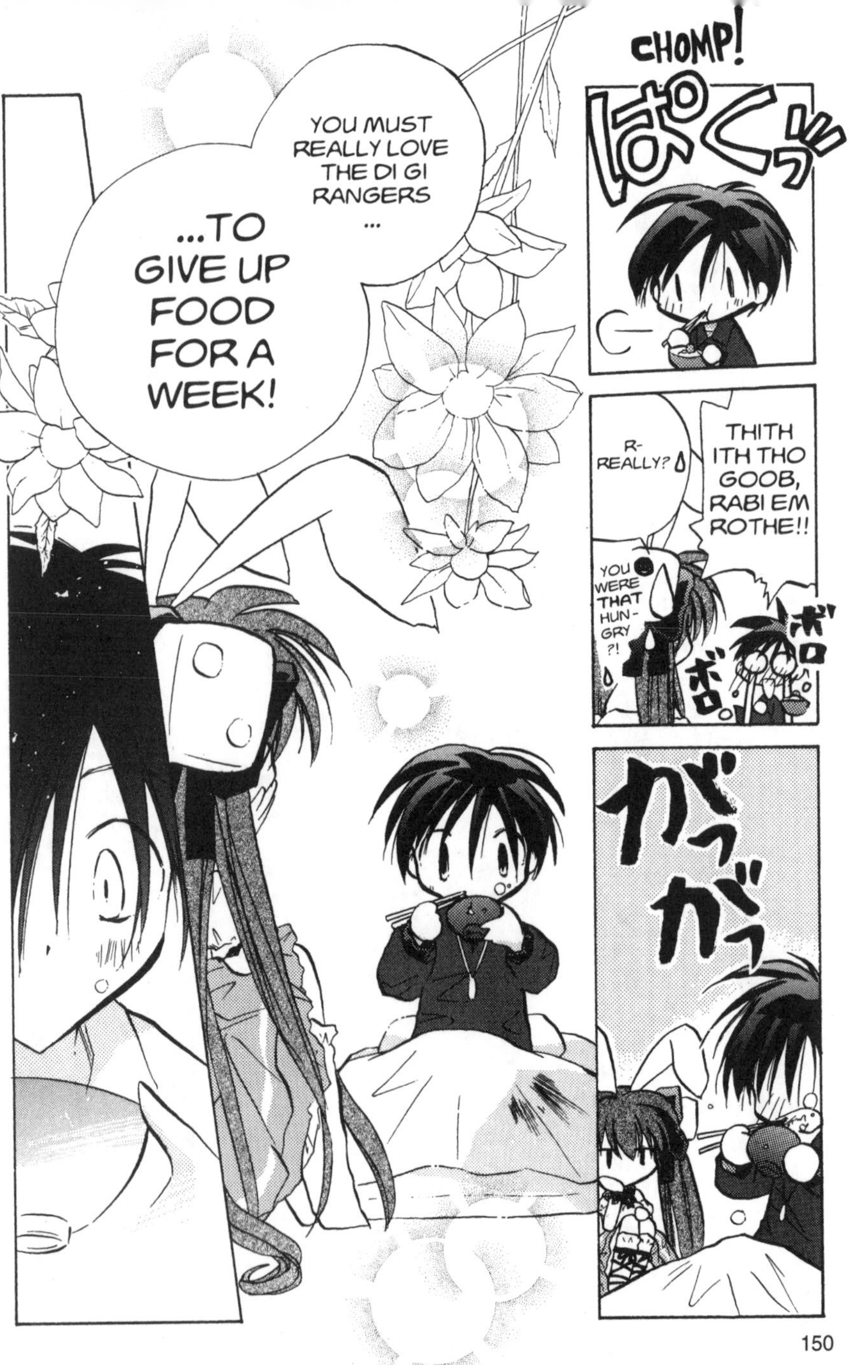
CHOMP!
ぱくっ
THITH ITH THO GOOB, RABI EM ROTHE!!
R-REALLY?
YOU WERE THAT HUN-GRY?!
ボロ
ボロ
がっ
がっ
YOU MUST REALLY LOVE THE DI GI RANGERS ...
...TO GIVE UP FOOD FOR A WEEK!

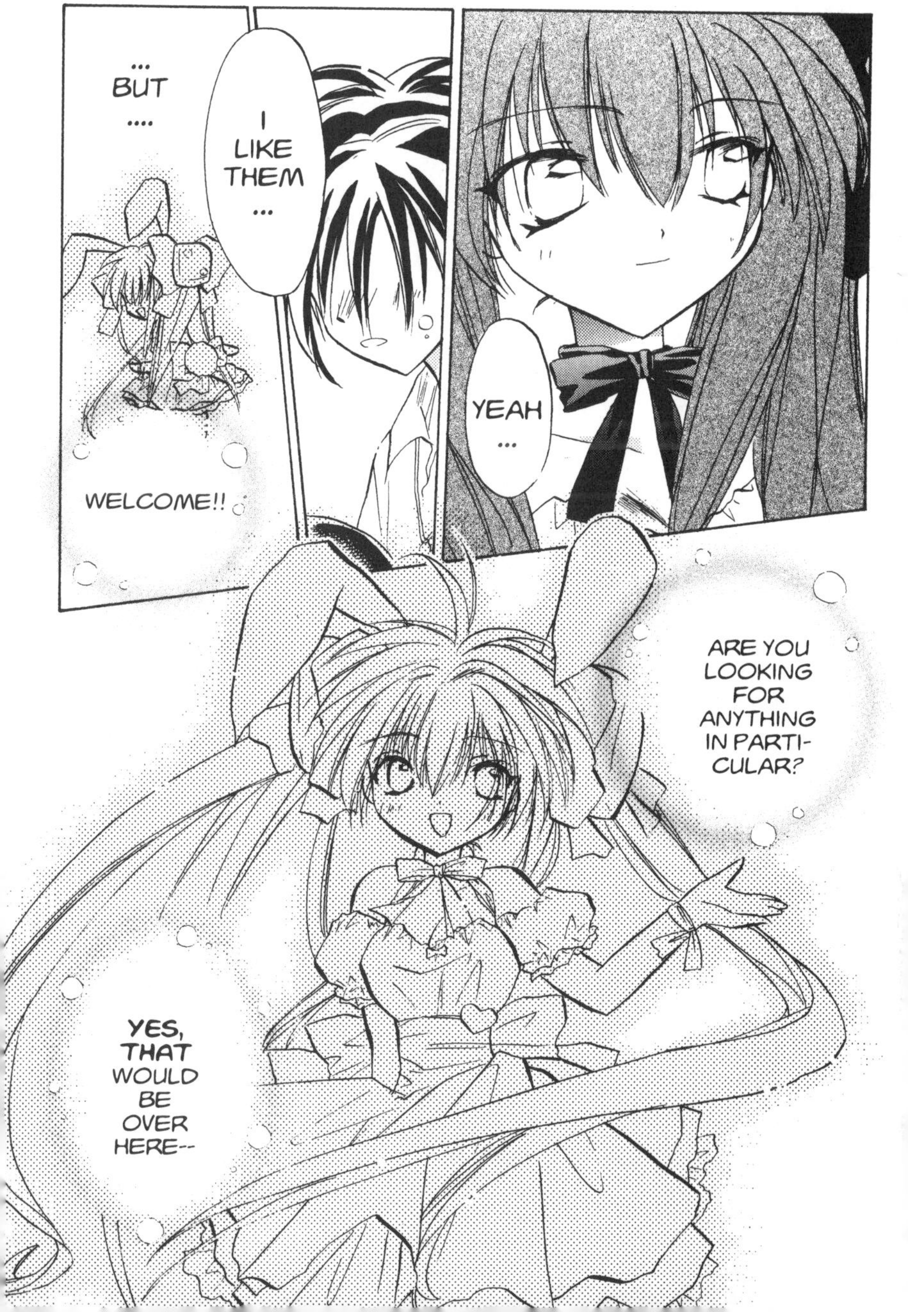
YEAH ...
I LIKE THEM ...
... BUT ....
WELCOME!!
ARE YOU LOOKING FOR ANYTHING IN PARTICULAR?
YES, THAT WOULD BE OVER HERE--

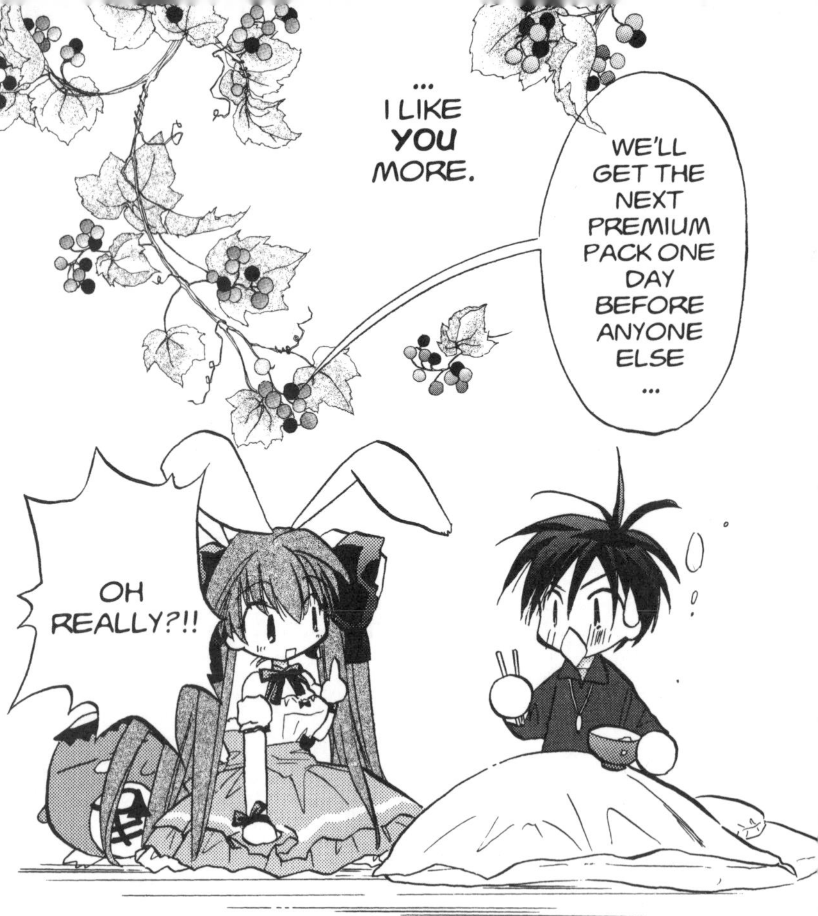
WE'LL GET THE NEXT PREMIUM PACK ONE DAY BEFORE ANYONE ELSE ...
... I LIKE YOU MORE.
OH REALLY?!!

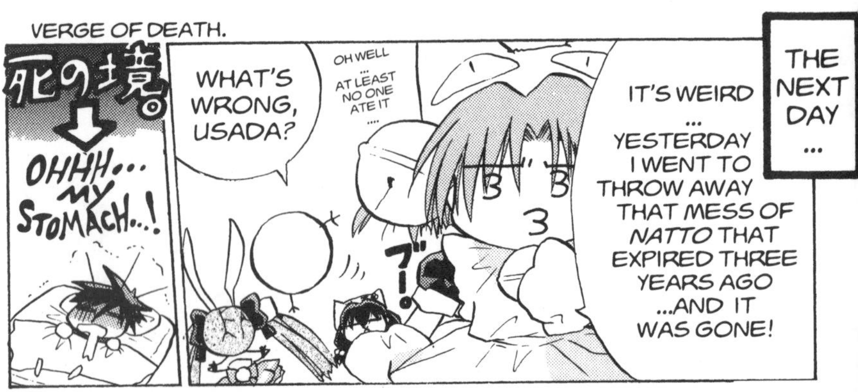
THE NEXT DAY ...
IT'S WEIRD ... YESTERDAY I WENT TO THROW AWAY THAT MESS OF NATTO THAT EXPIRED THREE YEARS AGO ...AND IT WAS GONE!
OH WELL ... AT LEAST NO ONE ATE IT ....
WHAT'S WRONG, USADA?
VERGE OF DEATH.
死の境
OHHH... MY STOMACH...!

END

WHAT WOULD YOU LIKE TO SEE HAPPEN AT GAMERS?

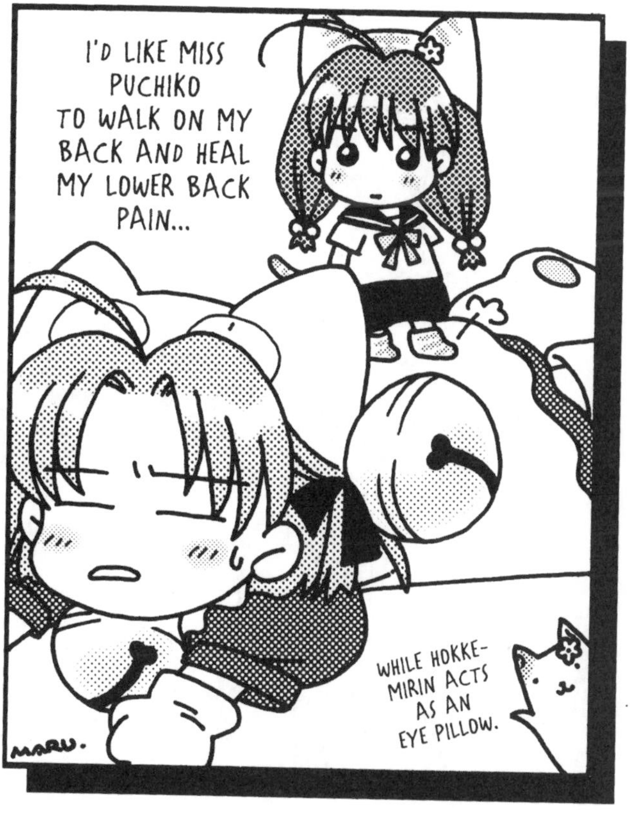
I'D LIKE MISS PUCHIKO TO WALK ON MY BACK AND HEAL MY LOWER BACK PAIN...
WHILE HOKKE-MIRIN ACTS AS AN EYE PILLOW.
MARU.

MARUMI YAMAMOTO

WHAT WOULD YOU LIKE TO SEE HAPPEN AT GAMERS?

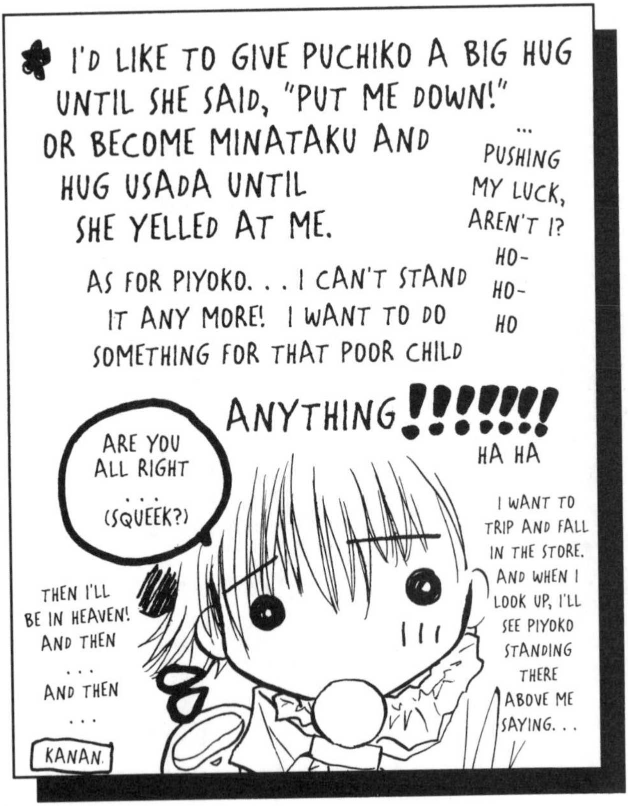
I'D LIKE TO GIVE PUCHIKO A BIG HUG UNTIL SHE SAID, "PUT ME DOWN!" OR BECOME MINATAKU AND HUG USADA UNTIL SHE YELLED AT ME.
... PUSHING MY LUCK, AREN'T I? HO-HO-HO
AS FOR PIYOKO. . . I CAN'T STAND IT ANY MORE! I WANT TO DO SOMETHING FOR THAT POOR CHILD
ANYTHING!!!!!!!
HA HA
I WANT TO TRIP AND FALL IN THE STORE. AND WHEN I LOOK UP, I'LL SEE PIYOKO STANDING THERE ABOVE ME SAYING. . .
ARE YOU ALL RIGHT . . . (SQUEEK?)
THEN I'LL BE IN HEAVEN! AND THEN . . . AND THEN . . .
KANAN.

KANAN

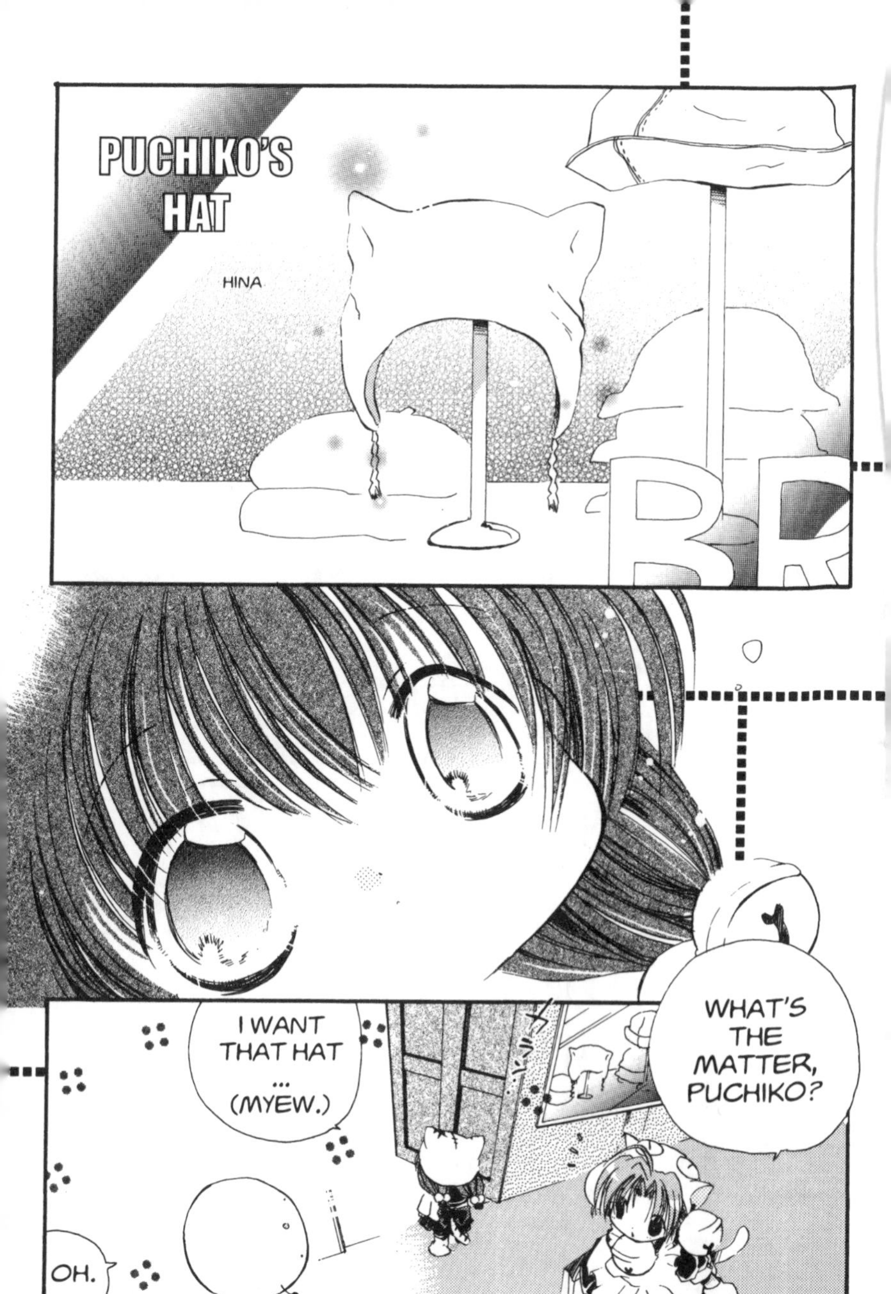
PUCHIKO'S HAT
HINA
BR
WHAT'S THE MATTER, PUCHIKO?
I WANT THAT HAT ... (MYEW.)
OH.

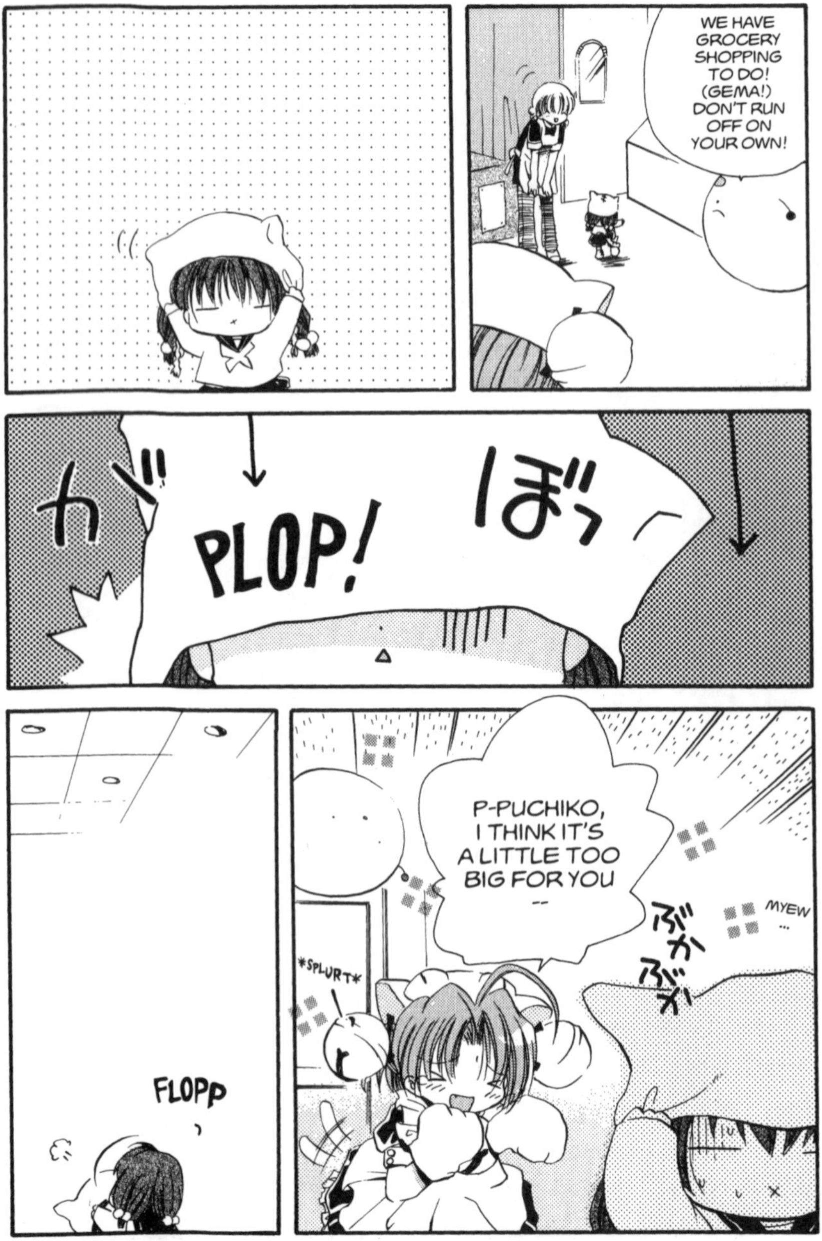
WE HAVE GROCERY SHOPPING TO DO! (GEMA!) DON'T RUN OFF ON YOUR OWN!
ぼっ
PLOP!
ガ
P-PUCHIKO, I THINK IT'S A LITTLE TOO BIG FOR YOU --
MYEW ...
ぶかぶか
SPLURT
FLOPP

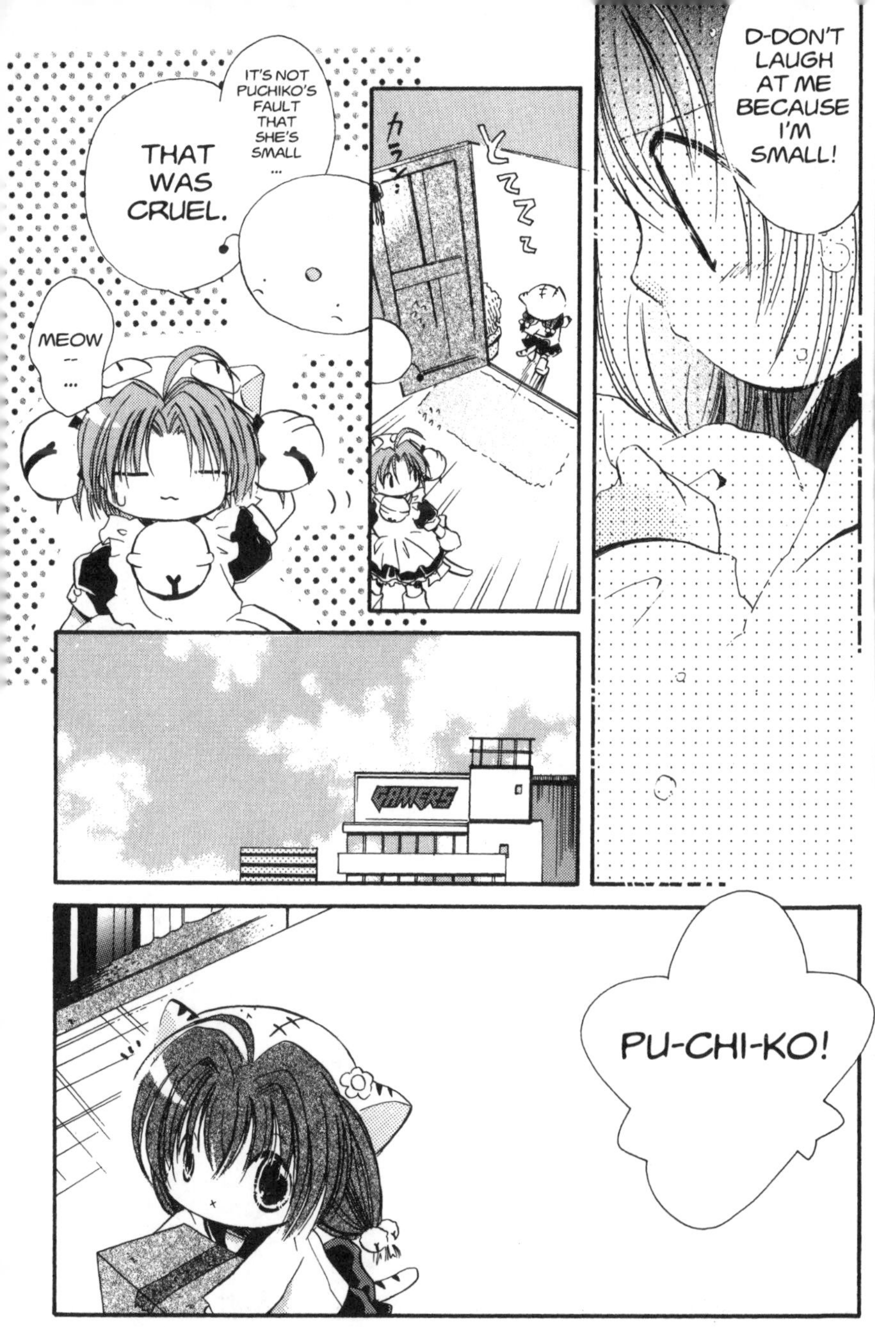
D-DON'T LAUGH AT ME BECAUSE I'M SMALL!
IT'S NOT PUCHIKO'S FAULT THAT SHE'S SMALL ...
THAT WAS CRUEL.
MEOW -- ...
GAMERS
PU-CHI-KO!

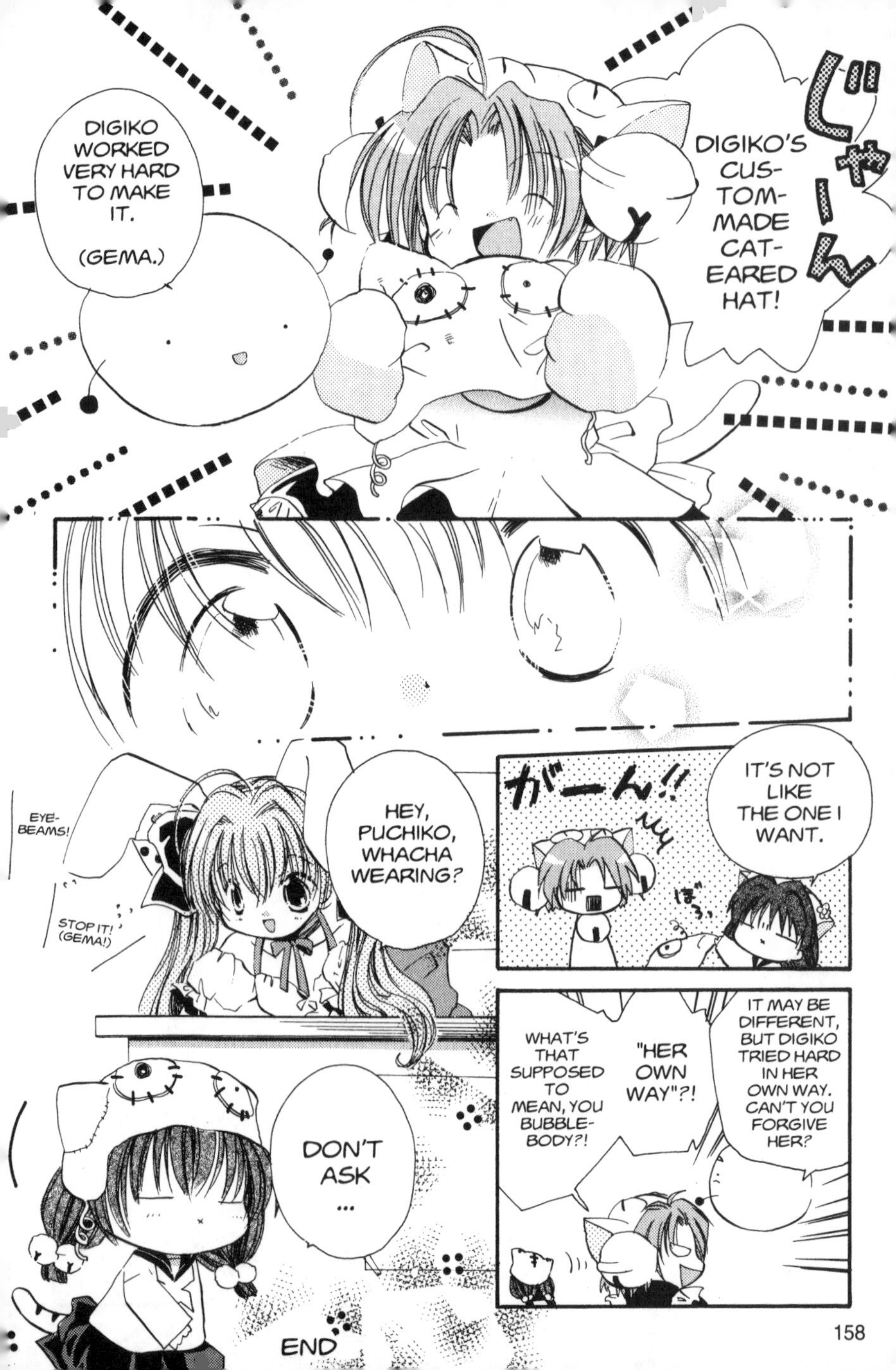
じゃーん
DIGIKO'S CUS-TOM-MADE CAT-EARED HAT!
DIGIKO WORKED VERY HARD TO MAKE IT.
(GEMA.)
がーん!!
IT'S NOT LIKE THE ONE I WANT.
HEY, PUCHIKO, WHACHA WEARING?
EYE-BEAMS!
STOP IT! (GEMA!)
IT MAY BE DIFFERENT, BUT DIGIKO TRIED HARD IN HER OWN WAY. CAN'T YOU FORGIVE HER?
"HER OWN WAY"?!
WHAT'S THAT SUPPOSED TO MEAN, YOU BUBBLE-BODY?!
DON'T ASK ...
END

WHAT WOULD YOU
LIKE TO SEE HAPPEN AT GAMERS?

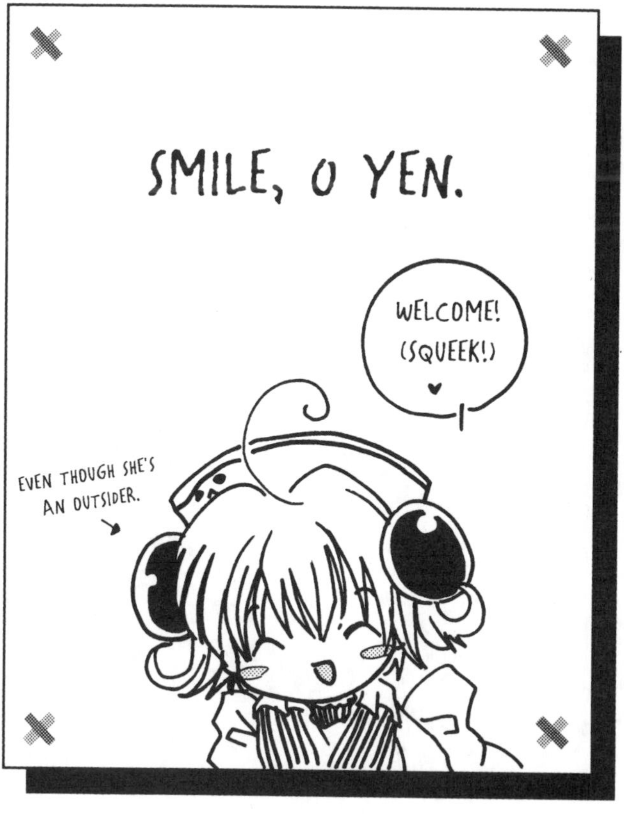
SMILE, 0 YEN.
WELCOME! (SQUEEK!)
EVEN THOUGH SHE'S AN OUTSIDER.

HINA.

WHAT WOULD YOU LIKE TO SEE HAPPEN AT GAMERS?

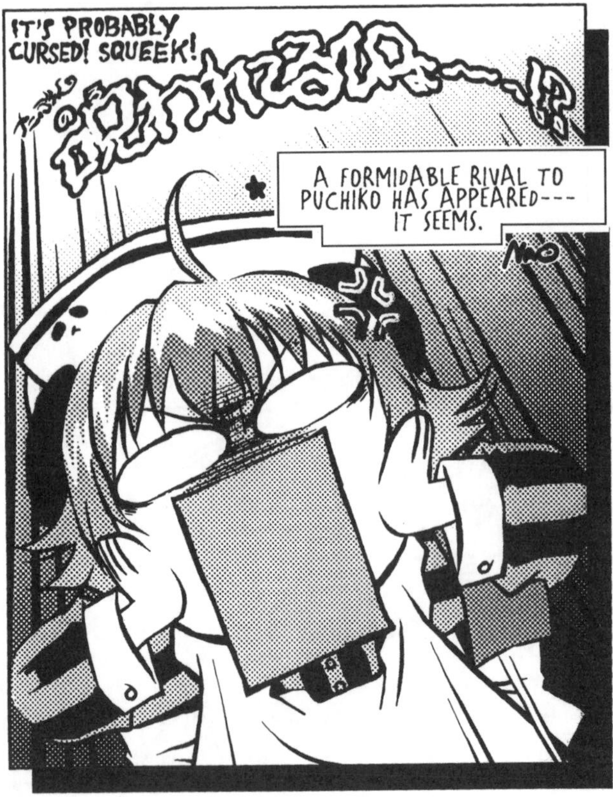

IT'S PROBABLY CURSED! SQUEEK!
A FORMIDABLE RIVAL TO PUCHIKO HAS APPEARED--- IT SEEMS.
NAO

NAO GOTO

The Di Gi Charat Guide to Sound Effects!

As you've undoubtedly noticed, most of the sound effects in ***Di Gi Charat*** are in Japanese. Seeing the various explosions, tantrums and incidental dialogue jump off the page in a foreign language offers a unique experience for readers familiar only with American comics.

Fans of Digiko, Usada and the rest of the gang may applaud our respect for the original source material. Others, however, may be confused by the wildly expressive *koukaon.*

Thus, in an attempt to satisfy everyone, we've compiled this handy glossary. On the following pages you'll find a panel-by-panel account of every Digiko burp and Gema hiccup. In the process, maybe you'll pick up a little bit of Japanese, as well.

---

4 CHARACTER: MA [upside down wish spell]

7.1 FX: PO- [sigh-]

8.4 FX: JII [stare]

9.2 FX: BUSU [jab]
9.4 FX: BASHI- [thwack-]
9.6.1 FX: TON TON [thump thump]
9.6.2 FX: KARARI [clatter]

10.2 FX: DE-N [ta-daa]

12.1.2 FX: HIKKU [hiccup]
12.5.1.2 FX: KI-!! [aargh-!!]
12.5.3 FX: MEW- [wail-]

14.1 FX: GA-N [d'oh]
14.2 FX: PU-N [waft]
14.5.1 FX: KYA- [aiee-]
14.5.2 FX: WA- WA- [chatter chatter]

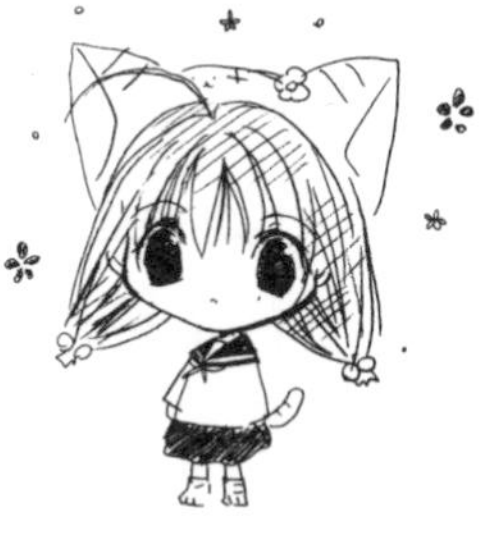

17.3	FX: KURA [stagger]
17.4	FX: DA- [dash-]
18.1	FX: DOSA DOSA [thud thud]
18.2	FX: DAA [dash]
20.1.1	FX: DO-N [d'oh]
20.1.2	SHIRT: MINATAKU
20.2	FX: JYARA JYARA [jangle jangle]
20.3	FX: DOKA-N [kaboom]
22.1	FX: KYORO KYORO [glance glance]
22.3	FX: GYU-GYU [squeeze squeeze]
23.5	FX: SAA [snatch]
23.6	FX: DODODODODODO [stampede]
24.1.1	FX: PI-HYARA DON DON [sound of flute and drums]
24.1.2	FX: POTSU-N... [gape...]
24.1.3.4	FX: WAI- WAI [chatter chatter]
24.5.1	FX: ME KARA BE-MU [eye beams]
24.5.2	FX: DOKA-N [kaboom]
27.4.1	FX: HYURURURURU [sound of fireworks being launched]
27.4.2	FX: KURUU [whirl]
28.1	FX: PA-N [fireworks exploding]
33.1	FX: BAN [slam]
33.3	FX: DON [blast]
33.4	FX: GAKUN GAKUN [shake shake]
34.2	FX: BORO... [tattered...]
35.4	FROCK: MANAGER
36.4	FX: DO-N [blast]
38.4	FX: BUN [hurl]
39.1	FX: GON [clunk]
39.2	FX: PAA [beam]

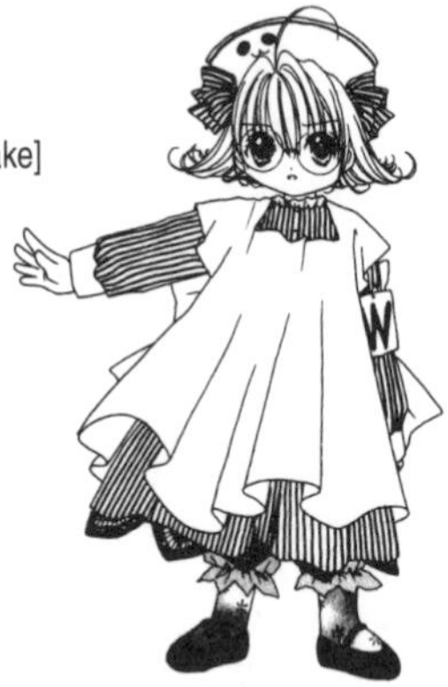
W

39.4.1   DIALOGUE FX: ARI-N [What's going on?]
39.4.2   FX: GOSO GOSO [rummage rummage]

40.4   FX: SHA- [hiss-]

42.2   FX: PINPO-N [ding-a-ling]

44.3   FX: BUTSUN [snap]

45.1   FX: DO-N [kaboom]

46.2   FX: PISHII [crack]
46.3   FX: DON [kaboom]

48.1   FX: PYOKOO [enter]

49.2   FX: ZORO ZORO [gather gather]

51.1   FX: ZUZUZUZUZU [slurp]

52.2   FX: DOKI DOKI [thump thump]

53.3   FX: HAA [sharp inhale]

56.5   SHIRTS: GE [for Gema]

58.3   DIALOGUE FX: HOW DID SHE KNOW—?! I'M WEARING A PERFECT
        DISGUISE!!

65.3   FX: HI HI HI [hee hee hee]

66.2   FX: BUKU BUKU [froth froth]
66.5   FX: MUKAA [irk]

67.1   APRON: MANAGER
67.2   FX: BUTSU BUTSU [mutter mutter]
67.3   FX: SUPANN [whap]
67.7   FX: GA-N [shock]
68.1   APRON: MANAGER
68.4   FX: GA-NN [d'oh]
68.6.1   FX: SHAKA SHAKA [rattle rattle]
68.6.2   DIALOGUE FX: GA-NN [d'oh]

69.2	FX: GU-... [growl-...]
69.3.1	FX: KARAA [empty]
69.3.2	DIALOGUE FX: MEW- [wail-]
70.2	FX: BISHI [point]
70.5.1	DIALOGUE FX: THIS MOUTH, EH.
70.5.2	FX: MYO-N [stretch]
70.5.3	DIALOGUE FX: AGAGA... [aargh...]
70.5.4	FX: PASHI [grab]
71.4	DIALOGUE FX: HO HO HO HO HO
71.5.1	FX: MUKA [irk]
71.5.2	FX: DOGEN [clobber]
72.3	DIALOGUE FX: MEW... [wail...]
73.2.1	FX: NITARI [evil grin]
73.2.2	FX: ZUZAA [shudder]
73.3	DIALOGUE FX: WAAH!
73.5	FX: PEH [blech]
74.3	FX: KAA [flash]
74.4	FX: PUSHU [sizzle]
76.2.1	FX: U-FU-FU [heh heh heh]
76.2.2	SIGN: BANK
76.2.3	FX: ZAWA ZAWA [whisper whisper]
80.1	FX: GESHI!! [boot!!}
80.2.1	FX: BOGO [body slam]
80.2.2	FX: GEHAA [spurt]
81.2	FX: GUSAA [stab]
81.3	FX: ZAN! [stomp!]
81.4	FX: DON [explode]
81.5	FX: GUO- [roar-]
81.6	FX: DOKA BAKI BAKO MEKYAA [clod crack thud]
82.2.1	BOOK: COMIKE PAMPHLET
82.2.2	APRON: MANAGER
82.4	APRON: MANAGER
82.5	APRON: MANAGER

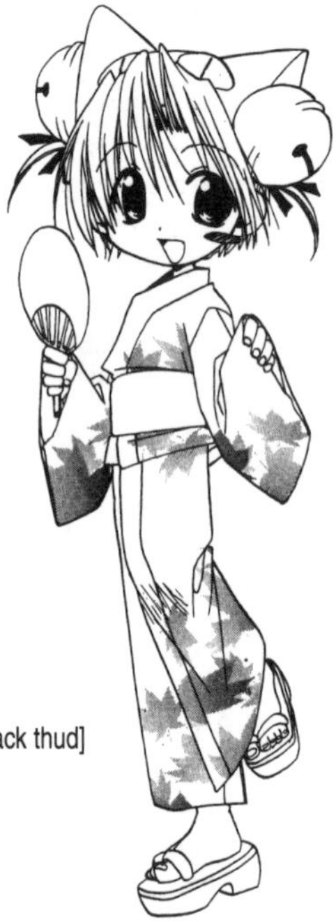

83.3	FX: KEKEKE [cackle cackle cackle]
83.5	FX: BUGYUU [shove]
84.8	FX: SHI-N [shocked silence]
85.5	APRON: MANAGER
85.7	APRON: MANAGER
89.1	FX: KUHA [yawn]
89.3	FX: ZU-N [heavy atmosphere]
90.1.1	FX: GAA [kick]
90.1.2	FX: GOO [thud]
90.1.3	FX: ZUNN [slam]
90.2.1	DIALOGUE FX: EYE BEAMS
90.2.2	FX: GOO [thud]
90.2.3	FX: A-CHACHACHA [ow-ouch ouch ouch]
90.4	FX: MUKUU [sit up]
91.1.1	FX: TOBO TOBOO [plod plod]
91.1.2	FX: HAH- [sigh-]
91.2	FX: KYUPI [tweet]
91.3.1	FX: KEH KEH KEH [cackle cackle cackle]
91.3.2	DIALOGUE FX: BOY, YOU ARE DUMB.
92.1	FX: MUHA- MUHA- [squeeze squeeze]
92.2.1	BOOK: KOGE-DONBO
92.2.2	BAG: USADA
92.2.3	BAG: GEMA
92.3.1	FX WITH ARROW: SOMEWHERE AROUND HERE
92.3.2	FX: ZUDO-N [blast]
92.4.1	DIALOGUE FX: PYO-
92.4.2	FX: CHIDO- CHIDO- [blast blast]
92.5.1	FX: PI-PO PI-PO [police sirens]
94	BOXES: GE
96.4	FX: MUKA MUKA [irk irk]
97.4	FX: KERII [kick]
98.1	FX: AWA... AWAWA... [stutter... stutter...]
98.3	FX: GAKUN [shudder]

98.5	FX: GO- [roar-]
99.4	FX: MUKURI [sit up]
100.2	FX: UA- [waaaah-]
102.2	FX: HYOO [hoist]
102.5	FX: SASAA [kneel]
102.6	DIALOGUE FX: HOW AMUSING.
104.3	FX: BAA [snatch]
105.2	DIAGLOGUE FX: PUCHIKO-CHA-N
106.2	FX: PUI [hmph]
108.2.1	FX: GUCHAA [smolder]
108.2.2	DIALOGUE FX: OH, DEAR—
108.3	FX: MUKI- [irk-]
108.5	FX: BAKKI [clobber]
109.2	FX: BUCHI-N [snap]
109.4	FX: KIRA-N [gleam]
111.1.1	FX: MOMI MOMI [knead knead]
111.1.2	FX: MOMI [knead}
116.4.1	FX: SUKAA [missed]
116.4.2	FX: CHOKOO [crouch]
116.4.3	FX: SHIKKA [grab]
116.4.4	DIALOGUE FX: HUH?
117.1	FX: TO-N [collapse]
119.6	FX: CHUDDON [blast]
122.1	FX: ZURA- [ta-daa-]
122.4	FX: KOKUN [nod]
123.3	FX: JI-N [throb]
129.6.1	CUP: FLAN
129.6.2	WRITING: DIGIKO'S

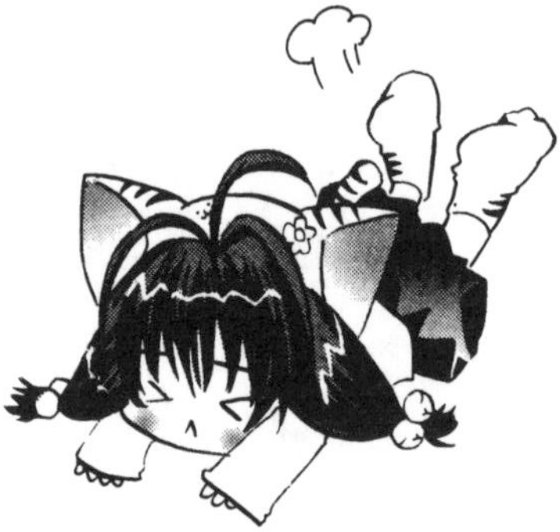

136.2.1	FX: BISHI! [point!]
136.2.2	DIALOGUE FX: WHAT?!
137.3.1	APRON: WIZARD
137.3.2	DIALOGUE FX: I'M NOT A SUSPICIOUS PERSON, I ASSURE YOU.
137.4	APRON: WIZARD
140.2.1	FX: WHOA—
140.2.2	FX: MUKAA [irk]
144.4	FX: GOSO GOSO [rummage rummage]
145.2	FX: DOSAA [thud]
145.4	FX: KA- KA- [caw caw]
145.5	FX: SHUN SHUN [steam steam]
146.6.1	FX: GU-! [growl-!]
146.6.2	FX: KYURURURU RURURU [rumble rumble rumble]
147.5	FX: KYUU KYUU [squeak squeak]
148.5.1	FX: KOTONN [clomp]
148.5.2	FX: HOKA HOKA [steam steam]
150.2	FX: BORO BORO [weep weep]
150.3	FX: GATSU GATSU [gulp gulp]
152.1	CHARACTER: MA [upside down wish spell]
152.2	FX: BU- [foo-]
155.3	FX: KARAN [sound of doorbell]
156.4	FX: BUKA BUKA [too big, too big]
157.2.1	FX: TOTETETE [dash]
157.2.2	FX: KARAN [sound of doorbell]
158.1	DIALOGUE FX: TA-DAA
158.3.1	FX: BOROO [sound of thread unraveling]
158.3.2	DIALOGUE FX: D'OH!!

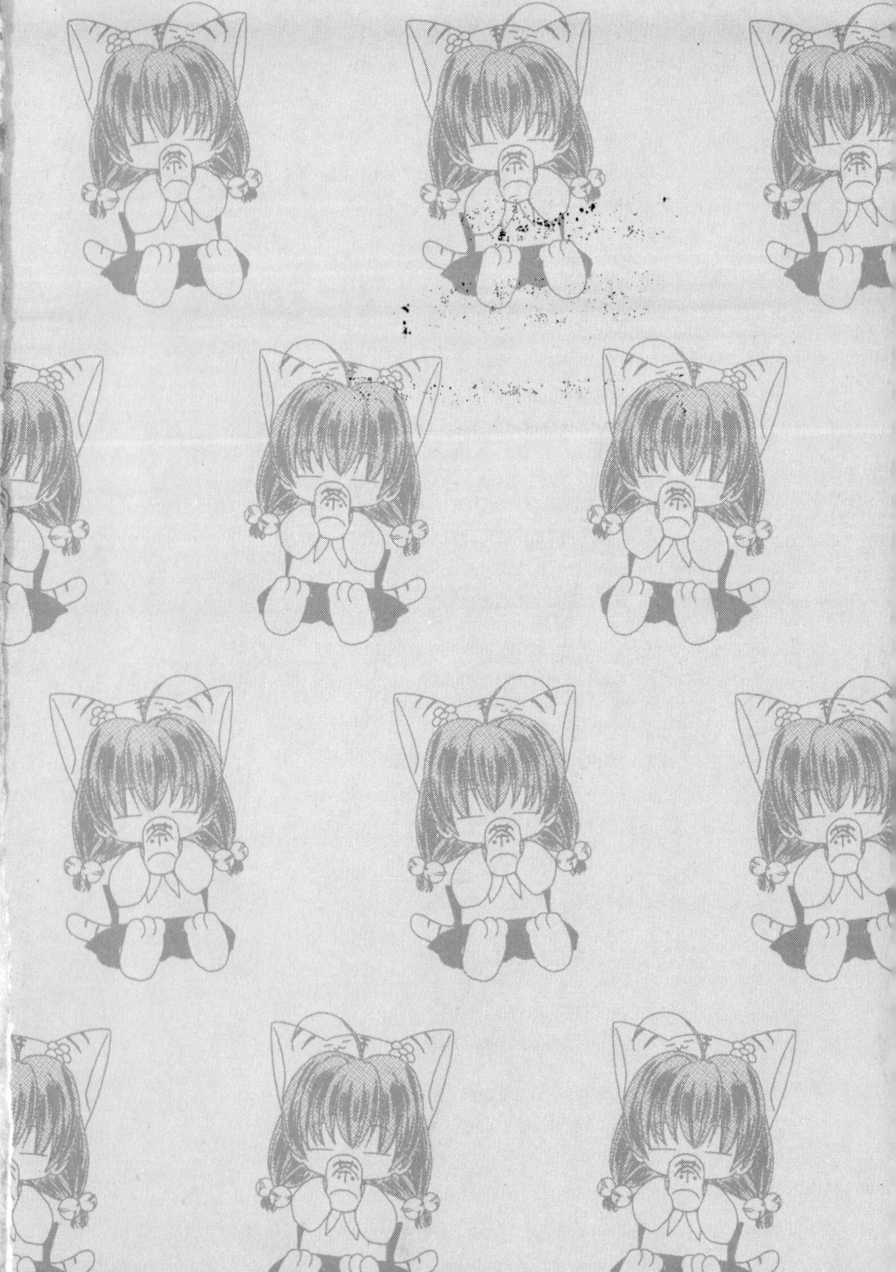